What others are saying about
LOOKING GOOD IN PRINT

"...a great find! Just what I needed. Thanks!"

J. Williams
Lompoc, California

"...Great book! Well worth the money!"

C. Conklin
Clay, New York

"I love the examples. I've been looking for a book like this for a long time!"

M. Rapson
Decatur, Illinois

"I was frantic until I found your book! Now I have what I need to keep me 'looking good in print'!"

B. Boyett
Irving, Texas

"...a fabulous book! Every page from the table of contents to the index is packed with helpful, useful information!"

P. Kearns
Moscow, Idaho

LOOKING GOOD IN PRINT

A Guide to Basic Design for Desktop Publishing

LOOKING GOOD IN PRINT

third edition

A Guide to Basic Design for Desktop Publishing

Roger C. Parker
Third Edition Updates by
Ventana Press Editorial Staff

VENTANA
PRESS

The Ventana Press Looking Good™ Series

Looking Good in Print: A Guide to Basic Design for Desktop Publishing, Third Edition

Library of Congress Cataloging-in-Publication Data
Parker, Roger C.
    Looking good in print : a guide to basic design for
  desktop publishing / Roger C. Parker. -- 3rd ed.
         p.   cm.
    Includes bibliographical references and index.
    ISBN 1-56604-047-7
    1. Desktop publishing. II. Title.
  Z253.53.P37 1993
  686.2'2544--dc20   93-10501
                                             CIP

Book design: Karen Wysocki
Cover design: Suzanne Anderson
Index service: Mark Kmetzko
Editorial staff: Ruffin Prevost, Pam Richardson
Production staff: Rhonda Angel, John Cotterman, Brian Little, Marcia Webb, Karen Wysocki
Proofreaders: Jean Kaplan, Jessica Ryan

Third Edition 9 8 7 6 5 4 3 2
Printed in the United States of America

Ventana Press, Inc.
P.O. Box 2468
Chapel Hill, NC 27515
919/942-0220
FAX 919/942-1140

Limits of Liability and Disclaimer of Warranty

ACKNOWLEDGMENTS

The author and publisher wish to express appreciation to the following illustrators, graphic designers, photographers and desktop publishers who assisted in the creation of many of the illustrations in this book:

Carolyn Bakamis
Todd Gilmore
Charlotte Kirchgessner
John Nedwidek
Ben Rayfield
Gary Rousseau
Holly Russell
Patrick Short
Teresa Smith
Southern Media Design and Production, Inc.
Shea Tisdale
Mary Votta
Susan Worsley

Many of the illustrations and other new material for the third edition was created by the Ventana Press staff, including John Cotterman, Brian Little, Marcia Webb, Karen Wysocki and Ruffin Prevost, who also wrote the new and updated chapters.

Thanks also to Hewlett-Packard for providing a ScanJet IIc color scanner for evaluation; Adobe Systems, for providing an evaluation copy of Photoshop 2.5 image editing software; and 3G Graphics, for providing an evaluation copy of the Images With Impact clip-art CD.

ABOUT THE AUTHOR

Roger C. Parker is author of *Newsletters From the Desktop*, *Desktop Publishing With WordPerfect* and *The Makeover Book: 101 Design Solutions for Desktop Publishing*, all published by Ventana Press. He has conducted numerous seminars and workshops on desktop publishing design. He is president of The Write Word, Inc., an advertising and marketing firm based in Dover, NH.

The author may be reached at

The Write Word
P.O. Box 697
Dover, NH 03820
603/742-9673

TRADEMARKS

Colophon

The third edition of *Looking Good In Print* was produced on a Macintosh Quadra 700, using Aldus PageMaker 4.2. Illustrations were created in a variety of programs, including Aldus FreeHand 3.0 and PageMaker 4.2 (Mac and Windows), Adobe Illustrator 3.0, Adobe Photoshop 2.5 and Quark XPress 3.0. Photographs and scanned illustrations were acquired using a Hewlett-Packard ScanJet IIc and Light Source's Ofoto Version 2. The color section was separated using Aldus PrePrint.

■

Page proofs were output on an Apple LaserWriter IIg, and final output was run directly to film using an Agfa Proset 9800.

■

All body type is set in Apple Palatino. Heads and subheads are set in Digital Typeface Corporation's Eras Book and Eras Bold. Sidebars are set in DTC Eras Book, and folios are set in DTC Mistral.

Contents

Building Blocks of Graphic Design **89**

XVIII   Looking Good in Print

Chapter Seven

Working With Color   **157**

Chapter Eight

Twenty-Five Common Design Pitfalls   **183**

Section Two: Putting Your Knowledge to Work

Putting Your Knowledge To Work

Section Three: Getting Down to Business

Designing Effective Newsletters   **255**

Sales Materials   **319**

Books, Documentation & Training Materials 335

Presentation Graphics: Projecting the Right Image 345

Response Devices—Forms, Coupons & Surveys

Graphics & Prepress Tips & Techniques

Photo & Clip Art Resources

Introduction

Until the mid-1980s, graphic design was the exclusive domain of art directors and design professionals whose livelihoods depended upon creating professional, effective graphic images. But desktop publishing changed all that.

By eliminating the traditional implements of design (T-squares, X-acto™ knives, rubber cement, etc.), desktop publishing has brought graphic design into the office and home. No longer must we commission professional design services. Everything from a business card to an annual report can be designed and laid out on your computer. However, for many people, graphic design is still a mystery.

Looking Good in Print is a design book for the rest of us—computer users with little or no design background who want to make the most of their desktop publishing investment. *Looking Good* outlines the skills necessary to create attractive, effective printed materials, such as newsletters, advertisements, brochures, manuals and other documents.

Regardless of your level of experience, you already may have more design skills than you suspect. In fact, you probably have an inherent, but as yet undeveloped, sense of good design—often referred to as taste!

Consider, for example, what your experiences as a reader and consumer reveal concerning the fundamentals of design:

- You subscribe to one newspaper or magazine rather than another of similar content.

■ You find it difficult to read your community group's newsletter but force yourself in order to find needed information.

■ While watching television, you pay attention to some commercials but hit the remote control to avoid watching others.

■ You're drawn to the colors used in an ad for a local retail business.

In such instances, your inherent sense of design helps you screen effective messages. This book teaches you how to consciously analyze your preferences and translate them into effective, good-looking printed materials.

EFFECTIVE GRAPHIC DESIGN—LUXURY OR NECESSITY?

Which is more important—the content of your message or its appearance?

The question is obviously rhetorical. Effective print communications depend on appearance as well as content.

Today, effective graphic design is more important than ever. Magazines and newspapers are crowded with ads. Mailboxes are stuffed with catalogs, newsletters and other direct-mail solicitations.

Consequently, your message has a lot of competition, increasing the need for a compelling graphic presentation.

In addition, because of the increasing complexity of products and services (coupled with recent changes in sales techniques), buying decisions are often based on information gleaned from brochures, proposals and other print communications rather than on direct hands-on, pre-purchase experience or person-to-person contact.

EFFECTIVE GRAPHIC DESIGN HELPS YOU SUCCEED

First impressions last. Effective graphic design favorably predisposes people to accept your product, service or point of view. Often buying decisions are based on emotional and intuitive feelings, which are highly influenced by the print communications that describe the product or service.

If your print communications fail to create a favorable first impression, the buying cycle may be short-circuited.

Because you never get a second chance to make a first impression, design is all-important to the power and success of your message.

WHO SHOULD READ "LOOKING GOOD IN PRINT"?

Looking Good in Print is a design guide, not for Madison Avenue art directors but for individuals discovering the challenges and joys of desktop publishing, including

- Retailers, entrepreneurs and other professionals who are producing their own printed materials.

- Managers who need to motivate personnel.

- Writers producing their own finished material.

- Educators who need to communicate on a large scale.

In short, anyone who wants to improve the appearance and effectiveness of his or her desktop-published projects—whether they are printed on a relatively inexpensive laser printer or a high-resolution imagesetter—will find *Looking Good in Print* a lasting reference tool.

HOW TO USE THIS BOOK

Looking Good in Print is organized into three sections.

■ Section One, "The Elements of Graphic Design," outlines the common graphics tools available in desktop publishing, the underlying principles of design and techniques for putting them into effect. We'll explore the most effective way to use photographs, illustrations and color.

■ Section Two, "Putting Your Knowledge to Work," features makeovers that demonstrate how the communicating power of a variety of different projects can be enhanced by simply rearranging the design elements in more effective ways.

■ In the final section, "Getting Down to Business," you will learn to apply the basic tools of graphic design to specific projects you're likely to undertake as you begin to put your desktop publishing hardware and software to work in the real world.

People new to desktop publishing should read the book from beginning to end, with special emphasis on Section One.

Intermediate and advanced users can probably skip Section One, but will gain valuable insights from reading the remaining two sections.

For those who want further material on the subject, an extensive bibliographical resource appendix contains outstanding ancillary reading material on graphic design, typography, printing, production and related subjects.

HOW WELL SHOULD YOU KNOW DESKTOP PUBLISHING?

This book assumes you're already comfortable with your desktop publishing hardware and software. It assumes your computer and printer are up and running, and that you've gone through the tutorials included with your software and are familiar with its basic commands.

While it's not a substitute for your software's documentation, *Looking Good in Print* will help you get the most from your program. You may find that techniques you once found intimidating—say, runarounds or drop shadows—are less formidable if you know when and how to use them.

Please note that throughout this book, the terms *publication* and *document* are used to refer to any desktop publishing project regardless of size or content: it may be as small as a business card or as large as a book!

HARDWARE/SOFTWARE REQUIREMENTS

Looking Good in Print is a generic guide, independent of any particular hardware or software. In other words, this book will be a valuable resource, regardless of whether you use a Macintosh or a PC, a dedicated page layout program like PageMaker or QuarkXPress, a state-of-the-art word processing program like WordPerfect or Microsoft Word for Windows, or any of the other fine software programs available. The elements of good design are constant and are achievable in any system.

All combinations of hardware and software are as capable of producing excellent results as they are mediocre results. The difference lies not so much in your system as in your willingness to develop your inherent talents and abilities and to learn new ones.

ABOUT THE DESIGN OF THIS BOOK

When producing *Looking Good in Print*, I was tempted to hire one of the nation's top graphic designers to create an award-winning statement on contemporary design.

I resisted for several reasons. The main reason is that a design showcase would defeat the basic premise of *Looking Good in Print*—that high-quality results are attainable by anyone who wants to learn the basics of good design. Second, today's design trends often are tomorrow's rejects.

A third reason is that I wanted the book to speak not just to those desktop publishers who are advancing the frontiers of design but also to newcomers to the field—those discovering for the first time the exhilarating freedom of expression that desktop publishing provides.

Consequently, the examples featured throughout this book were produced in a simple, unembellished style. As your design and desktop publishing skills grow, you undoubtedly will produce far more elegant materials than those found in this book. In the meantime, I hope *Looking Good in Print* will serve as a valuable stepping stone.

Let's get started.

Roger C. Parker
Dover, NH

Section One

The Elements of Graphic Design

Chapter One

Beginning Observations

Part of the challenge of graphic design is that it has no "universal rules." Everything is relative; it can't be reduced to a set of "if...then..." statements. Tools and techniques you use effectively in one situation will not necessarily work in another.

For example, framing an advertisement in a generous amount of white space may draw a lot of attention to the message and look striking. On the other hand, a large border of white space on a newsletter page may make the text look like an afterthought and create a sparse, uninviting look.

Or consider typeface choices. A combination of Palatino for text and Helvetica for headlines may look great for an instruction manual, but too bland for a flyer announcing a jazz concert in the park.

If design were governed by a set of hard-and-fast rules, computer programs would replace graphic artists—and every advertisement, book, brochure, newsletter and poster would look the same. The resulting uniformity would rob the world of the diversity and visual excitement that add so much to magazines, newspapers and even our daily mail!

Good design stems from a thorough knowledge of the building blocks of graphic design and specifying them appropriately, based on the format and function of an individual project.

Design techniques used effectively in one situation may not work in another.

Successful design also evolves from a mindset:

■ A willingness to experiment.

■ Confidence in your perceptions.

■ Recognition that effective design is a process, not an event.

■ Devotion to detail.

Part of the challenge of design is that it has no universal rules.

Because good design is often transparent, understanding the fundamentals of design—those building blocks that transform a scribbled note into a professional, attractive print communication—will give you the tools you need to use your desktop publishing system to full advantage.

First, let's examine some general principles and preliminary steps that will help you gain solid footing in designing your projects.

UNDERSTANDING YOUR MESSAGE

The design process is simply an extension of the organizing process that began as you developed the concept for your project.

To the extent that you can define your project's purpose and can prioritize the different parts of your message, you can create effective, good-looking print communications.

Effective design is often transparent.

If, however, you're unclear about the purpose and undecided about the sequence and relative importance of the information you want to communicate, you're in dangerous waters. You're forced to operate subjectively rather than objectively.

Let's say you're designing a layout for a newsletter article that includes a series of photographs. Unless you've thought through the role of the photographs in the article, you won't know how to position them. You'll be forced to be strictly subjective: "I think this photograph looks good here," etc.

But if you know how they relate to the story and each other, you can easily decide on the proper order and size for them.

In a sense, desktop publishing and the tools of graphic design are an extension of your communication skills. They make it easier for you to give visual organization and emphasis to your message.

However, they cannot compensate for a lack of initial planning or organization, which is why the success of your project hinges on this initial stage.

Before starting a project, ask yourself these questions:

- Who is the intended audience?

The more you define a project's purpose, the better you'll do.

- What is the basic message you're trying to communicate?

- In what format will readers encounter your message: book, newspaper, newsletter, magazine, brochure, mailer, slide presentation, etc.?

- What similar messages have your readers encountered from other sources or competitors?

- How does this publication relate to your other publications?

The more you define your project's purpose and environment, the stronger your design will be.

EXPERIMENT

Turn off your computer and start to experiment.

Let's dispel the myth that design solutions appear like magic in a burst of creative energy or like a light bulb illuminating over the head of a cartoon character. Successful graphic design usually emerges from trial and error. Solutions are the result of a willingness to try various design options until one looks right.

Although desktop publishing lets you produce graphics on your computer, it's often best to loosely sketch initial ideas and trial layouts with pencil and paper.

Try out ideas. When you finish one sketch, begin another. Let speed become a stimulant.

You'll find your ideas flow much faster—and you'll arrive at a design solution much quicker—if you sketch out alternative ways of arranging text and graphics by hand.

Effective design emerges from trial and error.

Don't bother with detail for now. Think big: use thin lines for text, thick lines or block lettering for headlines, and "happy faces" for art or photographs.

SEEK INSPIRATION

Train yourself to constantly analyze the work of others.

Sensitize yourself to examples of effective and ineffective design. If a direct-mail piece you like appears in your mail-box, examine it and determine why it appeals to you. If you see an advertisement in the newspaper that's confusing or too busy, dissect it and identify why it doesn't work.

Maintain a Clip File

Most experienced graphic artists maintain "inspiration" files containing samples they like.

When you get stuck on a project, spend a few moments reviewing your favorite designs on file. Chances are, they may serve as a catalyst for your design decisions.

If your projects will be printed in two-, three- or four-color, you may want to collect samples of color projects that you feel are particularly eye-catching.

Look Beyond Desktop Publishing

It's easy to become so involved with desktop publishing hardware and software features you lose sight of the fact that they're simply tools—that your real challenge is creating the overall design.

Keep a file of great designs for inspiration.

To focus on design without the technological trappings, skim professional design publications that showcase elegant, excellent design examples (see the "Bibliography").

Join a local advertising group, art directors club or communications forum. Even if you're not involved in the advertising or public relations fields, you as a desktop publisher share a common goal of informing, motivating and persuading others. You're likely to return from these meetings with a fresh perspective on your communication and design efforts.

RELEVANCE

Every graphic element should relate to its particular communications function and unique environment.

Just as in music, there's nothing right or wrong about notes such as Middle C or B-flat, there are no "good" or "bad" design elements—only appropriate or inappropriate ones.

A financial newsletter, for example, requires a totally different design than a gardening newsletter with lots of pictures and short articles.

There are no "good" or "bad" typefaces, only appropriate and inappropriate ones.

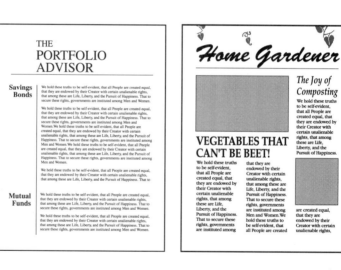

An image-building magazine ad requires a different design approach than a product- and price-oriented newspaper ad.

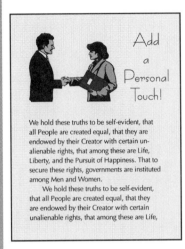

A letterhead for a prestigious law firm should be easily distinguishable from a letterhead for a rock music promoter.

Think of design as a means of communication rather than decoration.

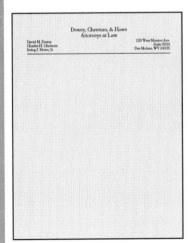

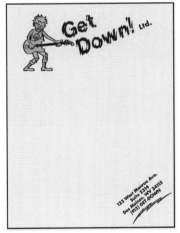

Successful graphic design is relevant. Each design should be judged on its ability to help the reader quickly and easily understand your message.

Form must always follow function. Think of graphic design as a means of communication rather than mere decoration.

And a word of caution: Don't let enthusiasm for the capabilities of your desktop publishing system get in the way of clear communication. Your message is the heart of your document. Design and technology should only enhance, not overshadow that message.

Clarity, organization and simplicity are as critical to design as they are to writing.

Always strive for cohesiveness between appearance and content. Important ideas, for example, should be made visually more prominent than secondary ideas or supporting facts and figures.

This should come as good news to those who have been intimidated by graphic design, thinking of it as an art practiced only by the gifted or the trained. If you use the appropriate tools, you should be able to produce effective, good-looking publications.

PROPORTION

The size of all graphic elements should be determined by their relative importance and environment.

Effective design depends on how well each piece of the puzzle fits with the other pieces.

Because there are no absolutes in graphic design, success is determined by how well each piece of the puzzle relates to the pieces around it.

For example, proper headline size is determined partly by its importance and partly by the amount of space that separates it from adjacent borders, text and artwork. A large headline in a small space looks "cramped."

DON'T CROWD ME OUT!

We hold these truths to be self-evident, that all People are created equal, that they are endowed by their Creator with certain unalienable rights, that among these are Life, Liberty, and the Pursuit

of Happiness. That to secure these rights, governments are instituted among Men and Women. We hold these truths to be self-evident, that all People are created equal, that they are

Likewise, a small headline in a large space looks "lost."

WHERE AM I?

We hold these truths to be self-evident, that all People are created equal, that they are endowed by their Creator with certain unalienable rights, that among these are Life, Liberty, and the Pursuit

of Happiness. That to secure these rights, governments are instituted among Men and Women. We hold these truths to be self-evident, that all People are created equal, that they are

The proper thickness of lines—called rules—should be determined by the size of the type and the surrounding white space.

Rules that are too thick can interfere with reading.

I Feel I'm Being Overwhelmed

Rules that are too thin can lack effectiveness.

WAR DECLARED

When working with groups of photographs or illustrations on a page also consider proportion. When one photograph is larger, it enhances interest and sends the reader a nonverbal message about the relative importance of the photographs.

Type size and the distance between lines should properly relate to the column widths that organize the type. As you'll see later, wide columns are generally preferable for large type. And narrow columns are appropriate for small type.

DIRECTION

Effective graphic design guides the reader through your publication.

Readers should encounter a logical sequence of events as they encounter and read your advertisement or publication. Graphic design should provide a road map that steers your readers from point to point.

The design of that map should follow the readers' natural tendency to read an advertisement or publication from upper left to lower right.

THIS DRIP IS
COSTING YOU
MONEY

Peter's Plumbing
112 E. South St.
Pipesville, PA 15223
(481) 553-2843

Reconcile the need for both variety and consistency.

CONSISTENCY

Consistency leads to an integrated style.

Style reflects the way you handle elements that come up again and again. Part of a document's style is decided from the beginning. The rest emerges as the document develops visually.

Consistency is a matter of detail. It involves using restraint in choosing typefaces and type sizes, and using the same spacing throughout your document.

One of your biggest challenges as a desktop designer is to reconcile the continuing conflict between consistency and variety. Your goal is to create documents that are consistent within themselves, without being boring. Boredom occurs when predictability and symmetry dominate a document.

Thus, your publications should be consistent within themselves and with your organization's other print communications, yet they should be visually distinct. If you use one-inch margins in the first chapter of a book, you should use one-inch margins in all chapters.

Page-to-page consistency can be provided in any of the following ways:

Predictability and symmetry result in visual boredom.

- Consistent top, bottom and side margins.

- Consistent typeface, type size and spacing specifications for text, headlines, subheads and captions.

- Uniform paragraph indents and spaces between columns and around photographs.

- Repeating graphic elements, such as vertical lines, columns or borders, on each page.

For example, you can create an "artificial horizon" by repeating a strong line or graphic on each page in your publication.

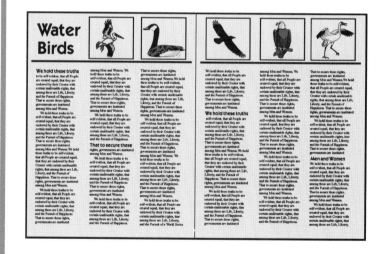

CONTRAST

Contrast provides dynamic interest.

Contrast gives "color" to your publication by balancing the space devoted to text, artwork and white space. When analyzing an attractive publication, compare "dark" areas—such as large, bold headlines, dark photographs or blocks of text—and notice how they're offset by lighter areas with little type.

High-impact publications tend to have a lot of contrast. Each page or two-page spread has definite "light" and "dark" areas, with lots of white space and illustrations.

Lively, attractive documents tend to have a lot of contrast.

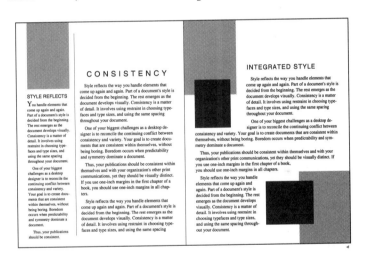

You can create publications low in contrast, where all pages and parts of pages are a uniform shade of "gray." Formal reports, policy statements, books and press releases often have low contrast.

Contrast enhances the communicating power of your publication.

Contrast can be observed by turning the publication upside down. Viewed from that perspective, your eyes aren't misled by the tendency to read individual words. Instead, you concentrate on the overall "color" of the publication.

Contrasting sizes can create visual tension, which can keep the reader interested. For example, you might have a headline set in a large size above a subhead set in the same typeface at a much smaller size.

Effective graphic design is based on balancing contrast and consistency. Your designs must be dynamic enough to keep the reader interested, yet consistent enough so that your advertisement or publication emerges with a strong identity.

THE TOTAL PICTURE

Think of graphic design as the visual equivalent of a jigsaw puzzle.

Your job is to assemble a total picture from a series of parts. No piece of the puzzle should be isolated from the others. The various parts must fit together harmoniously.

The "total picture" includes consideration of the environment in which your advertisement or publication will be distributed.

For example, when designing a newspaper advertisement, consider how it will look when surrounded by news items and other ads.

When planning a newsletter or direct-mail piece, imagine how it will look when it arrives in the recipient's mailbox. When designing a magazine cover, consider how it will appear surrounded by other magazines on the newsstand. When creating product literature, visualize it displayed in a brochure rack.

Inside a publication, the most important part of the total picture is the two-page spread. If you concentrate on designing each page as though it were a self-contained entity, you might end up creating two pages that look good individually, but don't work side by side. So, when designing multipage publications, such as newsletters, brochures or books, focus on two-page spreads instead of individual pages.

Designers assemble a total picture from individual parts.

This left-hand page is visually attractive and self-contained.

Design two-page spreads instead of individual pages.

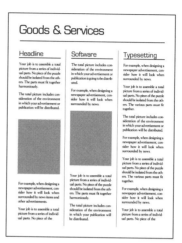

This right-hand page also works well on its own.

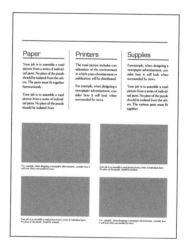

When viewed side by side, however, they "fight" each other and present a disorganized, difficult-to-read image.

Readers seldom encounter just one page, but see facing pages together.

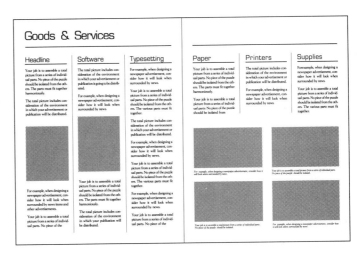

Remember that readers seldom encounter individual pages, but see left- and right-hand pages together.

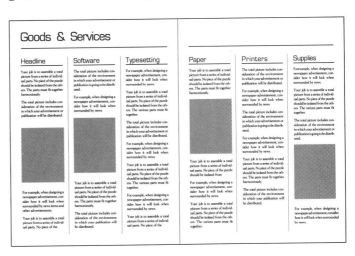

RESTRAINT

Strive for simplicity in design.

Restraint is probably the most difficult design principle to apply in a consistent manner. That's because desktop publishing presents you with tremendous design power—power which just a few years ago was limited to those who had years of training and tens of thousands of dollars worth of equipment.

With so much power at your fingertips, it's easy to forget that straightforwardness is a virtue and that graphic design should be invisible to the reader.

Restraint is the hardest design principle to apply in a consistent manner.

Restraint is exemplified by sticking to a few carefully chosen typefaces, styles and sizes.

In making design decisions, consider the degree to which design enhances the basic message you want to communicate.

Remember that emphasis can be effective only within a stable framework. Like the boy who cried "Wolf!" too often, excessive emphasis weakens your publication to the point where it loses all impact.

DETAIL

Success in desktop publishing is based on attention to detail.

Design is detail. And the smallest offending details can sabotage the appearance of an otherwise-attractive project.

Extra spaces after periods, for example, can create annoying rivers of white space in a text block. This can also be true of justified columns of text—in which all lines are the same length. Some lines are so sparse, huge gaps are created between words. These can be distracting and cause the reader's eyes to drag diagonally through a column.

Even the smallest offending detail can sabotage a project's design.

tivation analysis, the process that Nuclear Services primarily relies on for casework, involves exposing any type of material — liquid, gas or solid — to the reactor core, where the material is bombarded with thermal neutrons.

unfolding in which we have played a part."

**DANIEL BROWN
DIRECTOR, PCCU SOLID
WASTE SERVICES**

grams of its type and scope, officials say. The department operates behind secured doors in the basement of Burlington Laboratories, the destination of a myriad of materials — blood, coal, fish, skin tissues, fibers, water, featers and air particu-

Headlines and subheads placed at the bottoms of columns or pages set the readers up for disappointment, when the promised topic doesn't appear until the start of the next column or page.

Proofreading demands a lot of attention to detail.

Text placed in boxes should be indented on both sides. Otherwise, it may bump into the borders of the boxes.

Editorial tasks such as proofreading also require a lot of attention to detail. For example, correctly spelled, misused words sneak by spell-checking programs, which often can't differentiate spelling from usage.

The inns and outs of hotel/motel management opportunities.

Be careful not to let these and other errors go unnoticed until the presses are running.

EXAMINING PROOFS

Analyze reduced-size copies of your pages.

Most desktop publishing programs let you print out "thumbnail" proofs or a number of pages at a reduced size on a single sheet of paper. These programs typically organize facing pages next to each other, so you can see how spreads will look.

"Thumbnail" proofs reveal where design has been sacrificed for expediency.

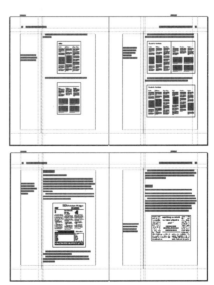

"Thumbnail" proofs let you see where good design has been sacrificed for expediency. Too much symmetry or too much contrast also becomes obvious.

Many desktop presentation programs that let you create slides and overhead transparencies offer a "handouts" feature. This lets you print the visuals for six or more slides or overheads in a reduced size on one page so that each audience member can take one along to use for future reference.

MOVING ON

These qualities—practicing restraint, concentrating on proportion, achieving a balance between consistency and contrast, and paying attention to detail—will ensure the effectiveness and attractiveness of your designs.

Now let's get down to the actual page makeup by exploring important organizational tools you'll use in creating your desktop-published projects.

Chapter Two

Tools of Organization

Effective graphic design is based on organization. It guides readers's eyes from one point to another in a document and alerts them to what's of primary importance and what is supplemental. It helps readers locate information quickly.

By applying various organizing tools, the two primary page elements, *graphics* and *type*, are given form, and the function of the document itself is defined.

In short, these "ingredients" are at the heart of page design and can be created by using your desktop publishing program's tools.

Graphic organizers are at the heart of effective page design.

PAGE ORGANIZERS

Fundamental to the overall page layout are page organizing tools. Different desktop publishing programs offer different ways of implementing those tools.

Grids

Grids establish the overall structure of a page by specifying the placement of text, display type and artwork.

Grids consist of nonprinted lines that show up on your computer screen but not on the finished publication. Grids determine the number of columns, margin size, placement of headlines, subheads, pull-quotes and other page ingredients.

They're valuable for a number of reasons: they set page-to-page or project-to-project consistency, as well as help you avoid reinventing the wheel each time you create another ad or newsletter issue. In other words, layout can be determined once and reused with slight variations.

Grids set up page-to-page and project-to-project consistency.

Desktop publishing programs differ in their ability to create grids. Some programs provide you with ready-made grids you can modify.

Many programs use a series of horizontal and vertical lines that define columns and page margins.

By creating grids, layout can be determined once and reused later.

Other page-layout programs are based on setting text into boxes, or frames.

Many word processing programs also let you format pages by setting parameters that define column placement and margins, even though the column boundaries aren't always visible on-screen.

One way or another, all programs let you establish formats that are automatically maintained from page to page or throughout a series of documents.

Styles

Styles provide the "memory bank" for desktop publishing, giving you instant access to the design specifications on a project.

Keeping track of all these organizers—column specifications, headline font and size, caption placement and size, the picas between a subhead and the text—is too daunting for those of us not blessed with a photographic memory. Fortunately, desktop publishing programs offer the ultimate organizer—styles.

Each specification concerning type or format in your document can be defined as part of your document's styles. Once defined, the style can be conveniently applied as you create your document.

Styles are of paramount importance if you're creating a multipage document or a standard format that will be repeated frequently on future projects. After you've finalized your document design, setting up styles is probably the most important part of production planning.

Columns

The most fundamental part of a grid, columns organize text and visuals on a page.

Text and visuals rarely extend in an unbroken line from the left side of the page to the right. They're usually arranged in *columns,* or vertical blocks. For most documents, column formats range from single-column to seven-column page layout.

Column width affects readability.

The greater the number of columns on a page, the narrower the column and the shorter the line length. And column width has a profound influence on a publication's readability. Remember that readers scan groups of words rather than individual letters. Narrow columns can be difficult to read because the readers' eyes have to shift to the next line more often than with longer line lengths.

The wider the column, the more difficult it is for the readers' eyes to make a smooth transition from the end of one line to the beginning of the next without getting lost.

Readers tend to scan groups of words rather than individual letters.

8-point text placed on a 23-pica column is very difficult to read. 8-point text placed on a 23-pica column is very difficult to read. 8-point text placed on a 23-pica column is very difficult to read. 8-point text placed on a 23-pica column is very difficult to read. 8-point text placed on a 23-pica column is very difficult to read. 8-point text placed on a 23-pica column is very difficult to read. 8-point text placed on a 23-pica column is very difficult to read. 8-point text placed on a 23-pica column is very difficult to read. 8-point text placed on a 23-pica column is very difficult to read.

Column width affects the type size of the text. Narrow columns work best with small type sizes.

But 8-point text in a 12-pica column is readable. But 8-point text in a 12-pica column is readable. But 8-point text in a 12-pica column is readable. But 8-point text in a 12-pica column is readable.

Wider columns usually require larger type sizes.

12-point type looks good when placed in 23-pica columns. 12-point type looks good when placed in 23-pica columns. 12-point type looks good when placed in 23-pica columns. 12-point type looks good when placed in 23-pica columns.

Not all columns on a page have to be the same width. Good-looking publications can be created by varying column widths based on an established multicolumn grid.

For example, the five-column grid lends itself to a variety of arrangements.

Attractive documents can be created by varying the widths of columns.

In a five-column format, subheads and illustrations can be laid out side by side in a narrow column adjacent to one or two wide columns of text.

Variations on the above are permissible within a document, but should always conform with the overall column scheme. A two-column photo, "A," on a five-column grid looks good when its edges are aligned with column guides.

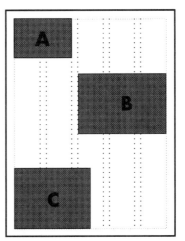

Likewise, a three-column photograph, "B," on a five-column grid works well when the edges of the photograph are lined up with the column guides.

The distance between columns also affects the "color" of a publication.

Closely spaced columns "darken" a document.

But, a two-and-a-half-column photograph, "C," on a five-column grid creates unsightly "half-columns" of white space or short columns of type.

Just as establishing the number of columns influences the "color" of a publication, so does the space between columns.

Closely spaced columns "darken" a document and often make it more difficult to read—the reader's eye tends to jump the gap between columns.

Extra space between columns "lightens," or opens up, a page and clearly separates one column from another.

Gutters

In designing multipage documents, pay particular attention to the gutter, or inner space of facing pages.

The width of a gutter depends upon a project's binding method.

Gutter size depends primarily on the type of binding you plan to use. For example, perfect binding—a method in which all pages are glued together—used in this and most books will reduce the size of the inner margin. It's usually a safe bet to leave a traditional gutter margin of a 1/2-inch to accommodate this type of binding.

T ext and visuals rarely extend in an unbroken line from the left side of the page to the right. They're usually arranged in one or more columns, or vertical blocks. For most documents, column formats range from single-column to seven-column page layout. ■ The greater the number of columns on a page, the narrower the column and shorter the line length. And column width has a profound influence on a publication's readability. Remember that readers scan groups of words rather than individual letters. Narrow columns can be difficult to read because the readers' eyes have to shift to the next line more often than with longer line lengths. The wider the column, the more difficult it is for the readers' eyes to make a smooth transition from the end of the next without getting lost. Column width affects the type size of the text. Narrow columns work best with small type sizes. Wider columns usually require larger type sizes. The greater the number of columns on a page, the narrower the column and shorter the line length. And column width has a profound influence on a publication's readability. Remember that readers scan groups of words rather than individual letters. Narrow columns can be difficult to read because the readers' eyes have to shift to the next line more often than with longer line lengths. ■ The wider the column, the more difficult it is for the readers' eyes to make a smooth transition from the end of one line to the beginning of the next without getting lost. ■ Column width affects the type size of the text. Narrow columns work best with small type sizes. Wider columns usually require larger type sizes. Text and visuals rarely extend in an unbroken line from the left side of the page to the right. They're usually arranged in one or more columns, or vertical blocks. For most documents, column formats range from single-column to seven-column page layout. The greater the number of columns on a page, the narrower the column and shorter the line length. And column

F or most documents, column formats range from single-column to seven-column page layout. The greater the number of columns on a page, the narrower the column and shorter the line length. And column width has a profound influence on a publication's readability. Remember that readers scan groups of words rather than individual letters. ■ Narrow columns can be difficult to read because the readers' eyes have to shift to the next line more often than with longer line lengths. The wider the column, the more difficult it is for the readers' eyes to make a smooth transition from the end of one line to the beginning of the next without getting lost. Column width affects the type size of the text. Narrow columns work best with small type sizes. Wider columns usually require larger type sizes. ■ The greater the number of columns on a page, the narrower the column and shorter the line length. And column width has a profound influence on a publication's readability. Remember that readers scan groups of words rather than individual letters. Narrow columns can be difficult to read because the readers' eyes have to shift to the next line more often than with longer line lengths. The wider the column, the more difficult it is for the readers' eyes to make a smooth transition from the end of one line to the beginning of the next without getting lost. Column width affects the type size of the text. ■ Narrow columns work best with small type sizes. Wider columns usually require larger type sizes. Text and visuals rarely extend in an unbroken line from the left side of the page to the right. They're usually arranged in one or more columns, or vertical blocks. For most documents, column formats range from single-column to seven-column page layout. The greater the number of columns on a page, the narrower the column and shorter the line length. ■ And column width has a profound influence on a publication's readability. Remember that readers scan groups of words rather than individual letters. Narrow

|←—X—→|

For ring binding, reserve a 5/8- to 3/4-inch gutter. Most plastic spiral bindings don't require such wide gutters, but it's best to choose a particular binding first and design your gutter width around it.

Margins

Margins determine the space between columns and/or the borders and edge of a page.

The larger the margin, the "lighter" the publication.

Effective design allows "breathing room" between the live area and the physical boundaries of a page, referred to as trim size.

The larger the margin, the "lighter" the publication. Thinner margins result in "darker" publications.

TEXT ORGANIZERS

Text organizers include headlines, subheads, captions and more.

Often referred to as display type, these organizing tools highlight your message and help readers understand it quickly and easily.

Headlines

Use headlines to invite readers to become involved in your advertisement or articles in your publication.

The most basic text-organizing tool, headlines help readers decide whether to read a document. They should be as short and concise as possible so they can be quickly read and understood.

Effective headlines are clearly differentiated from text.

To be effective, headlines should be clearly differentiated from text, which can be done in two ways.

In addition to setting them in a large type size, you can add emphasis to headlines and give contrast to your page by setting them in a different typeface than the one used for the text.

For example, headlines set in sans-serif type are often used with text set in a serif typeface—a popular font combination for documents such as advertisements, books, brochures and newsletters. (See page 52 in Chapter 3, "The Architecture of Type," for a review of serif and sans-serif type.)

Alternately, you can emphasize headlines by setting them in the text typeface, but in a larger size and/or heavier weight.

Headlines should be designed for impact and readability.

The greater the size difference between headline and text, the easier it is for readers to identify and read your headline.

Even though headlines should be designed for impact, make them as readable as possible. For example, avoid setting long headlines in uppercase type. Not only do long, uppercase headlines occupy more space, they slow readers down because they're difficult to read.

It's best to limit uppercase headlines to several words. This adds impact without slowing down the reader.

The most readable type scheme for headlines is to use uppercase only for the first letter of each word (other than articles and short prepositions).

Long headlines can look too complex and wordy.

**Set Your Headlines
With Initial Caps**

Use headlines to invite readers to become involved in your advertisement or articles in your publication.

The most basic text organizing tool, headlines help readers decide whether to read a document. They should be as short and concise as possible so they can be read and understood quickly.

To be effective, headlines should be clearly differentiated from text, which can be done in two ways.

In addition to setting headlines in a large type size, you can add emphasis to them and give contrast to your page by setting headlines in a different typeface than the one used for the body copy.

For example, headlines set in sans-serif type are often used with text set in a serif typeface–a popular technique for documents such as advertisements, books, brochures and newsletters.

To be effective, headlines should be clearly differentiated from text, which can be done in two ways.

In addition to setting headlines in a large type size, you can add emphasis to them and give contrast to your

page by setting headlines in a different typeface than the one used for the text.

For example, headlines set in sans-serif type are often used with text in a serif typeface–a popular technique for documents such as advertisements, books, brochures and newsletters.

Alternately, you can emphasize headlines by setting them in the same typeface as text, but in a larger size and/or heavier weight. Use headlines to invite readers to become involved in your advertisement or articles in your publication.

The most basic text organizing tool, headlines help readers decide whether to read a document. They should be as short and concise as possible so they can be read and understood. Use headlines to invite readers to become involved in your advertisement or articles in your publication.

The most basic text organizing tool, headlines help readers decide whether to read a document. They should be as short and concise as possible so they can be read and understood quickly.

To be effective, headlines should be clearly differentiated from text, which can be done in two ways.

Try to limit headlines to three lines. Long headlines of four or more lines can look too wordy and complex to read at a glance. Also, avoid centering headlines that contain more than two lines. Long, centered headlines slow readers down because they have to search for the beginning of each line.

Centering long headlines forces readers to search for the beginning of each line.

**Sleet and Snow Storms
Predicted to Occur Over
the Next Several Days
in the Midwest**

Use headlines to invite readers to become involved in your advertisement or articles in your publication.

The most basic text organizing tool, headlines help readers decide whether to read a document. They should be as short and concise as possible so they can be read and understood quickly.

To be effective, headlines should be clearly differentiated from text, which can be done in two ways.

In addition to setting headlines in a large type size, you can add emphasis to them and give contrast to your page by setting headlines in a different typeface than the one used for the text.

For example, headlines set in sans-serif type are often used with text set in a serif typeface–a popular technique for documents such as advertisements, books, brochures and newsletters.

To be effective, headlines should be clearly differentiated from text, which can be done in two ways.

In addition to setting headlines in

a large type size, you can add emphasis to them and give contrast to your page by setting headlines in a different typeface than the one used for the text.

For example, headlines set in sans-serif type are often used with text set in a serif typeface–a popular technique for documents such as advertisements, books, brochures and newsletters.

Alternately, you can emphasize headlines by setting them in the same typeface as text, but in a larger size and/or heavier weight. Use headlines to invite readers to become involved in your articles in your publication.

The most basic text organizing tool, headlines help readers decide whether to read a document. They should be as short and concise as possible so they can be read and understood. Use headlines to invite readers to become involved in your advertisement or articles in your publication.

The most basic text organizing tool, headlines help readers decide whether

Flush-left headlines, on the other hand, let readers move directly down to the first words of the following paragraph.

Kickers

Lead into your headline with a kicker, a short summary phrase.

Kickers can introduce the headline by relating it to other articles or existing information. Kickers also can categorize an article.

Profile of a Modern Hero:

Fireman Risks Life to Save Cat Caught in

We hold these truths to be self-evident, that all People are created equal, that they are endowed by their Creator with certain unalienable rights, that among these are Life, Liberty, and the Pursuit of Happiness. That to secure these rights, governments are instituted among Men and Women. We hold these truths to be to be self-evident, that all People are created equal, that they are endowed by their Creator with certain unalienable rights, that among these are Life, Liberty, and the Pursuit of Happiness. That to secure these rights, governments are instituted among Men and Women. We hold these truths to be self-evident, unalienable rights, that among these are Life, Liberty, and the Pursuit of Happiness. That to secure these rights, governments are instituted among Men and Women. We hold these truths to be self-evident, that all People are created equal, that they are endowed by their Creator with certain unalienable rights, that among these are Life, Liberty, and the Pursuit of Happiness. That to secure these rights, governments are instituted among Men and Women. We hold these truths to be self-evident,

Subheads

Subheads clue readers into the content organization within an article.

Subheads placed between the head and the text improve the appearance of a page by providing a transition between headlines and text. They give visual contrast and offer readers more detailed information about the text.

Subheads placed within a document, instead of following the headline, let readers quickly locate information and break text into manageable segments.

Compare these two examples. In the left-hand example, you're faced with a long expanse of type. Because the page is so "dark" and you don't have a clue to its contents, reading it is a chore.

Subheads can provide a transition between headlines and text.

Don't Make Reading A Chore

Subheads clue readers into the content organization within an article. Subheads break text into manageable segments, improve the appearance of a page and enhance readership by providing a transition between headlines and text. They also provide visual contrast and identify the subject of the text. They let readers locate information.

Subheads can be set apart from text by using various techniques. For example, they can be placed inside or next to the text. Subheads should always be closely associated with the text they introduce. There should be more space above the subhead than below it to link it with the text.

Like headlines, subheads tend to stand out when set in a larger type size than the text and in a typeface that contrasts with the text. Subheads can be set centered, flush-left or flush-right.

As with other organizing tools, uniformity is important. Subheads should be treated consistently.

Subheads clue readers into the content organization within an article. Subheads break text into manageable segments, improve the appearance of a page and enhance readership by providing a transition between headlines and text. They also provide visual contrast and identify the subject of the text. They let readers locate information.

Subheads can be set apart from text by using various techniques. For example, they can be placed inside or next to the text. Subheads should always be closely associated with the text they introduce. There should be more space above the subhead than below it to link it with the text. Like headlines, subheads tend to stand out when set in a larger type size than the text and in a typeface that contrasts with the text. Subheads can be set centered, flush-left or flush-right.

As with other organizing tools, uniformity is important. Subheads should be treated consistently. Subheads clue readers into the content organization within an article. Subheads break text into manageable segments, improve the appearance of a page and enhance readership by providing a transition between headlines and text. They also provide visual contrast and identify the subject of the text. They let readers locate information. Subheads can be set apart from text by using various techniques. Subheads should always be closely associated with the text they introduce. There should be more space above the subhead than below it to link it with the text.

Don't Make Reading a Chore

Open up Your Pages

Subheads clue readers into the content organization within an article. Subheads break text into manageable segments, improve the appearance of a page and enhance readership by providing a transition between headlines and text. They let readers locate information.

Subheads can be set apart from text by using various techniques. For example, they can be placed inside or next to the text. Subheads should always be closely associated with the text they introduce. There should be more space above the subhead than below it to link it with the text.

Like headlines, subheads tend to stand out

when set in a larger type size than the text and in a typeface that contrasts with the text. Subheads can be set centered, flush-left or flush-right. Subheads clue readers into the content organization within an article. Subheads can be placed inside text.

Add Subheads Frequently

Subheads can be set apart from text by using various techniques. For example, they can be placed inside or next to the text. Subheads should always be closely associated with the text they introduce. There should be more space above the subhead than below it to link it with the text. Subheads should contrast with the text they introduce.

Use Various Subhead Techniques

Subheads can be set centered, flush-left or flush-right.

As with other organizing tools, uniformity is important. subheads should be treated consistently throughout your document.

Subheads clue readers into the content organization within an article. Subheads break text into manageable segments, improve the appearance of a page and enhance readership by providing a transition between headlines and text. They also provide visual contrast and identify the subject of the text. They let readers locate information.

Subheads can be set apart from text by using various techniques.

The right-hand example is more inviting because the page is more "open" and you can easily decide whether the text relates to your interests.

There are various ways to set subheads apart from text. For example, they can be placed inside or next to the text.

Don't Make Reading a Chore

Open up Your Pages

Subheads clue readers into the content organization within an article. Subheads break text into manageable segments, improve the appearance of a page and enhance readership by providing a transition between headlines and text. They also provide visual contrast and identify the subject of the text. They let readers quickly locate information.

Subheads can be set apart from text by using various techniques. For example, they can be placed inside or next to the text. Subheads should always be closely associated with the text they introduce. There should be more

space above the subhead to link it with the text.

Add Subheads Frequently

Subheads should always be closely associated with the text They introduce. There should be more space above the subhead than below it to link it with the text. Subheads should always be closely associated with the text Subheads can be set apart from text by using various techniques. For example, they can be placed inside or next to the text. Subheads should be closely associated with the text they introduce. There should be more

Use Various Subhead Techniques

Subheads can be set centered, flush-left or flush-right. As with other organizing tools, uniformity is important. subheads should be treated consistently. Subheads clue readers into the content organization within an article. Subheads break text into manageable segments, improve the appearance of a page and enhance readership by providing a transition between headlines and text. They also provide visual contrast and identify the subject of the text. Subheads can be set apart from text by using various techniques.

Don't Make Reading a Chore

Open up Your Pages

Add Subheads Frequently

Subheads clue readers into the content organization within an article. Subheads break text into manageable segments, improve the appearance of a page and enhance readership by providing a transition between headlines and text. They also provide visual contrast and identify the subject of the text.

They let readers locate information. Subheads can be set apart from text by using various techniques. For example, they can be placed inside or next to the text. Subheads should always be closely associated with the text they introduce. There should be more space above the subhead than below it to link it with the text.

Like headlines, subheads tend to stand out when set in a larger type size than the text and in a typeface that contrasts with the text. Subheads can be set centered, flush-left or flush-right. Subheads break text into manageable segments, improve the appearance of a page and enhance readership by providing a transition between headlines and text.

Use Various Subhead Techniques

They also provide visual contrast and identify the subject of the text. They let readers quickly locate information. Subheads can be set apart from text by using various techniques. For example, they can be placed inside or next to the text. Subheads should always be closely associated with the text they introduce. There should be more space above the subhead than below it to link it with the text. Subheads should contrast with the body copy.

Subheads should always be closely associated with the text they introduce. Leave more space above the subhead than below it to link it with the text.

Subheads should be visually linked with the text they introduce.

Subheads clue readers into the content organization within an article. Subheads break text into manageable segments, improve the appearance of a page and enhance readership by providing a transition between headlines and text.

Subhead Linked to Text Mystery

Subheads can be set apart from text by using various techniques. For example, they can be placed inside or next to the text. Subheads should always be closely associ-

Subheads clue readers into the content organization within an article. Subheads break text into manageable segments, improve the appearance of a page and enhance readership by providing a transition between headlines and text.

Subhead Linked to Text Mystery

Subheads can be set apart from text by using various techniques. For example, they can be placed inside or next to the text. Subheads should always be closely associ-

Incorrect   Correct

Like headlines, subheads tend to stand out when set in a larger type size and a different typeface than the text.

Subheads clue readers into the content organization within an article. Subheads break text into manageable segments, improve the appearance of a page and enhance readership by providing a transition between headlines and text.

Missing Contrast Is Suspected

Subheads can be set apart from text by using various techniques. For example, they can be placed inside or next to the text. Subheads should always be closely associated with the text they introduce. There should contrast between the subhead

Subheads clue readers into the content organization within an article. Subheads break text into manageable segments, improve the appearance of a page and enhance readership by providing a transition between headlines and text.

Correct Contrast Has Been Located

Subheads can be set apart from text by using various techniques. For example, they can be placed inside or next to the text. Subheads should always be closely associated with the text they introduce. There

Subheads tend to stand out when set in a different type than the text.

Subheads can be set centered, flush-left or flush-right.

Subheads clue readers into the content organization within an article. Subheads break text into manageable segments, improve the appearance of a page and enhance readership by providing a transition between headlines and text.

Subheads Offer Great Variety

Subheads can be set apart from text by using various techniques. For example, they can be placed inside or next to the text. Subheads

Subheads clue readers into the content organization within an article. Subheads break text into manageable segments, improve the appearance of a page and enhance readership by providing a transition between headlines and text.

Subheads Offer Great Variety

Subheads can be set apart from text by using various techniques. For example, they can be placed inside or next to the text. Subheads should always be closely associated with the

Subheads clue readers into the content organization within an article. Subheads break text into manageable segments, improve the appearance of a page and enhance readership by providing a transition between headlines and text.

Subheads Offer Great Variety

Subheads can be set apart from text by using various techniques. For example, they can be placed inside or next to the text. Subheads should always be closely associated with the

Horizontal rules above or below subheads can add emphasis.

Subheads clue readers into the content organization within an article. Subheads break text into manageable segments, improve the appearance of a page and enhance readership by providing a transition between headlines and text.

THE RULES OF SUBHEADS

Subheads can be set apart from text by using various techniques. For example, they can be placed inside or next to the text. Subheads should always be closely associated

As with other organizing tools, uniformity is important. Remember to treat subheads consistently throughout your desktop-published document.

Captions

Use captions to tie photographs and illustrations into the rest of your publication.

Studies show that headlines and captions are more likely to be read than any other part of a publication. Accordingly, use captions to summarize important points.

Captions can be placed in a variety of ways. They can be placed next to the artwork they describe or can be placed above the artwork.

Next to headlines, captions are the most widely read part of a publication.

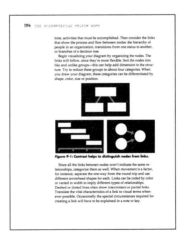

Most often, captions are placed below the artwork.

Another alternative is to place the caption inside the artwork (see page 213).

When set above or below the artwork, captions can be centered or aligned with the left- or right-hand edge of the visual.

Caption width should be in a pleasing proportion to the width of the photograph or illustration and to surrounding white space and text.

This caption is too long.

This caption is too short.

But this caption is just right.

Regardless of their position or alignment, captions should be treated the same way throughout a publication. Thus, if you align captions with the left-hand edge of photographs on Page 5, align them the same way on Page 20.

Headers & Footers

Information at the top or bottom of each page in a newsletter, book or training manual can be used to reinforce the publication's identity as well as serve as a road map to help readers locate the information they seek.

Header information at the top of a page can include publication, section title and chapter title, chapter number and page number.

Headers serve as road maps that help readers quickly locate information.

Alternately, this space can be used to summarize the content of each page, helping readers quickly locate information. Can you imagine how hard it would be to locate a specific word in a dictionary without the aid of headers?

Footers can include the same information as the header but at the bottom of a page.

Pull-Quotes & Sidebars

Pull-quotes and sidebars give your pages editorial diversity and add visual interest to your layouts.

In addition to subheads, you can add graphic interest to your page by using pull-quotes—a sentence or two extracted from the text and set in display type within the text column or in a side margin.

Pull-quotes should occupy only a few short lines, making it easy for the reader to glance at them quickly. They should be written in a concise, pithy style, to invite interest in the related text.

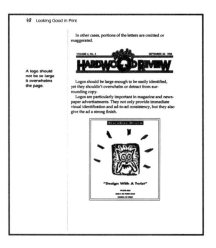

Another page element you may want to use is the sidebar—a block of copy set apart from but related to the rest of the text on a page. This is an ideal format for supplemental information, such as a biographical sketch of an individual important to a major article.

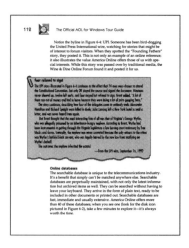

Bullet Lists

To add emphasis to a list, use bullets or icons to mark each item.

Often, you'll want to list items in a long column instead of running them in with the text. By inserting a bullet (usually a boldface dot or square) or other icon, the list takes on a new importance and invites readership. This technique is particularly effective in advertising.

Checkmarks, triangles and other symbols (known as dingbats) used for bullet lists can add a more sophisticated look to a page.

Jumplines

Use jumplines to inform readers when articles are continued from one page to another.

By continuing articles on inside pages, you can offer readers a wider variety of editorial material on the front page of your publication. As the number of articles included on Page 1 increases, so does the likelihood you'll interest the reader.

Continuing articles on other pages also allows for more flexibility in laying out a long story that won't fit on a page. The jumpline eliminates any confusion readers may have about where to read next.

Jumplines elimi-nate confusion about where to read next.

Nameplates & Logos

Establish the identity of your publication with a distinctive and prominent nameplate.

A nameplate is a distinctive type treatment of your publication's title. As the first item on the first page, it should be prominent enough to immediately establish a lasting visual identity and should remain the same from issue to issue.

Although large and recognizable at a glance, a nameplate should not overshadow the headlines on a page.

Use your firm's logo as a "signature" on your document.

A logo is a graphic symbol that relates to your firm's type of business.

A logo reflects the nature and philosophy of a business.

It also can reflect your firm's philosophy.

Often, the letter-spacing has been specially modified to create a distinct effect called *logo type*.

Sometimes the letters touch or overlap.

In other cases, portions of the letters are omitted or exaggerated.

A logo should not be so large it overwhelms the page.

Logos should be large enough to be easily identified, yet they shouldn't overwhelm or detract from surrounding copy.

Logos are particularly important in magazine and newspaper advertisements. They not only provide immediate visual identification and ad-to-ad consistency, but they also give the ad a strong finish.

MOVING ON

By now you have an understanding of some of the organizing tools that form the foundation of a well-designed document. In the next two chapters, you'll learn how to manipulate text and graphics to further enhance the communicating power of your printed materials.

Chapter Three

The Architecture of Type

Typography—the design of the characters that make up text and display type (headlines, subheads, captions, etc.) and the way they're configured on the page—influences the appearance of your print communications more than any other single visual element.

The typeface you choose sends an important message *about* your message. It conveys mood, communicates attitude. Therefore, type choices can help, or hinder, your readers' ability to understand your message.

However, many other factors must be considered in choosing type: column alignment, column width and spacing. These decisions rank right along side determining type family, size, style and weight.

In addition, your desktop publishing system may give you such options as rotating or distorting type, as well as wrapping type around visuals and composing it to fit the available space.

Establishing a grid for your document is the first step in creating a page layout; developing the typographic treatment follows closely behind.

The type you choose can help or hinder readability.

TYPEFACE

Choose a typeface that "speaks" to your readers in the tone most appropriate to your publication.

Typeface refers to the design of letters, numbers and other characters. Thousands are available, each representing its designer's unique approach to clarity and expressiveness.

Each typeface influences the tone of a publication. For example, some are authoritative (Kabel Bold):

Recall Demanded

Others convey friendliness (Bookman Bold):

Sunny Weekend

Others look decorative (Vivante):

Your Dream House

Still others possess a classy look (Mona Lisa):

Symphony Performance

Typeface design generally falls into two broad categories: serif and sans-serif.

Serif Type

Serif typefaces are commonly used for text.

Serif type is categorized by small strokes at the ends of each letterform. These strokes, called serifs, serve both decorative and functional purposes: they add visual character to the

Typefaces set the tone of a document and "speak" to the reader.

letters and guide the reader's eye movement from letter to letter, helping the reader see your message in terms of words and sentences instead of as individual letters.

Typefaces with rounded serifs tend to be friendly (Letraset Rialto):

Serifs help guide readers from letter to letter.

Yard Work Made Easy

Typefaces with squared serifs look official or architectural (Square Serif):

Tax Form Enclosed

Times Roman, one of the most frequently used serif typefaces, is a resident font in most laser printers. Other frequently used serif typefaces include

New Century Schoolbook
Bookman ▪ Palatino

Sans-Serif Type

Sans-serif type is ideal for display type—headlines, subheads, pull-quotes, captions, etc.

Sans-serif type is just what the name says: type without serifs. Here's an example (Univers Bold)

No Serifs Here!

The simplicity and elegance of sans-serif typefaces make them ideal for large headlines and other display treatments.

In small doses, sans-serif type adds impact to a document.

Serif type, on the other hand, works well in smaller sizes, particularly for a text face, and can look busy and cluttered when set in large sizes for display purposes.

However, while sans-serif type in small doses can add impact to a document, it's often difficult to read in long blocks of text. Serifs help the reader recognize the shapes of the letters. Take away the serifs and there's less letter-to-letter differentiation.

Sans-serif typefaces look best when surrounded by plenty of white space, as in headlines or widely spaced lines of display type, as shown in the sidebar below.

Sans-serif type looks best when surrounded by white space.

Helvetica, the best-known sans-serif typeface, is built into most laser printers.

Other popular sans-serif typefaces include

Optima

AaBbCcDdEeFfGgHhIiJjKkLlMm
NnOoPpQqRrSsTtUuVvWwXx
YyZz 0123456789

Futura

AaBbCcDdEeFfGgHhIiJjKkLlMm
NnOoPpQqRrSsTtUuVvWwXx
YyZz 0123456789

Gill Sans

AaBbCcDdEeFfGgHhIiJjKkLlMmNn
OoPpQqRrSsTtUuVvWwXxYyZz
0123456789

Because they contain enough letter-to-letter differences to enhance legibility, Frutiger and Stone Sans—two contemporary sans-serif typefaces—can safely be used for text (if line spacing is increased). Both can add a fresh look to your publication.

Frutiger

"Home is a place where, when you have to go there, they have to take you in."
Robert Frost

Stone Sans

"Home is a place where, when you have to go there, they have to take you in."
Robert Frost

Decorative & Script Fonts

Choose decorative or script typefaces for situations in which type is more ornamental—and mood evoking—than informative.

Decorative and script fonts work well for some advertisements, invitations, menus and posters. These fonts are also ideal for creating logos and other applications in which style and emotional response are more important than the reader's ability to easily decipher each letter.

Revue

The year in Revue.

Dom Casual

Clothes for comfort - Dom Casual.

Beesknees

GETTING DOWN TO BEESKNEES.

Harlow Solid

Hardy Salad or Harlow Solid?

Script fonts can offer an atmosphere of either elegance or informality. Often, the letters are connected, echoing the appearance of caligraphy or more basic handwriting.

Script fonts can offer a tone of elegance or informality.

Mistral

The Mistral sang sweetly.

Palette

Color your life with Palette.

Although you wouldn't want to read long blocks of text set in a decorative typeface, when used appropriately these fonts can draw attention and provide a pleasing contrast to more conventional serif or sans-serif type.

Dingbats

Use asterisks, bullets and other dingbats, or symbols, for visual punctuation and interest.

Dingbats—decorative marks such as bullets, check marks and square boxes—can be used to embellish page design or call attention to items in a list in which all items are equally important.

Consider the following cool-season bloomers for your autumn garden:
- ✿ Chrysanthemum
- ✿ Flowering Kale
- ✿ Asters

If you plant seeds in late summer, your flowers will bloom continuously until the first frost.

Dingbats can be used for end signs, symbols that indicate the ends of articles.

Dingbats can be used to embellish page design.

> People are created equal, that they are endowed by their Creator with certain unalienable rights, that among these are Life, Liberty, and the Pursuit of Happiness. ☙
>
> ## Women in Multimedia
>
> That to secure these rights, governments are instituted among Men and Women. We hold these truths to be self-evident, that all People are created equal, that they are

Symbols can further reinforce publication identity: for example, a gavel for a newsletter distributed to judges or a small airplane for an aviation pamphlet.

> The seminar will consider ideas and methods for increasing safety levels in the aviation environment, such as
>
> ✈ Structures
> ✈ Performance
> ✈ Power Plants
> ✈ Navigation
> ✈ Airports

Other typefaces are available for engineering, mathematical, architectural and other technical applications. These faces include specialized symbols and fractions.

Enviro

ABCDEFGHIJKLMNOPQRSTUV
WXYZ 0123456789

Universal News & Greek Pi

AαBβΨψΔδEεΦφΓγHηIιΞξKκΛλMμ
NνOoΠπΘϑPρΣσTτΘθΩωϬφXχ
YυZζ "+−×÷=±∓°′

Composers can even choose typefaces that create musical notes! Some software programs allow you to create your own custom equations and symbols.

TYPE STYLE

Type style refers to the variations in weight and stroke that lend contrast or emphasis to each typeface.

On most desktop publishing systems, style options include bold, italic, bold italic and small capitals.

Bold • *Italic* • ***Bold Italic*** • SMALL CAPS

Shadow, outline and underline styles are also offered as styles for some typefaces, but should be used with restraint since they are more difficult to read.

GHOST STORIES ARE <u>SCARY</u>

Characters set in boldface type have thicker strokes and add authority or emphasis to a typeface. Bold type is also frequently used for subheads that break up long expanses of text.

Type styles lend contrast or emphasis to a particular typeface.

Lend Contrast to Your Publication

Sans-serif type is, literally, what the name says: type without serifs. The simplicity and elegance of many sans-serif typefaces make them ideal for large headlines and other display treatments.

Serif type, on the other hand, works well in smaller sizes, particularly for a text face, and can look busy and cluttered when set in large sizes for display purposes. For this reason, you rarely encounter serif type on road signs.

Add Authority to Your Page
However, while sans-serif type in small doses can add impact to documents, it's often difficult to read in long blocks of text. Serifs help the reader recognize the shapes of the letters. Take away the serifs and there's less letter-to-letter differentiation.

Sans-serif typefaces look best when surrounded by plenty of white space, as in headlines or widely spaced lines of text.

Sans-serif type is, literally, what the name says: type without serifs. The simplicity and elegance of many sans-serif typefaces make them ideal for large headlines and other display treatments.

Break Up Long Blocks of Text
Serif type, on the other hand, works well in smaller sizes, particularly for a text face, and can look busy and cluttered when set in large sizes for display purposes. For this reason, you rarely encounter serif type on road signs.

However, while sans-serif type in small doses can add impact to documents, it's often difficult to read in long blocks of text. Serifs help the reader recognize the shapes of the letters. Take away the serifs and

there's less letter-to-letter differentiation.

Use Boldface Type Carefully
Sans-serif typefaces look best when surrounded by plenty of white space, as in headlines or widely spaced lines of text.

Serif type, on the other hand, works well in smaller sizes, particularly for a text face, and can look busy and cluttered when set in large sizes for display purposes. For this reason, you rarely encounter serif type on road signs.

However, while sans-serif type in small doses can add impact to documents, it's often difficult to read in long blocks of text. Serifs help the reader recognize the shapes of the letters. Take away the serifs and there is less letter-to-letter differentiation.

Boldface type must be used carefully and sparingly. A lot of boldface type darkens a page, making it look too dense and uninviting.

A lot of bold type can darken a page.

Bold Not Always Better

Characters set in boldface type have thicker strokes and add authority or emphasis to a typeface. Bold type is frequently used for subheads that break up long expanses of text.

Close-Up of Typefaces
Boldface type must be used carefully. In small sizes, the counters- enclosed spaces within letters like e and o – often become filled in on laser printed output. A lot of boldface type also darkens a page.

Setting isolated words in boldface type in the middle of a block of text can draw more attention to a word than it warrants and can also create a "checkerboard" appearance on the page. Characters set in boldface type have thicker strokes and add authority or emphasis to a typeface. Bold type is frequently used for.

Letters Move In
Setting isolated words in boldface type in the middle of a block of text can draw more attention to a word than it warrants and can also create a "checkerboard" appearance on the page.

Characters set in boldface type have thicker strokes and add authority or emphasis to a typeface. Bold type is frequently used for subheads that break up long expanses of text.

Boldface type must be used carefully. In small sizes, the counters - enclosed spaces within letters like e and o - often become filled in on laser printed output. A lot of boldface type also darkens a page.

Setting isolated words in boldface type in the middle of a block of text can draw more attention to a word than it warrants and can also create a "checkerboard" appearance on the page. Characters set in boldface type

have thicker strokes and add authority or emphasis to a typeface. Bold type is frequently used for subheads that break up long expanses of text. Boldface type must be used carefully. In small sizes, the counters often fill in on laser printed output. Characters set in boldface type have thicker strokes and add authority or emphasis to a typeface. Bold type is frequently used for subheads that break up long expanses of text.

Boldface type must be used carefully. In small sizes, the counters - enclosed spaces within letters like e and o - often become filled in on laser printed output. A lot of boldface type also darkens a page.

Setting isolated words in boldface type in the middle of a block of text can draw more attention to a word than it warrants and can also create a "checkerboard" appearance on the page.

Also, be careful when setting isolated words in boldface type in the middle of a block of text. The bold type can draw more attention to a word than it warrants and create a "checkerboard" look to the page.

Type style refers to the modifications that lend *contrast* or emphasis to each typeface. On most desktop publishing systems, *style options* include bold, italic, bold-italic and small capitals. Shadow, outline and underline styles are also offered.

Use *italic* for emphasis or when irony or humor is intended. It can also imply a conversational *tone* or indicate a quote. It's often used to set *captions.* Use ***bold italic*** to make a point really stand out.

Italics can be used to imply a conversational tone.

Use italic type for emphasis or when irony or humor is intended. It can also imply a conversational tone or indicate a quote. It's often used to set captions.

He was not one hour late, he was *three hours* late.

Use bold italic to make a point really stand out.

And he forgot it was their ***anniversary!***

Small caps are approximately 20 percent smaller than regular uppercase type. Small caps let you emphasize words without darkening the page with boldface or drawing attention with large caps.

REGULAR CAPS vs. SMALL CAPS

You can use large and small caps together to indicate sentence beginnings and or abbreviations.

KEEP OUT is not a message most of us like to hear. We are by nature, creatures of curiosity, and we enjoy exploring the unknown.

Shadowed and outlined type should be used with discretion—and rarely in small sizes, since these styles can seriously hinder legibility.

LOOKS GREAT!
But, not so great in small sizes.

Likewise, underlining interferes with the reader's ability to recognize letterforms by obscuring descenders, the stems of letters such as g, j, p, q that dip below the text baseline.

Lines of emphasis can become lines of annoyance.

TYPE WEIGHT

Weight—letter width and stroke thickness—gives you further flexibility in lightening or darkening your page.

For example, in the Helvetica family, Helvetica Black has more impact than Helvetica Bold. Helvetica Black is an ideal choice for short, high-impact headlines.

BOLD WINS

Helvetica Light gives headlines a gentler look, "lightening" the page in comparison to the heavier Helvetica Black.

Lighten up and live longer.

Condensed weights offer a narrower "footprint." This increases the number of letters that can fit on a line. Helvetica Condensed, for example, preserves the essential attributes of Helvetica, but the letters are narrower. It's ideal for business forms where space is at a premium.

Combinations are also available. Helvetica Condensed, for example, is available in both Light and Black variations.

Condensed type increases the number of letters that can fit on a line.

Helvetica Condensed
Helvetica Condensed Light
Helvetica Condensed Black

These typeface variations offer you extra flexibility in giving your publication a "voice" without having to introduce entirely different typefaces.

Stress

Stress refers to variations in the thickness of the strokes that make up a letter.

Serif type tends to have more stress than sans-serif; that is, it usually contains vertical and horizontal strokes of varying thickness.

Times Roman is characterized by moderate amounts of stress. Notice how the vertical strokes are thicker than the horizontal strokes.

Different strokes…

Bookman, another frequently used serif typeface, has strokes of a more even thickness.

for different folks.

By contrast, most sans-serif typefaces tend to exhibit the same thickness at all points of a character (although there are some notable exceptions). Univers, for example, lacks stress.

Stress-free strokes.

TYPE SIZE

Type size should be proportionate to both the importance of the message and its surroundings.

When choosing type size, consider the amount of white space available. In selecting a type size for text, consider the width of the column and the number of columns

Serif type tends to have more stress than sans-serif faces.

(see "Columns" in Chapter 2, "Tools of Organization," for a review). The best measure for setting text type size is achieving a comfort level that makes the material easy and inviting to read.

For display type size, bear in mind that small type adrift in a sea of white space appears to be lost.

> Where am I?

Type size should be proportionate to the importance of the message.

Conversely, large type squeezed into a small area is hard to read and is visually disturbing and claustrophobic.

> # Over Here, Taking Up All Available Space

Strive for the balance that calls attention to the message by both having the appropriate type size and giving it sufficient breathing room.

> ## Type that looks and feels good.

Type is measured in points (72 points to the inch). Most desktop programs let you adjust type size in half-points.

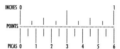

X-Height

Alphabets set in different typefaces in the same type size can vary widely in apparent size and in line length.

Consider these two typefaces. Both are set in 18-point type. One looks significantly larger than the other. In addition, its lowercase alphabet occupies far more space than the other.

Now may be the time.
Now may be the time.

Classical Sans in the top example has a larger x-height—the height of lowercase letters that don't have ascenders (for example, a, o, e and, of course, x).

You can manipulate type to create special effects.

low x-height   high x-height

X-height plays a major role in the density, or grayness, of pages containing a lot of text. Alphabets with a low x-height increase word density while preserving "lightness," because of the extra white space between the top of the ascender and the main body of the letter.

> Keep out is not a message most of us like to hear. We are by nature, creatures of curiosity, and we enjoy exploring the unknown.
>
> Keep out is not a message most of us like to hear. We are by nature, creatures of curiosity, and we enjoy exploring the unknown.

This is why you often want to increase leading between lines of type with high x-heights.

On the other hand, typefaces with a large x-height may enhance legibility, enabling you to use a smaller type size.

ALIGNMENT

Lines of type can be set justified (flush-left/flush-right); flush-left with a ragged-right margin; flush-right with a ragged-left margin; or centered.

The type of alignment you choose influences the "color" and tone of your publication, as well as the cost. Readability studies tend to favor flush-left/ragged-right alignment, meaning the first letters of each line are lined up with each other, but the lines themselves are of irregular length. The irregular line endings create a ragged margin of white space, giving publications a lighter look. In addition, the even word spacing enables readers to easily recognize word groups.

Flush-left/ragged-right alignment provides an "open," informal feeling.

Flush-left/ragged-right type gives a publication an informal, contemporary, "open" feeling. The space between each word is the same. Flush-left/ragged-right lines generally end where words end. Only long words that fall at the end of lines are hyphenated.

> "This country, with its institutions, belongs to the people who inhabit it. Whenever they shall grow weary of the existing government, they can exercise their constitutional right of amending it, or their constitutional right to dismember or overthrow it."
>
> *Abraham Lincoln*

Justified type produces lines of equal length. Type is aligned on both left and right margins. Word spacing is adjusted automatically to create the even line endings.

Because of the uniform line length, justified columns lack the white space created with ragged alignment, and thus tend to "darken" a publication. In addition, justified type is sometimes considered more difficult to read because more words are hyphenated and large gaps can develop between words.

Nevertheless, many magazines, newspapers and books use justified alignment because the word density is higher. As a result, less space is needed to communicate the same amount of information, which can reduce the number of pages in a document and result in cost-savings.

Justified columns of type can "darken" a page.

> "This country, with its institutions, belongs to the people who inhabit it. Whenever they shall grow weary of the existing government, they can exercise their constitutional right of amending it, or their constitutional right to dismember or overthrow it."
>
> *Abraham Lincoln*

For display type, centering is another alignment scheme that's particularly useful for short headlines that span more than one column of type. Centering text lends a formal tone to a document; it's frequently used for wedding invitations and official announcements.

Centering lends a formal tone to a document.

> *William and Mary*
> *invite you to join them*
> *in the celebration of their marriage.*
>
> *Saturday, April 12, 1992*
>
> *The Harcourt Gardens*

However, avoid centering long blocks of type, even for a three- or four-line headline. Because readers have to search for the beginning of each line, centered type is more difficult to read.

> **The Secret to the Chef's New Masterpiece may be Licorice— a love-it-or-leave it flavor.**

Type also can be set flush-right/ragged-left. But, like centered type, flush-right alignment forces the reader to slow down to find the beginning of the next line, and therefore should be used with discretion.

> **The Secret to the Chef's New Masterpiece may be Licorice—a love-it-or-leave it flavor.**

Setting short headlines flush-right is a way to lock them to text-heavy columns.

KERNING, TRACKING & LETTER-SPACING

Kerning is the adjustment of space between selected pairs of letters. Tracking automatically governs the amount of space placed between each character throughout a block of text. Letter-spacing can be used for special effects.

Adjusting space between letters often improves readability.

Certain pairs of letters sometimes appear to be separated by too much space. This effect is particularly apparent in a headline with an uppercase T next to a lowercase o, or an uppercase W next to a lowercase a, etc.

| WA | | Want |
| WA | | Want |

| Tonight | | any. |
| Tonight | | any. |

Kerning reduces the space between individual pairs of letters to improve readability. It can also be used to add space between certain letter pairs. This is often done to improve legibility when setting white type against a black background.

Most desktop publishing systems have a default tracking that determines the amount of space between each character. However, tracking can be adjusted.

By tightening tracking, you increase the density of your text, fitting more words into the same amount of space. This tends to "darken" a publication.

> **Usually, if you've set reasonable parameters for justification in your program, the very worst offenders in hyphenation will be lines with bad breaks, caused by long single-syllable words or words with**

Conversely, loose tracking lightens a page.

> **Usually, if you've set reason-able parameters for justifica-tion in your program, the very worst offenders in hy-phenation will be lines with bad breaks, caused by long**

Letter-spacing can transform a word into a graphic element.

Letter-spacing, or stretching a word across a space (such as the top of a column or page) can transform that word into a graphic element. Letter-spacing is often used to create department headings, identifying standard recurring features in periodicals.

WORD SPACING

The amount of space between words affects word density and the readability of a publication.

When word spacing is tight, more words can be included on each line. In certain situations, this reduces the number of hyphenated—or split—words.

> Licorice may be a love-it-or-leave-it flavor, like sarsaparilla or horehound, and an acquired taste, like turnips, caviar or single-malt Scotch, but to those who know it well, it is a convection with a Proustian pull and a complexity that invites connoisseurship.

> Licorice may be a love-it-or-leave-it flavor, like sarsaparilla or horehound, and an ac-quired taste, like turnips, caviar or single-malt Scotch, but to those who know it well, it is a convection with a Proustian pull and a complexity that invites connoisseurship.

Word spacing and tracking are often adjusted simulta-neously.

However, word spacing should be adjusted with care. If you reduce word spacing too much, the text becomes difficult to read and the publication looks too dark.

Tracking and word spacing are often adjusted simultaneously. One common technique, especially with high-x-height typefaces (see page 66), is to slightly reduce letter spacing and increase word spacing.

When experimenting with tracking and word spacing, be sure to review proofs before deadline time to ensure you've achieved the right balance.

PARAGRAPH SPACING, TABS & INDENTS

Use tabs, indents or extra space between paragraphs to enhance readability. Tabs and indents also can be used to effectively set off lists and quotations.

Be sure to make spacing at the beginning of paragraphs consistent in your documents. Generally, two types of spacing schemes are used: a two- to five-space indent at the beginning of the first line of each paragraph or extra spacing between paragraphs, with the first line being set flush-left.

Adding space between paragraphs makes each paragraph appear more like a self-contained unit. It also adds an openness to a publication by breaking up the "grayness" of large expanses of text.

Increasing paragraph spacing can add an openness to a page.

To increase paragraph spacing, always use your desktop publishing program's paragraph-spacing command, rather than using two carriage returns, which can result in far too much space between paragraphs. The paragraph-spacing command lets you add just enough white space between paragraphs to add interest without creating a page filled with distracting parallel bands of white space.

also adds an openess to a publication by breaking up the "grayness" of large expanses of text.

To increase spacing between paragraphs, always use your desktop publishing program's paragraph-spacing command, rather than using two carriage returns, which can result in too much space between paragraphs.

The paragraph-spacing command lets you add just enough white space between paragraphs to add interest without creating a page filled with distracting parallel bands of white space.

Extra space between paragraphs enhances readability. Adding additional space between paragraphs makes each paragraph appear

also adds an openess to a publication by breaking up the "grayness" of large expanses of text.

To increase spacing between paragraphs, always use your desktop publishing program's paragraph-spacing command, rather than using two carriage returns, which can result in too much space between paragraphs.

The paragraph-spacing command lets you add just enough white space between paragraphs to add interest without creating a page filled with distracting parallel bands of white space.

Extra space between paragraphs enhances readability. Adding additional space between paragraphs makes each paragraph appear more like a self-contained unit. It

Tabs can be used in conjunction with extra space between paragraphs to further "open up" a publication.

Indention can be used to draw attention to quotations.

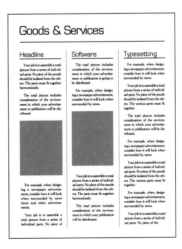

Indents can be used to call attention to quotations in a publication by moving a text block in from the left- and right-hand margins. Indents also can set a list off from the body copy.

According to Dr. Ignatz P. Daley, of the Virtual Reality Institue in Racida, CA, virtual reality is only beginning to come into its own.

"The future remains to be seen through the eyes of virtual reality."

Daley says the Institute, renowned as one of the world's foremost VR research centers, has been struggling with the issue of how to bring virtual reality to the mass market at reasonable

LINE SPACING

Adjust leading—the space between lines of type—to improve the appearance and readability of your publication.

Leading is the space above and below a line of type. It's a critical factor in determining legibility. Leading, like type size, is measured in points (72 points equal one inch).

The default (or automatic) line spacing found on most desktop publishing systems is approximately 20 percent greater than the type size being used. Thus, the default leading for 10-point type is 12 points.

The spacing between lines affects overall legibility.

Headlines often improve in appearance and readability when leading is reduced between lines. Tighter leading integrates the words into a distinct visual unit instead of a series of seemingly unrelated lines.

Latest Business Research Provides Explanation for Increase in Log Home Sales

The most recent issue of *Log Home Digest* published a survey which indicated that more people are buying log homes because "they like the way they look." Industry sources say a drop in log

Latest Business Research Provides Explanation for Increase in Log Home Sales

The most recent issue of *Log Home Digest* published a survey which indicated that more people are buying log homes because "they like the way they look." Industry sources say a drop in log prices may also be contributing to the trend.

On the other hand, extra leading often improves the appearance of text. It opens up the page, making it seem less "gray."

Extra leading is usually called for when sans-serif type-faces (see page 53) are used for text.

People are created equal, that they are endowed by their Creator with certain unalienable rights, that among these are Life, Liberty, and the Pursuit of Happiness. ❧

Women in Multimedia

That to secure these rights, governments are instituted among Men and Women. We hold these truths to be self-evident, that all People are created equal, that they are

People are created equal, that they are endowed by their Creator with certain unalienable rights, that among these are Life, Liberty, and the Pursuit of Happiness. ❧

Women in Multimedia

That to secure these rights, governments are instituted among Men and Women. We hold these truths to be self-evident, that all People are created equal, that they are

Be careful to avoid leading so generous that readers get lost when their eyes leave the end of one line and try to find the beginning of the next line.

Leading should be proportionate to line length. In general, use minimal leading for short lines of type. Increase leading as line length increases.

Extra leading can make a page look less "gray."

Leading also can be used as a design tool for special effects. You may sometimes want to tighten leading so that descenders (letter stems such as g and p that drop below the invisible line text rests on) from one line of type touch the ascenders (rising stems of letters such as b and d) from the line below. That lets you create special effects, particularly in designing logos and nameplates.

One of the advantages of using uppercase letters for headlines is that you can substantially reduce leading, since capitals lack descenders.

Happy Birthday | HAPPY BIRTHDAY
to all employees | TO ALL EMPLOYEES

SPECIAL TYPE EFFECTS

Computers offer limitless ways to transform type into a special graphic element.

Special type effects should never make your message unreadable.

Desktop publishing has liberated designers' imaginations letting them fulfill their most inspired visions of how type can be shaped, altered and manipulated. As tempting as a creative type treatment may be, there should always be a reason for it. Legibility is paramount—if your type can't be read, your message isn't getting across.

Reversing & Screening Type

By reversing and screening type, you can achieve the effect of color without the expense.

Two simple type effects can be easily achieved by reversing type out of a black background or screening it in a lighter shade of gray (or color).

Using these techniques, you can add enough visual contrast to your pages to achieve a "color" effect with only black ink and white paper.

When screening type against a background, be sure to create sufficient contrast to ensure that your type is clearly legible.

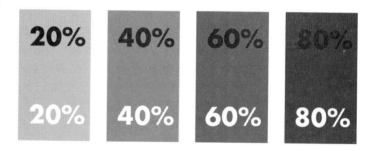

Use white type against dark-gray backgrounds and black type against light-gray backgrounds; otherwise the type may be obscured.

You can also screen type you want to highlight or draw attention to, such as in sidebars or logos.

Draw attention to type in headlines and subheads by using screens.

When using screens, always consider the limitations of your output device. The average 300 dpi laser printer produces a coarse, grainy screen. If possible, send desktop publishing files that contain screens to a service bureau to be output on a high-resolution imagesetter. The results will be much smoother and more professional looking.

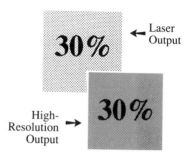

Similar to screened type, reversed type is usually white (or zero percent black) letters reversed out of a solid (or 100 percent black) background. Reversing type is a great way to draw attention to headlines, subheads and other important display copy.

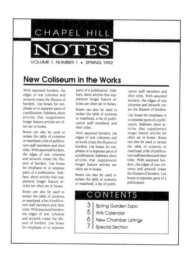

Reversing works best with single words or small phrases set at large size—lots of small reversed copy can be difficult to read.

Tons of Fun!

We hold these truths to be self-evident, that all People are created equal, that they

Use bold, sans-serif type for the most legible reverses.

It's also best to use clean, bold, sans-serif typefaces when reversing type. Serif type, particularly ornate scripts, tend to break up when reversed.

More effects can be achieved through screening and reversing colored type. For more details, see Chapter 7, "Working With Color."

Stretching & Compressing Type

Most programs give you the capability to stretch or compress type.

Most basic desktop publishing and graphics software packages let you stretch or compress individual letters, words and sentences to create interesting designs.

Distorted type is an option for words that are "recognized" instead of "read."

STRETCH   COMPRESS

As with other special effects, stretch or compress type with caution. Too much of it can overwhelm a document.

Rotating Type

Type can be rotated to run at an angle on the page.

Most desktop publishing software offers some degree of type rotation capabilities. For example, a program may allow rotation in 45- and 90-degree increments, which will come in handy for setting photo credits or copyright notices.

Use rotated type sparingly for maximum effect.

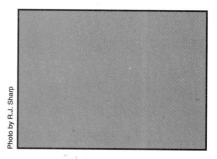

Photo by R.J. Sharp

Other programs let you rotate type in nearly any fraction of a degree across all 365 degrees. You can achieve some interesting effects with this feature.

Rotating type can be used effectively for attention-getting display type.

Setting Type Along a Path

Forcing type to follow a path offers several design options.

By flowing type along a path, whether it's a geometric shape (circular or diamond path) or a custom-drawn line, you can realize results that take traditional typesetters hours of tedious work to achieve. This technique works well when combined with simple graphics to create illustrations and logos that draw and hold the reader's interest.

Filling Type

Filling letters can change their tone, shape and impact.

Another eye-popping effect involves filling letters with a pattern or image. It's best to limit this to easily recognized words; complex messages are not legible under this treatment. You should also use bold, sans-serif faces for optimum impact.

When filling letters, use words that are easily recognized.

Other Effects

You can achieve a variety of special type effects with most desktop publishing programs.

You can apply dozens of other custom treatments to type, depending on the software you're using.

As enticing as these effects can be, remember to rely on them only when they are appropriate to the subject at hand. Never let special effects stand between your message and the reader—legibility is more important than novelty and design for the sake of design. But when used carefully, these typographic enhancements can create compelling graphics.

TYPOGRAPHIC REFINEMENTS

Attractive desktop-published documents rely on typographic consistency and restraint.

The keys to effective typography are based on consistency, restraint and attention to detail. When choosing typefaces for a project, keep in mind that each font sets a tone, sends a message. Mixing fonts should be done with care.

In general, avoid using more than two typefaces on a page—three if you include a symbol typeface for lists and end signs. Many great-looking documents are based on a single sans-serif typeface for heads and subheads with a second serif typeface for text and captions.

Refining Punctuation

Replace "typewritten" characters with "typeset" punctuation whenever possible.

For example, replace two hyphens with a single long dash called an em dash.

```
"I am in earnest -- I will not
equivocate -- I will not excuse --
I will not retreat a single inch --
and I will be heard!"
          Salutatory Address of
               The Liberator
```

"I am in earnest—I will not equivocate—I will not excuse—I will not retreat a single inch—and I will be heard!"
Salutatory Address of
The Liberator

You also may want to replace a single hyphen—used for compound words—with an en dash, which is slightly longer than a hyphen.

Effective typography is based on restraint and consistency.

Also, be sure to use "open" and "close" quotation marks instead of vertical ones. Some programs automatically make the substitution; others rely on you to do it.

MOVING ON

Typography is a time-honored craft and an important one for every desktop publisher to learn.

By taking advantage of the wide variety of typeface alternatives available on desktop publishing systems and using the full range of spacing controls at your disposal, you can avoid a "desktop-published" look, and more closely approximate the work of traditional typesetters.

Strive to approximate the look of traditional typesetting.

In the next chapter, we'll explore some of the most important graphic tools essential to successfully executed typography and overall design.

Chapter Four

Building Blocks of Graphic Design

The building blocks of graphic design add interest and color to your document, thereby enhancing its power to communicate.

Adding rules (solid or screened lines) to a layout or framing a message in enough white space to draw readers' attention can separate great design from the ho-hum. However, these tools must be used with restraint. Otherwise, the exceptional becomes the norm, making it difficult to separate the important from the unimportant.

WHITE SPACE

White space provides a resting point for readers' eyes.

White space—or blank space free of text or artwork—is one of the most undervalued tools of graphic design.

White space provides contrast, as well as a resting point for readers' eyes, as they begin moving through the publication. White space can take many forms:

A The open area surrounding a headline. The attention-getting power of a headline may be enhanced more by extra white space around it than by larger type.

B The page margins of an advertisement or publication. Wide margins direct the readers' attention into the center of the page.

C The vertical space between columns of type. The wider the columns, the more space needed between them.

D The space created by ragged line endings of unjustified type. This space relieves the monotony of large expanses of evenly measured text.

E Paragraph indents and extra line space between paragraphs. These small but effective increments of space can open up a page layout.

F Leading between lines of type. Tightly packed lines of type "darken" a publication page.

Note that "white space" doesn't have to be white. If your publication is printed on colored paper stock (e.g., ivory or tan), white space lets more of the background color appear.

White space is one of the most undervalued tools of graphic design.

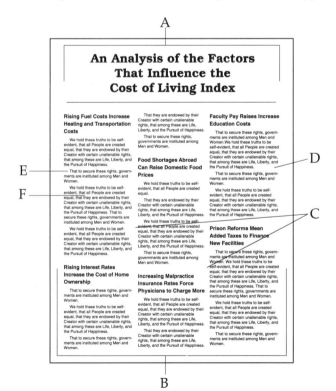

Sinks

One of the easiest ways to enliven your publication is to include a sink—a band of white space, also called a "drop"—at the top of each page.

This white space draws attention to the text below by adding contrast. It can also dramatize headlines.

A sink calls attention to the text below.

You can place photographs to slightly extend into the sink, rather than align with the top text margin.

A consistent sink provides important page-to-page continuity throughout your publication. Notice how publication unity is destroyed when the text begins at a different level on each page.

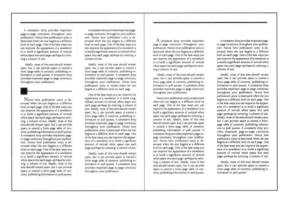

Vertical White Space

One of the best ways you can improve the appearance of a newsletter is to build a significant amount of vertical white space into each page—perhaps by omitting a column of text.

Ideally, most of this area should remain open, but it can provide space to extend a front-page table of contents, publishing information or pull-quotes.

Vertical white space can open up a page.

RULES

Rules are lines that can be used to emphasize or frame various page elements (headlines, pull-quotes, headers, etc.) or to separate items or parts of a publication from one another.

Rules can be horizontal or vertical, thick or thin.

Use rules to organize text and emphasize subheads.

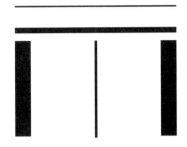

Vertical rules, called downrules, are often used to separate columns, particularly when type isn't justified.

Horizontal rules can be used to separate topics within a column or to draw attention to subheads.

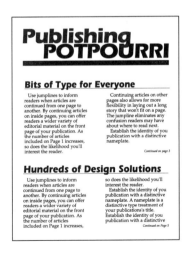

Horizontal rules often are used to draw attention to "pull-quotes" (short sentences or phrases that summarize the key points of an article).

Choose rules that harmonize with the "color" of your document.

Choose rules that harmonize with the "color" of your document. Thick rules "darken" a document and are most effective when set off by white space.

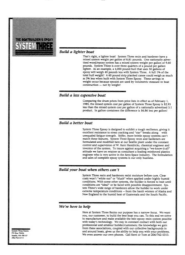

Thin rules are often appropriate for documents with a lot of copy.

Thick rules are most effective when set off by white space.

Another useful technique is to use rules similar in width to the thickness of the strokes of the letterforms used in a newsletter nameplate or an ad headline. This can add an interesting graphic element to the type treatment.

BORDERS

Use borders to frame and draw attention to the "live area"—the space in which text, display type and artwork appear.

Borders work with white space to determine publication "color" and "tone." Borders can be tangible or assumed. Tangible borders are rules or graphics that outline a document. Assumed borders aren't visible but are created subconsciously as the reader encounters the edge of the live area of a document.

The basic tangible border is a large frame surrounding the contents of a page. With most desktop publishing programs, it's easy to create one by using the box-drawing tool. Either single or double lines, thick or thin, can be used.

All four borders don't have to be the same, however. Different styles of rules can be used for the vertical or horizontal sides.

Borders can frame the "live area" of a page.

Thick borders can be created by using the box-drawing tool and filling the frames with solid (100 percent) black or shades of gray (see pages 101-102).

Assumed borders are created in the mind's eye.

Borders don't have to extend the full height or width of a publication's "live area."

With assumed borders, the edges of text columns and artwork create the illusion of borders.

BOXES

Boxes can be used to emphasize or separate parts of a publication.

Sidebars (short articles that supplement longer feature articles) are often set in boxes.

A box can distinguish a list from the other text on a page.

Boxes can also be used to isolate the table of contents or masthead (a list of publication staff members and their titles).

Boxes can be used to create reader-response coupons. Most desktop publishing programs let you create boxes with dashed borders to clearly identify the coupon.

Boxes can define the boundaries of a visual, especially important when the edges of the photograph or illustration are light-colored or indistinct. Remove the thin box from the photograph below, and the photograph looks unfinished, blending into the background.

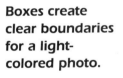
Boxes create clear boundaries for a light-colored photo.

Box borders can be as thick or thin as you like. Avoid thick boxes, however; they darken the page and tend to look like obituaries.

DROP SHADOWS

Drop shadows can draw attention to boxes or visuals.

Skillfully used, drop shadows can create attention-getting three-dimensional effects. They can help emphasize a photo or illustration by isolating it from its background.

Drop shadows can create dramatic, 3D effects.

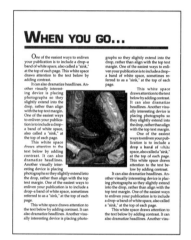

However, like all desktop publishing tools, drop shadows should be used with discretion. Because they are easily created, they tend to be overused.

SCREENS

Screening adds contrast and defines various elements of a document such as sidebars or boxes that contain important information.

Screens can make or break a page layout. Experiment with the percentage of black (or color) to find the screen that best suits your needs.

Screens add contrast, turning text into a graphic element.

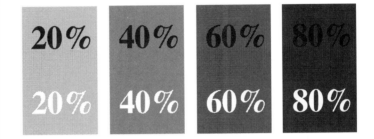

Screens can be effective in adding "color" to a page, breaking up the monotony of black and white. Adding a screened rule to an ad, for instance, breaks up the type block and makes the document more visually appealing.

Solar Soak your cares away!

Relaxing in your own backyard, we hold these truths to be self-evident, that all People are created equal, that they are endowed by their Creator with certain unalienable rights, that among these are Life, Liberty, and the Pursuit of Happiness. That

Solar Soak Hot Tubs • 1-800-U2SOLAR

Screening a sidebar or a chart sets that information apart from the rest of the text and draws attention to it.

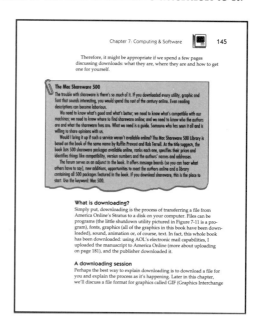

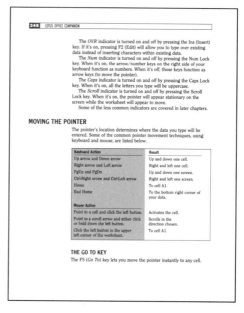

BLEEDS

A printed image that extends beyond the text margin to the edge of a page is called a bleed.

Bleeds add impact to page design by emphasizing building blocks such as text, visuals or graphics.

An oversize initial cap, or chapter number, can bleed to the top or side edges of a title page of a manual or book.

Bleeds can add emphasis to text and visuals.

A photograph can gain "motion" when it extends to the edge of a page.

A photo gains motion when it bleeds to the edge of the page.

Horizontal rules that bleed to one, or both, sides of a page can add continuity to the pages.

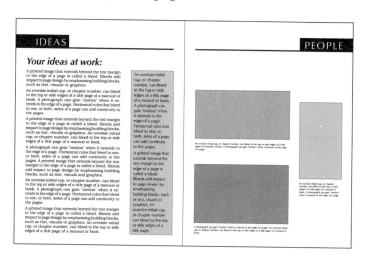

A nameplate gains impact when its background bleeds to the top of a page.

Newsletter nameplates gain impact when their backgrounds bleed to the top and/or sides of the page.

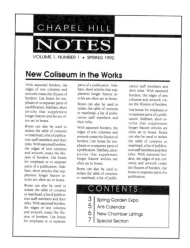

Bleeds work particularly well with two-color brochures, in which the entire front and back covers are printed in a second color, with headlines reversed out. (See Chapter 7, "Working With Color," for more.)

Check your budget and hardware resources before using bleeds. Because your commercial printer has to use an oversize sheet of paper and trim it to actual publication size after printing, bleeds increase costs. In addition, the printing area of most laser printers is approximately a quarter-inch smaller than the physical size of the paper. (High-resolution output devices do not have this limitation.) If necessary, you can print your pages at a slightly reduced size and instruct your printer to increase them.

MOVING ON

Now that you've learned the basics of layouts, type and graphic elements, let's explore the types of illustrations you can add to your documents. The next chapter addresses the importance of such visuals as illustrations, clip art, charts and graphs that can be used to emphasize and/or enhance your message.

Working With Illustrations

Visual images in a document communicate your message at a glance.

Using professional illustrations and information graphics in your documents can significantly enhance the effectiveness of your message and the overall attractiveness of your page.

Desktop publishing offers numerous features that can help you manipulate and modify your artwork to suit your page layout and overall design.

Artwork enhances the attractiveness of your page.

USING ILLUSTRATIONS EFFECTIVELY

Illustrations can make or break a layout, depending on how they're used.

Designers often fall into the trap of using illustrations when they don't really need to. It's tough to resist the temptation to add artwork to a layout to fill up a page, break up copy or generally add spice or visual appeal to a document.

But adding an inappropriate illustration—or using a graphic in a way that doesn't serve the reader—is as bad (or worse) as having no artwork at all.

Easter Parade Scheduled

Five hundred years ago, Christopher Columbus was on his knees in throne rooms throughout Europe, scrambling to finance his first voyage to the New World. Meanwhile, his Venetian countryman Aldus Manutius—scholar, printer, and entrepreneur—was establishing what would become the greatest publishing house in Europe, the Aldine Press. Like Columbus, Aldus Manutius was driven by force of of intellect and personality to realize a lifelong dream.

Aldus' greatest passion was Greek literature, which was rapidly going up in smoke in the wake of the marauding Turkish army. It seemed obvious to Aldus that the best way to preserve this literature was to publish it—literally, to make it public. The question was, how?

Although it had been forty years since the advent of Gutenberg's perss, most books were still being copied by scribes, letter by letter, a penstroke at a time. Because of the intensity of this labor, books were few and costly. They were also unwieldy. Far too large to be held in the hands or in the lap, books sat on lecterns in private libraries and were seen only by princes and the clergy.

One day, as he watched one of his workers laboring under the load of books he was carrying, Aldus had a flash of insight: Coopuld books from the Aldine Press be made small enough to be carried without pulling a muscle? And could he produce the elegant, lightweight volumes he imagined and still sell them at an attractive price?

The first problem was how to print more legible words.

Illustrations Versus Photographs

Follow your instincts when choosing between illustrations and photos.

Choosing between a photo or illustration is largely a matter of personal preference.

Designers with years of experience can (and often do) disagree over whether a particular layout calls for a photo or an illustration. Like most other aspects of graphic design, there are no hard and fast rules, and the issue usually comes down to the individual preference of the designer.

Photos are generally used to report or document an event or realistically portray an individual or group of people. Illustrations are the logical choice to evoke a particular mood or depict a complex object. While recent advances in computer imaging are blurring the line between photos and illustrations, they are treated as separate subjects in this book.

For more on selecting and using photos in your documents, see Chapter 6, "Working With Photographs." Many of the design concepts covered in that chapter hold true for working with illustrations as well as photos, but there are also a few commonsense guidelines you can follow that will help you effectively integrate your illustrations into an attractive layout:

Rules about graphic design were made to be broken.

- Don't crowd your artwork. Leave generous borders around illustrations so the eye flows to them naturally.

- Vary illustration size and shape. Running lots of illustrations at roughly the same size and shape gets boring. Be creative with the size, shape and placement of each image.

- Be consistent. Using a vastly different range of illustration styles in a document can make it seem disjointed or poorly planned.

- Less is more. It's usually the case that running fewer illustrations at a larger size yields a higher visual impact than lots of smaller ones—it also gives you more bang for your illustration buck.

Rules were made to be broken, and that's certainly true in graphic design. You can achieve specific and unique effects by following steps that might normally yield ugly pages. But in general, crowded, repetitive illustrations make for an unattractive document. For more on designing with illustrations and photographs, see Chapter 4, "Building Blocks of Graphic Design."

Illustrious Possibilities

Illustrations consist of drawings, either hand- or computer-generated.

Illustrations offer far more opportunities for interpretation than photos do. The artist can selectively organize and emphasize information. Therefore, artwork can convey accuracy and atmosphere or substitute accuracy for aesthetics.

Illustrations can place aesthetic considerations before accuracy.

For example, a draw-type program can be used to render an image of a person's hand, either literally or abstractly.

In this age of computer graphics, cutaways (line diagrams) of objects are often used in technical manuals and documents. These illustrations can show the structure of an object with more clarity than photographs of the various components of the object.

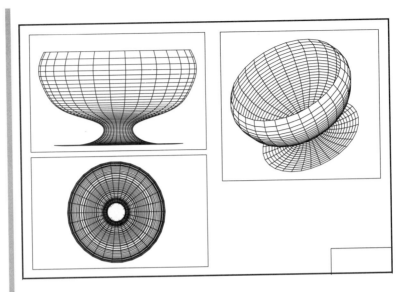

Though many graphic artists prefer to work with pen and paper, right up until the final comp, designing with computers offers a number of luxuries and capabilities simply not available to conventional designers.

READY-MADE ART

Use ready-made art to save time and to try out a number of illustrations in a page layout program before making a final choice.

Using a page layout program, you can try out any number of different illustrations on a page before making a final choice. And with the wide proliferation and low cost of electronic clip art, background textures, patterns and other forms of pre-created digital art, designers have never had more options to choose from:

- Clip art comes on both floppy disk and CD-ROM, and offers the designer nearly unlimited access to digitized art ranging from the simple to the masterful.

- Background textures and patterns are packaged much like clip art, but they are meant to be used as a backdrop for type or graphics, not as the main visual attraction.

■ Dingbat sets are fonts that contain numerous images accessible via keystrokes that would ordinarily yield letters. Instead of printing letters, these special fonts yield dingbats, bullets, icons or other pictures.

Clip Art

Use clip art to add pizazz and professionalism to ads, brochures, menus and newsletters.

Clip art consists of files of existing artwork that can be dropped into your desktop-published documents. Clip art can save you lots of time and money by letting you "brighten" your publication without having to create your own illustrations.

"Canned" art can save you the time and money involved in creating original artwork.

A variety of clip art is available in digital format (on both floppy and CD-ROM) for just about every occasion. For example, some clip-art packages are based on holiday or party themes, graduations and other special events.

Other clip-art files are available in practically any format and in any subject category you might be interested in. There are collections that reflect occupational categories or particular fields of interest. Special packages are available for financial, legal, medical and religious publications.

Maps are also a popular and useful form of clip art.

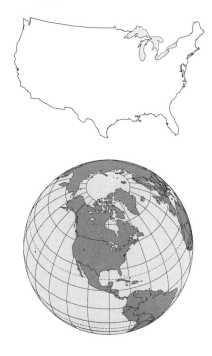

Clip art is often used for borders. There are hundreds of unique and specific clip-art border treatments.

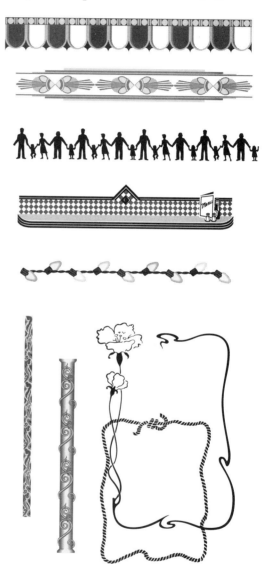

And there are tens of thousands of other clip-art files available to suit any conceivable subject or interest.

Clip art doesn't have to be used "as is." You can often disguise its origins by using some special techniques.

For example, you can use just a portion of a clip-art image, but greatly increase its size.

Another technique involves combining several clip-art images. For example, individual clip-art items can be brought together to form a dynamic visual, such as the still life superimposed on a geometric feature in the following example.

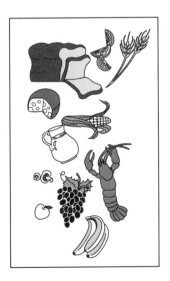

For more on manipulating clip art, see the section "Manipulating Illustrations," later in this chapter.

Background Textures & Patterns

You can achieve impressive results with patterns and textures.

Another kind of ready-made art, much like clip art but different in some important ways, has become popular among desktop designers lately. Background textures and patterns—which are either created by professional graphic artists or scanned or photographed from actual objects like marble or fabric—can be used to lend a touch of elegance or respectability to a layout.

Patterns and textures lend elegance and respectability to layouts.

Unlike clip art, background textures and patterns are used more to lend color or weight to a document, not to illustrate a particular part of the text. They are especially effective for ads, brochures, invitations and flyers. Another popular application for this kind of art is to use it as a backdrop over which text is placed.

As with clip art, you don't have to use textures or patterns as they originally appear. A little editing and manipulation goes a long way toward making commercially created artwork look like a unique graphic.

For more on editing textures and patterns, see "Manipulating Illustrations" later in this chapter.

Dingbat Sets & Picture Fonts

Image fonts are an often overlooked source of illustrations.

Although most designers don't turn to fonts when they're looking for a particular illustration, a host of companies produce dozens of non-text fonts that can be used to illustrate everything from books to flyers. Most designers are familiar with dingbat collections, such as the popular Zapf Dingbats, named after Hermann Zapf, who also created the typeface Palatino.

Dingbat sets and picture fonts make integrating text and graphics easy.

Dingbat sets are useful sources for clean, effective bullets, slugs, icons and other small pictures. And since they are actually fonts, dingbats are conveniently imbedded in lines of text, so there's no placing or importing to worry about when using page layout programs. But bullets and slugs are just the beginning. You may be able to solve many of your illustration needs using only picture fonts.

Shopping for Ready-Made Art

It's important to know what you need and can use before buying commercial graphics.

There's no shortage of sources for clip art and graphics, and each vendor offers a huge array of products. But to make sure you're buying the right graphic for the job, there are a few guidelines you should follow:

- Graphics come on floppy disk, CD-ROM and even via online services. Make sure the source medium a graphics vendor uses is compatible with your system.

- Be sure to find out how many images are included on each disk or CD—that way you can estimate how much you're paying per image.

- Graphics are saved in a number of file formats. Images saved in TIFF or EPS formats are usually compatible with any machine or platform.

- Some graphics are in a form that you can edit with a paint or draw program, while others aren't. If you plan to alter individual objects in an image, make sure your software is capable of working with it.

Check out the details before buying and using ready-made art.

MANIPULATING ILLUSTRATIONS

Illustrations can be manipulated in a number of dramatic ways.

Most page layout, paint and draw programs let you enlarge, reduce and stretch an image.

You can edit images for dramatic effects.

There are a number of special techniques (besides the simple cut-and-paste and cropping techniques discussed in the "Clip Art" section of this chapter) that you can use to manipulate or otherwise change an illustration to suit the needs of a specific layout. Many software packages allow you to edit images in a variety of dramatic ways.

Generally, computer-generated illustrations are created using either a paint program or a draw program.

Images in "paint" formats are bitmaps—a huge collection of tiny squares that make up the larger picture. Enlarging a bitmapped image causes the individual squares to become more clearly visible, yielding jagged or chunky results.

Enlarging bit-mapped graphics usually makes the image jagged or chunky.

You can't normally manipulate individual objects or single items in a bitmapped graphic, although some programs provide tools that emulate this capability. You can however, use special techniques and filters to change the appearance of the entire bitmapped graphic.

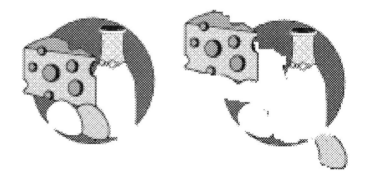

Images in "draw" formats, on the other hand, are composed of a series of lines, curves or objects that you can usually edit using a draw program. Because draw programs use equations to define the curves and lines in individual objects, the resulting images print smoothly at practically any size.

Using a draw program, you can isolate and edit specific objects in a larger image, while leaving the rest of the graphic unchanged.

Draw programs let you edit individual objects within a larger image.

The kind of effects you can create using ready-made art depend largely on the software at your disposal and the format of the image itself, but nearly every program that handles graphics will allow you to stretch, size and crop an image, regardless of its format.

INFORMATION GRAPHICS

Information graphics can inform and draw attention to trends, comparisons and organizational structures.

Information graphics combine the communicating power of charts, diagrams and tables with the aesthetic appeal of drawings. They can be created easily using clip art and your desktop publishing program's drawing tools. Or, you can create them with separate drawing programs.

Information graphics combine communication with aesthetics.

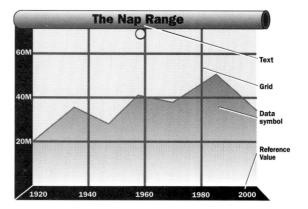

The widespread use of information graphics in publications such as *USA Today* and *Time* has shown that charts, diagrams and tables can be presented in visually exciting ways. As multicolor printing becomes easier and more affordable, you're likely to be using information graphics more and more in your publications and presentations.

You'll be surprised at the way you can assemble impressive graphics from nothing more than combinations of circles, straight lines, fill patterns (such as parallel lines or dots) and clip art.

Charts & Diagrams

Charts translate numbers and values into images.

Charts quickly communicate comparisons, relationships and trends. The first step in choosing the appropriate type of chart is to define its purpose and identify the most effective chart to present that concept to the reader or viewer.

Pie charts display part-to-whole relationships.

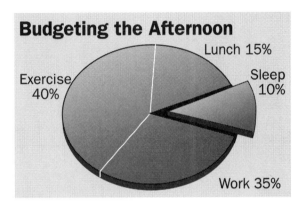

Charts quickly convey trends and comparisons.

Bar charts make comparisons.

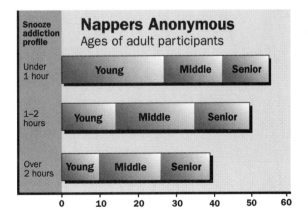

Line charts show trends.

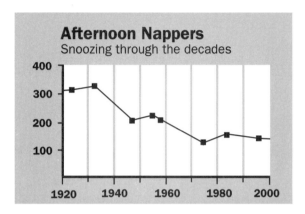

You can also combine chart types. Compound charts can show both total yearly sales and departmental contributions to the total.

Diagrams communicate relationships rather than numbers.

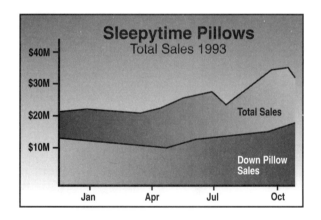

Choose diagrams rather than charts when you want to emphasize relationships and sequences, rather than numbers.

Organizational diagrams are one of the most frequently encountered types of diagrams. These display dominant/subordinate, "who reports to whom," relationships.

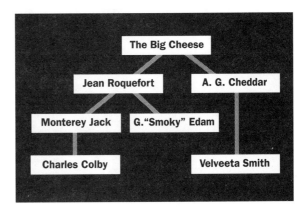

Flow, or process, diagrams are used to display sequences—what must be done first, what must be done second, and so on.

Flow diagrams display a sequence of events.

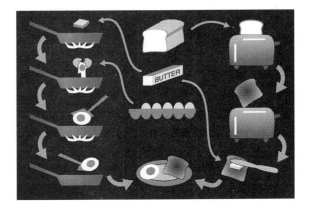

Choose a PERT—Program Evaluation Review Technique—diagram when you want to display both sequence and the length of time it will take to accomplish each step. PERT diagrams communicate both sequence and time because all elements are drawn to the same scale.

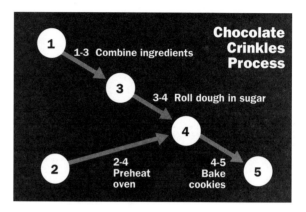

Timelines help you visually communicate historical perspectives. You can show when certain events occurred as well as how much time elapsed between them.

Timelines convey a historical perspective.

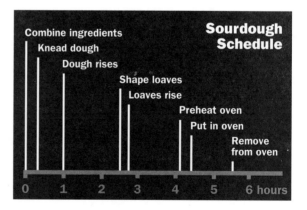

Diagrams can also be used to display spatial relationships. Floor plans, cutaway product drawings and maps are examples.

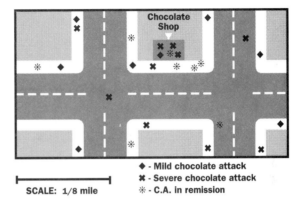

◆ - Mild chocolate attack
✖ - Severe chocolate attack
✳ - C.A. in remission

SCALE: 1/8 mile

Add impact to your diagrams by using size and color. Size can be used, for example, to indicate time, and color can be used to draw attention to critical parts. You can also enhance your drawings by "exploding" them—isolating the most important part.

Use size and color to add impact to a diagram.

"Chunky Chocolates"
The ultimate cookie

3/8 inch

Detail of Chip

0   1   2   3   4 inches

You can increase the impact and communicating power of your charts and diagrams by adding the following.

- A title that summarizes the purpose or importance of the information being displayed. This title lacks impact:

1992 Sales by Region

But this title commands more attention:

Projected 1992 Sales Increases

- Labels to indicate the exact amounts displayed in each chart segment or bar graph column.

Grids provide a frame of reference by showing numeric divisions.

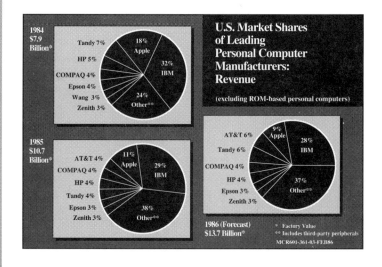

■ Background grids that provide a frame of reference by indicating the major numeric divisions.

■ Tick marks that define subdivisions.

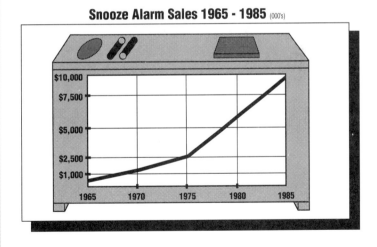

- A legend that identifies symbols, units of measure, etc., used in a chart or diagram.

- Shades, patterns and colors that complement each other. Avoid adjacent colors that "fight" or blend together.

Legends indicate symbols and units of measure.

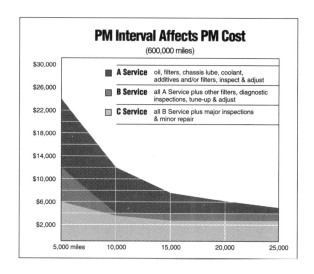

Also, keep in mind three-dimensional effects, which can draw the reader's attention to charts and diagrams.

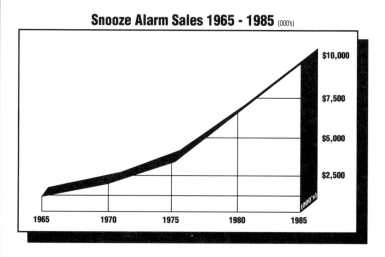

Tables

Tables present a lot of information in a concise and orderly way.

Tables are useful when you want to focus your reader's attention on the data itself rather than on representations.

Tables focus on data rather than graphic representations of it.

Preferred Morning Beverage (1,000s)				
COFFEE	**1960**	**1970**	**1980**	**1990**
Instant	540	562	580	590
Perk	453	444	420	410
Drip	622	690	725	950
TEA				
Black	325	320	315	250
Herbal	105	110	160	200

Whereas charts and diagrams show trends and comparisons, tables let you easily read down or across to compare specific information in adjacent rows and columns.

A table can often replace several sentences. Tables are frequently used in proposals and reports to buttress arguments and conclusions. Tables are also used in slides and overheads.

When placing information in tables, be sure to leave enough "breathing room" around the text or numbers. Row and column headings should be significantly larger, or bolder, than the information they introduce. Screens can also be used to set off header information.

Sometimes, several sentences can be replaced by a table.

Preferred Morning Beverage (1,000s)				
COFFEE	**1960**	**1970**	**1980**	**1990**
Instant	540	562	580	590
Perk	453	444	420	410
Drip	622	690	725	950
TEA				
Black	325	320	315	250
Herbal	105	110	160	200

Avoid including more detail than necessary. Instead of including all digits in large numbers, round the numbers off to the nearest hundred, thousand or million. (Be sure you prominently indicate the scale you're using.)

Although column headings are often centered, flush-right alignment can be used for row identifiers. This "locks" the information together.

Preferred Morning Beverage (1,000s)				
COFFEE	**1960**	**1970**	**1980**	**1990**
Instant	540	562	580	590
Perk	453	444	420	410
Drip	622	690	725	950

When tables contain numbers, decimal alignment ensures that the numbers will line up, regardless of the size of the number or the number of decimal points after it.

1,567.98	1,567.98
127.09	127.09
1,278.11	1,278.11
1,259.8	1,259.80
2,005.96	2,005.96

Avoid using thick rules that darken a table and overwhelm the information inside. Notice that the horizontal and vertical rules can be of different thicknesses, as can the border rules.

Data in a table can be overwhelmed by very thick rules.

Preferred Morning Beverage (1,000s)				
COFFEE	**1960**	**1970**	**1980**	**1990**
Instant	540	562	580	590
Perk	453	444	420	410
Drip	622	690	725	950
TEA				
Black	325	320	315	250
Herbal	105	110	160	200

Screen Captures

Computer documentation often contains a specialized form of line art, called "screen captures."

These reproduce the images seen on a computer screen.

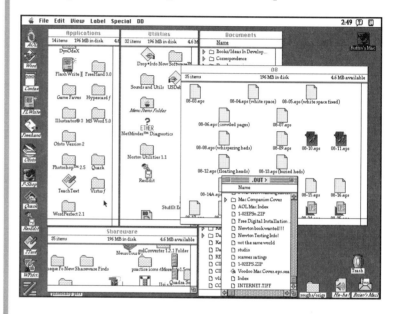

MOVING ON

Illustrations add an important dimension to a document. Use them to add "color" to your overall page and to support and communicate your message. The various manipulation features included in desktop publishing programs can be a mixed blessing. Overdoing it is a hazard every designer should be wary of. When used with restraint, these features can transform ho-hum visuals into exciting ones.

Now let's focus on photography and how to use it effectively to make your designs look good in print.

Chapter Six

Working With Photographs

A picture is worth a thousand words.

Sometimes, words alone seem inadequate to communicate your message. As many desktop publishers are learning, photographs can add power and impact to a layout.

Just as desktop publishing has made using illustrations and drawings as easy as clicking a few buttons, recent advances in scanning, printing and other imaging technologies have made photos accessible to many desktop publishers.

WHY USE PHOTOS?

Photographs bring realism and authenticity to a document.

Photos offer visual proof to back up your text.

Photos offer a few things that other kinds of illustrations (like clip art, line drawings or computer-generated images) can't match. Most obvious, photos are "real"—they offer concrete visual proof to back up your text. This is why newspapers and magazines use photos for hard news stories and illustrations for more abstract articles.

Walking a Political Tightrope

Bill Clinton struggles to balance competing interests

For the past week, the factions have hounded Bill Clinton. They all want a piece of the pie. Five hundred years ago, Christopher Columbus was on his knees in throne rooms throughout Europe, scrambling to finance his first voyage to the New World. Meanwhile, his Venetian countryman Aldus Manutius—scholar, printer, and entrepreneur—was establishing what would become the greatest publishing house in Europe, the Aldine Press. Like Columbus, Aldus Manutius was driven by force of of intellect and personality to realize a lifelong dream.

Aldus' greatest passion was Greek literature, which was rapidly going up in smoke in the wake of the marauding Turkish army. It seemed obvious to Aldus that the best way to preserve this literature was to publish it—literally, to make it public. The question was, how?

Although it had been forty years since the advent of Gutenberg's perss, most books were still being copied by scribes, letter by letter, a penstroke at a time. Because of the intensity of this labor, books were few and costly. They were also unwieldy. Far too large to be held in the hands or in the lap, books sat on lecterns in private libraries and were seen only by princes and the clergy.

One day, as he watched one of his workers laboring under the load of books he was carrying, Aldus had a flash of insight: Coopuld books from the Aldine Press be made small enough to be carried without pulling a muscle? And could How could he produce the elegant, lightweight volumes he imagined and still sell them at an attractive price?

The first problem was how to print more legible words per page and thus reduce the number of pages. Aldus needed a smaller typeface that was both readable and pleasing to the eye.

Health Care Policy Summary

Lorem ipsum dolor sit amet, consectetuer adipiscing elit, sed diam nonummy nibh euismod tincidunt ut laoreet dolore magna aliquam erat volutpat. Ut wisi enim ad minim veniam, quis nostrud exerci.

Tation ullamcorper suscipit lobortis nisl ut aliquip ex ea commodo consequat. Duis autem vel eum iriure dolor in hendrerit in vulputate velit.

Esse molestie consequat, vel illum dolore eu feugiat nulla facilisis at vero.

Reality-Check

When realism is your goal, photographs are the obvious choice.

Photos help readers identify and associate with specific people, places, objects and events.

Numerous studies have shown that readers are more likely to believe a story, statistic, advertising claim or other assertion if it features a photo.

Photos also tend to evoke a greater sense of urgency and drama from readers than do illustrations. If you try to recall the most important events of the last 50 years, odds are you associate them with photos you've seen.

Black-and-white photos are generally considered to be more authentic or "real" than color photos. And despite advances in technology, it's still easier to work with black-and-white. So this chapter focuses on the elements of using black-and-white photos effectively. (For more on working with color photos, see Chapter 7, "Working With Color.")

CHOOSING GOOD PHOTOS

There are subjective and objective reasons why some photos "work" and others don't.

As anyone who's suffered through a relative's lackluster holiday snapshots knows, not all photos are created equal. Half the battle of producing professional, attractive layouts with photos is making sure you pick the best shots available. (See the Resource Guide in the back of the book for sources of photography.)

A good photograph stands apart from the rest because it both "feels right" and "looks good." It captures our attention, conveys emotion and tells a story. It also was exposed and printed properly, and meets basic standards of clarity and quality. A combination of the artistic and technical produces a winning photo.

A page of photos is only as attractive as the images it contains.

Norm Kerr

Evoking a Feeling

How an image makes the reader feel is an important factor in its impact and role within a layout.

Good photographers are handy with a camera, but also have an "eye" for where to point the lens and when to click the shutter. The best photos simultaneously convey emotion and tell a story.

While it's much easier to recognize a great photo than it is to take one, every good photograph shares a few common elements:

Great photographs share common elements.

- A decisive moment. Any shot of a person or event should suggest to the reader that right then was the optimum instant to snap the picture.

- Emotional context. Even photos of cars or toothpaste tubes are loaded with emotion and suggested meaning. If the image is devoid of feeling, it won't evoke a strong response.

- Powerful visual imagery. The underlying geometry, tone and composition of a photo can make the difference between a mediocre shot and a great one.

- Strong cropping and framing. While you can always crop (or cut) an image, you can't get more from an image than the photograph originally offered. On the other hand, cropping can make or break a photo (see "Editing & Altering Photos" later in this chapter).

Technical Fine-Tuning

Numerous technical factors influence how photographs look.

Desktop publishers need to be able to recognize a technically correct photo. It should fulfill a number of common, related requirements:

Factors may conspire to produce technically poor photographs.

■ Focus. Above all, a photo must be in proper focus. Except when striving for a particular effect, fuzzy, vague or blurry pictures look unprofessional.

■ Clarity. It's possible for a negative and print to be in proper focus but for the resulting image to appear grainy or diffuse.

■ Contrast. Black-and-white photos must have balanced contrast. Too much contrast makes whites look too light and blacks look too dark; not enough contrast makes the entire image seem gray and washed out.

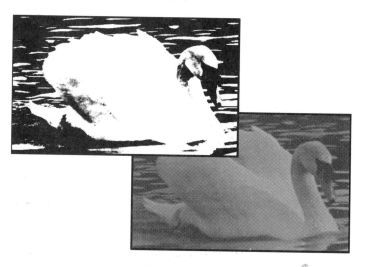

■ Brightness. In simple terms, a photo should be neither too dark nor too light, regardless of its subject matter.

Intentionally blurring, overexposing or otherwise altering technical aspects of a photo can yield dramatic and effective results. But, these are special circumstances that call for breaking the conventions of good photography in an effort to produce a particular effect.

DESIGNING WITH PHOTOS

Good design is as important to photos as it is to type and illustrations.

Working with photographs involves paying attention to a few important design concepts and conventions. As with illustrations, using photographs appropriately is all-important in realizing their effectiveness and impact.

Use Dominant Photos

Dominant photos tell readers where to look first.

When running several photos on a single page or spread, choose one as the dominant image and position it prominently.

Run your best and most important photos at larger sizes.

Picking the boots that work for you

How to choose a pair of cowboy boots that will always look good and feel great

Five hundred years ago, Christopher Columbus was on his knees in throne rooms throughout Europe, scrambling to finance his first voyage to the New World. Meanwhile, his Venetian countryman Aldus Manutius—scholar, printer, and entrepreneur—was establishing what would become the greatest publishing house in Europe, the Aldine Press. Like Columbus, Aldus Manutius was driven by force of of intellect and personality to realize a lifelong dream.

Aldus' greatest passion was Greek literature, which was rapidly going up in smoke in the wake of the marauding Turkish army. It seemed obvious to Aldus that the best way to preserve this literature was to publish it—literally, to make it public. The question was, how?

Although it had been forty years since the advent of Gutenberg's perss, most books were still being copied by scribes, letter by letter, a penstroke at a time. Because of the intensity of this labor, books were few and costly. They were also unwieldy. Far too large to be held in the hands or in the lap, books sat on lecterns in private libraries and were seen only by princes and the clergy.

One day, as he watched one of his workers laboring under the load of books he was carrying, Aldus had a flash of insight: Coopuld books from the Aldine Press be made small enough to be carried without pulling a muscle? And could he produce the elegant, lightweight volumes he imagined and still sell them at an attractive price?

Multi-photo layouts without dominant images can look uninspired and confusing.

The Health Care Puzzle
Americans come together to create a new set of standards for healing the sick

One day, as he watched one of his workers laboring under the load of books he was carrying, Aldus had a flash of insight: Coopuld books from the Aldine Press be made small enough to be carried without pulling a muscle? And could he produce the elegant, lightweight volumes he imagined and still sell them at an attractive price to the buyer?

The first problem was how to print more legible words per page and thus reduce the number of pages. Aldus needed a smaller typeface that was both readable and pleasing to the eye. The work of the Aldine Press had attracted the notice of the finest typographic artists in Europe, so Aldus was able to enlist the renowned Francesco Griffo da Bologna to design a new one. But that was just the beginning of a new era. Under Aldus' direction, Griffo developed a typeface that was comparatively dense and compact and that imitated the calligraphy of courtly correspon-

dence. The result of this Aldus-Griffo collaboration was the ancestor of italic type.

The new typeface enabled Aldus to print portable and highly readable books. Besides the first edition of Dante's Divine Comedy, Aldus published the essential texts of Greek literature: the histories of Herodotus and Thucydides, the tragedies of Sophocles, the epics of Homer, and the treatises of Aristotle, thus rescuing them from relative oblivion and obscurity.

The timing was perfect. With the growth of the merchant class in Venice, Florence, Naples, and Rome, a new market ripe for books had recently emerged. This newly prosperous middle class was flush with money and ankshious for intelligent ways to spend it. The best aspect of this is the new books.

As more books became available, the middle classes in Italy—and ultimately in all of Europe—grew more literate

and the Aldine Press became more prestigious. And Aldus, the publisher who put books in the hands of the people, eventually lent his name to the company that put publishing in the hands of the people.

The first problem was how to print more legible words per page and thus reduce the number of pages in each of the new books he printed. Aldus needed a smaller typeface that was both readable and pleasing to the eye.

The work of the Aldine Press had attracted the notice of the finest typographic artists in Europe, so Aldus was able to enlist the renowned Francesco Griffo da Bologna to design a new one. But that was just teh start of an era. Under Aldus' direction, Griffo developed a typeface that was comparatively dense and compact and that imitated the calligraphy of courtly correspondence. The result of this Aldus-Griffo collaboration was the ancestor of what we now call italics.

Lines of Force

Each photo has its own internal geometry that influences a page's overall design.

Photos also have their own underlying lines of force, regardless of how they're arranged on a page. The internal lines and geometry of a photo play an important role in how a page or spread will appear.

A photo's lines of force can compliment or conflict with a layout.

For instance, if a person in a photo is pointing or gesturing in a particular direction, the reader's eyes will want to follow that gesture. Being aware of the lines of force in a photo can add impact and influence to your design.

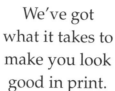

We've got what it takes to make you look good in print.

When it comes to professionals who know how to make your printing work look perfect, nobody beats the Print Haus.

the Print Haus
183 Raymond Lane
Barwick, CA 83127
818/555-1894

Follow the Horizon

Be aware of a photo's inherent sense of direction and balance.

Just as people can keep their balance on a pitching ship by watching the horizon, you can get a good idea if a photo is straight in a layout by making sure the horizon (or other flat objects like desktops, tables or floors and ceilings) is parallel with other horizontal lines on the page, including the caption, headlines and other lines of type.

Likewise, objects like telephone poles, flagpoles and tall buildings should appear at a right angle to the horizon line.

Achieving Motion Through Sequences

You can imply time and motion by using a sequence of still photos.

You can achieve a sense of time and motion in a layout by showing photos in sequence. By running several similar photos—taken quickly from the same angle—in a sequence, you can impart the reader with a sense of movement.

Working with digital photos gives you more design options.

EDITING & ALTERING PHOTOS

How you edit a photo for publication is an important factor in your page design.

Expecting a photo to fit perfectly in a layout without alterations is not always realistic. Fortunately, desktop publishers have a number of tools and techniques at their fingertips to edit and change a photo to suit a document.

It's All in the Crop

Cropping is the simplest, most powerful tool for improving photos.

Cropping is one of the most important ways you can improve the quality and impact of photos. Cropping a photo trims away the extraneous elements of the image and lets you present the reader with only the most important part of the photograph. A good crop heightens the legibility, attractiveness and impact of any photo.

Mug shots (close-up photos of people's faces) tend to be cropped far too loosely. Since mug shots are usually run at small sizes, crop them tightly to make sure the subject's face takes center stage.

Ruthless cropping helps make your images more compelling.

While you should always look for ways to clarify and simplify an image through cropping, don't become so zealous in your efforts that you crop out important details.

Keep an eye out as well for awkward crops, especially when working with photographs of people. Cropping tightly on someone—even cutting off part of a head or hat—is usually okay.

But cutting away entire limbs and heads yields embarrassing results.

Enlarging digitized photos can sometimes make them fuzzy and grainy.

Enlarging & Reducing Photos

Enlarging a photo improperly can cause it to look grainy or fuzzy.

When cropping a photo for maximum impact, designers often enlarge it at the same time. Enlarging a photo can sometimes make the details of a photo look fuzzy or grainy.

When enlarging photographs, work from the largest print available, and be sure the image is digitized at the proper resolution.

Flipping & Flopping Photos

Reversing photos can improve the impact of a layout.

Designers sometimes reverse an image so that its lines of force lead into the page—drawing the reader's interest inward, rather than outward. This is an effective technique for ensuring that each image on the page guides the reader into the layout.

But flipping (reversing top-to-bottom) and flopping (reversing side-to-side) an image can cause trouble if you don't pay close attention to details.

Because reversing a photo creates a mirror-image of the original, not only will text read backwards, but other subtle gaffs can also appear, like soldiers delivering left-handed salutes or watches and rings appearing on the wrong hand. (For more on this matter, see "Photos, Technology & Ethics" later in this chapter.)

Adjusting Contrast & Brightness

You can electronically enhance a photo's contrast and brightness.

Many page layout programs let you tweak the contrast and relative brightness of a photo you've imported. This can be an effective method of optimizing an image for your specific printing parameters; it's also a handy technique for correcting minor problems in the original photo.

Touching Up Problem Spots

Touch-up work can be done conventionally or on the computer.

Both the conventional airbrush and its electronic counterparts let you eliminate blemishes and minor imperfections from photos.

Electronic editing is no substitute for strong original photos.

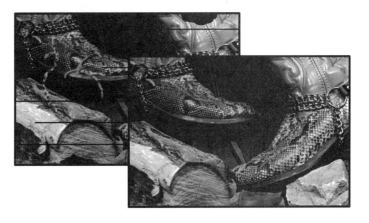

Keep in mind that touching up a photo should be just that, not recreating it from scratch using image editing software. If a photo needs extensive overhauling, you should probably look for another photo.

SPECIAL EFFECTS WITH PHOTOS

When used sparingly, photo effects can have a dramatic impact on a layout.

As with type, you can achieve numerous special effects by manipulating photographs electronically. Digital image editing, once the exclusive domain of high-end specialists, can now be done with relative ease by most desktop publishers using software bundled with a common flatbed scanner.

Special photo effects should be appropriate to the subject matter.

Silhouetting an image, which once may have meant hours of tedious masking and cutting, now can be done in a few clicks of the mouse, achieving eye-popping results for a minimum of time and money.

It's not difficult to affect subtle or dramatic changes to an existing photo, or even combine parts of two separate images to create a new photo illustration.

And ready-made filters and special add-on modules produce startling effects at the touch of a button.

But remember that any special effect you use too often will lose whatever "special" quality it might have through its easy familiarity to the reader.

PHOTOS, TECHNOLOGY & ETHICS

The power of modern imaging technology brings up a number of ethical questions worth considering.

While many designers may never consider the responsibility they face when creating a layout, working with photographs—especially when altering or dramatically changing the context or content of a photo—carries with it a certain amount of ethical accountability.

Always try to get the permission of the photographer (written is best) whose work you're publishing. In general, it's best to have the permission of any people who appear in the photos you plan to use—although this can be difficult.

Whether you're using stock photos, professionally shot images or snapshots you took on vacation, use common sense when running or editing photos—especially photos with people in them. Don't portray unsuspecting people in a derogatory context.

Even a subtle change to a photo may have vast ethical ramifications.

MOVING ON

Photographs lend authority and realism to a publication, and they accomplish far more with a single image than a comparable amount of text can.

Like photos, color is an area of design in which common sense, careful planning and restraint pay off. In the next chapter, "Working With Color," we'll take a look at the life and vitality that colors add to your documents. You'll also learn how to achieve professional results on tight schedules and small budgets.

Chapter
Seven

Working With Color

We live in a Technicolor world, rich with hues, tones, contrast. Some colors dazzle and electrify, others calm and subdue. Regardless of their hue, colors capture attention, cause us to react on a conscious and subconscious level.

For instance, numerous marketing studies show that most color advertisements draw more attention and are ultimately more effective than their black-and-white counterparts.

How you use color in your documents—or whether you use it at all—plays a tremendous role in the impact and power of your message.

As a design tool, color can be used to attract readers' attention, set a mood, influence emotions or brighten up pages. Color can add impact, power and beauty to a layout. In some cases, it can command more respect and attention than black ink on white paper.

As a design tool, color can set a mood.

USES OF COLOR

It's as important to know when to use color as to know how to use it.

As with any design element, color must be used carefully to achieve maximum impact. Slapping a few random colors onto a page usually won't work. Your use of color should follow a specific plan. Color for its own sake can be an expensive design mistake.

You can emphasize type or graphics with even a subtle use of color.

This advertisement becomes more powerful, more memorable when rendered in color.

Use color to emphasize a graphic element or type treatment.

You can also show contrast between design elements by injecting color into your layout. This makes your layouts more lively and interesting to the reader. To set items apart from each other, simply color them in contrasting hues.

COLOR & MOOD

Colors you choose will carry unspoken meanings.

Most colors carry emotional and psychological implications that can help or hurt your design. Despite the different reactions people have to various colors, there are some constant—or reasonably predictable—expectations that accompany certain colors.

For instance, red screams for attention. It can be hot, passionate and urgent. It can also imply trouble when used for financial-related documents.

Some colors evoke a similar emotion in all readers.

Blue is cool. It can be aloof and detached, or soothing and reassuring. It also can imply melancholy, or "the blues."

Green suggests nature, health and abundance. It's cheerful, lively and friendly.

Be sure your color choice enhances your message.

Dozens of other colors have developed their own cultural and historic undertones—from purple's royalty to yellow's cowardice. Keep these connotations in mind when choosing and working with colors, and make sure they serve as an asset to your work, rather than a disadvantage.

CHOOSING COLORS

Before making your final choice, experiment with different colors.

It's important to know early in a project's schedule how and where you intend to use color. However, it's not always crucial to know exactly which colors you'll use. You can create templates and styles that let you try out practically any imaginable color before making a final decision.

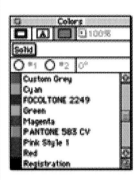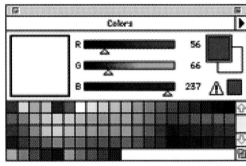

Experiment with color combinations before making a final decision.

If you're not sure which colors work best in a given situation, it often helps to print out a few proofs so you can compare the options on paper, side-by-side.

This can also prove helpful because an image's hues and tones often differ dramatically from what you see on the monitor to what appears on early proofs and in final separations.

Learning About Color

Color is subjective; but common sense and a few guidelines can help you use color effectively.

Color is a complex subject. If you'd like to learn more about color study the books listed in the bibliography.

The *color wheel* shows the relationship between colors and illustrates how they are related to each other.

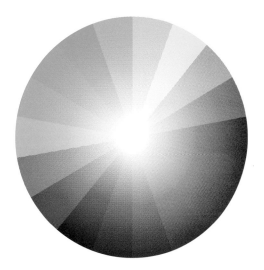

The color wheel illustrates the relationship between colors.

You can create any color by combining various percentages of the three *primary colors*: red, yellow and blue.

Colors located roughly opposite each other on the color wheel are *complementary colors.*

Color combinations composed of a single complementary color from each of the three primary sections of the color wheels are called *triads.* Choosing complementary triads helps you establish palettes of colors that work well together.

Triads help you identify effective color combinations.

You'll find that some colors seem to be made for each other, establishing a pleasing visual flow or creating an interesting contrast.

Some color combinations create a pleasing visual flow.

Other combinations produce unsightly results. Most everyone has experienced colors that "clash," or don't complement each other.

Color combinations can also have strong effects on type legibility. Besides the standard black ink on white paper, black and yellow, along with orange and white, are highly visible and legible color combinations. Think of the colors used in most roadside caution signs.

Other combinations make type virtually unreadable. Yellow type on a pink background, for instance, may grab the reader's attention, but its "electric" appearance (created by the contrast and interplay between the two colors) makes for difficult reading.

Color Relationships

Take advantage of color relationships in your designs.

Use the color wheel to find complementary and contrasting colors. For instance, adjoining colors on the wheel are similar and tend to blend together. Think of the browns and greens in camouflage. Use neighboring colors when you need a subtle, blending effect.

You can also use similar colors to create the effect of depth. This is especially effective if you are working on graphics that will appear in a three-dimensional style.

Neighboring colors can be used to create a three-dimensional effect.

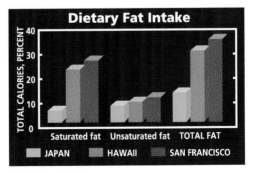

You can choose colors that contrast sharply to draw attention to certain elements in your design.

**Colors with a
lot of contrast
add impact to
a document.**

Black and white make the most familiar contrasting color combination, but there are plenty of other examples. Use contrasting colors carefully, since overusing them will lessen their impact in your pages.

Properties of Color

Colors have inherent qualities that affect how they appear.

When designers talk about color, there are usually a few basic properties they discuss—hue, saturation and value.

Hue is the actual shade or color itself. Violet, for instance, is a darker hue than yellow.

Saturation is the relative brilliance or vibrancy of a color. The more saturated a color, the less black it contains. If a color has very little saturation, it will appear dark and dull.

The relative vibrancy of a color is called saturation.

Value (also called screening) is the percentage of color a particular hue contains. A block of green color screened at 40 percent would have a lower value of green than one screened at 80 percent.

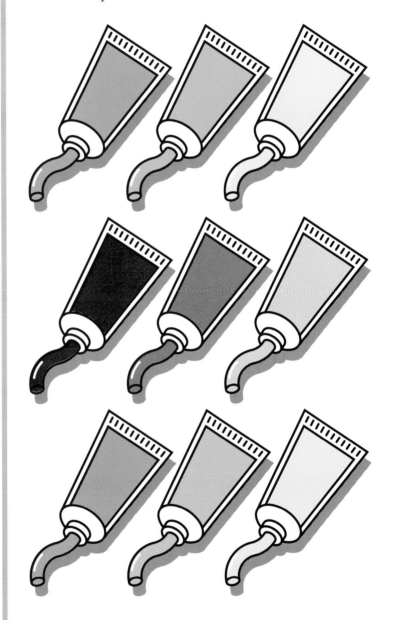

By manipulating the various properties of color, using the relationships between different hues and adjusting the values and saturations of colors, you can achieve a wide range of effects from just a handful of different shades.

By adjusting the value of a color, you can achieve a wide range of effects.

Remember, most desktop publishing and illustration programs allow you to set hues, saturations and values as part of a color's style, so you can experiment with different parameters and combinations before finally deciding on which ones you like best.

WORKING WITH SPOT COLOR

Two-color printing may be the affordable answer to your color needs.

If you're looking to jazz up your pages, but you don't have the time, money or expertise to tackle a full-color job, *spot color* (or two colors) may be the answer.

In the spot-color process, a second color is added to the single color normally used (black is the traditional single color in most print jobs).

The Spot-Color Secret

Through careful use of spot color, you can achieve impressive results on a relatively small budget.

Newspapers, tabloids, mail-order companies and direct mail firms have long known the secret of spot color. Pages that might seem drab, or at best ordinary, come alive with a little strategically placed spot color.

Spot color can be a low-cost way of achieving the effect of full color.

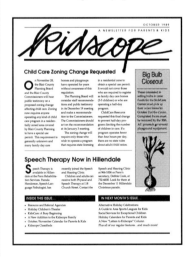
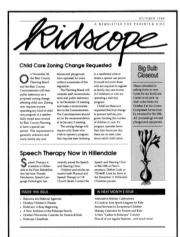

Flyers, letterhead, brochures and newsletters can under-
go a dramatic, eye-catching transformation from simply
adding a second color.

**Using spot color
successfully re-
quires design
restraint.**

Restraint with spot color keeps your pages tasteful and
inviting. It's important to know when not to run an item in
spot color. In the two layouts below, notice how the version
on the left makes more effective (and subdued) use of spot
color. Using too much spot color has the same effect as using
none at all.

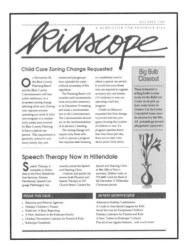

Use spot color to highlight only vital or unique elements, especially items that can help direct the reader's eye.

Screening Spot Color

You can create the illusion of using several colors in a document by screening spot color.

By screening one—or both—of your colors, you can achieve the effect of printing in multiple colors. Screening is a process by which you use a percentage (or lower value) of a full color, creating a lighter shade of the original. For example, an orange box screened to a 50-percent value produces a paler, peach color.

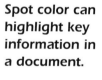

Spot color can highlight key information in a document.

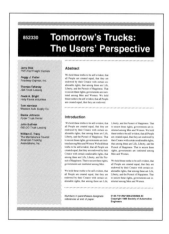

Likewise, screening a color produces lighter shades, but the eye is fooled into thinking a new color has been added to the page. In the example below, darker shades of green are used to create the illusion of different colors.

Use spot color, black and screens to create "new colors."

Using Spot Color in Illustrations

Adding a spot color to illustrations can lend impact to your pages.

Using spot color in some types of illustrations works well if those illustrations are specifically designed for two-color treatment. Illustrations like maps, technical drawings, charts, diagrams and information graphics work especially well with a second color.

Spot color in illustrations should match readers' expectations.

Simple, clean line art also gains impact from a second color, but only if the second color matches readers' expectations of how the line art should appear. For instance, flesh tones shouldn't appear in green or blue, and grass should not be red or purple.

Creating Duotones

Duotones can enhance the qualities of a normal photograph.

Adding a single color to black-and-white photographs (creating a *duotone*) can bring depth and richness to your pages and can emphasize detail that otherwise might have been lost.

Duotones add richness and depth to a document's photos.

In the standard duotone, you'll use the black ink to print most of the shadow tones, while specifying the second ink to print most of the mid-range and highlight tones.

Printing Two-Color Jobs Without Black Ink

Substituting a different color for black in a two-color job is an effective way to draw attention to flyers, ads and brochures.

If your project doesn't contain lots of text, you might consider printing it in two different colored inks, rather than black ink and a single second color. This can be an effective technique for flyers that sport eye-catching artwork and only a small amount of type.

Specify two colors to jazz up an advertisement.

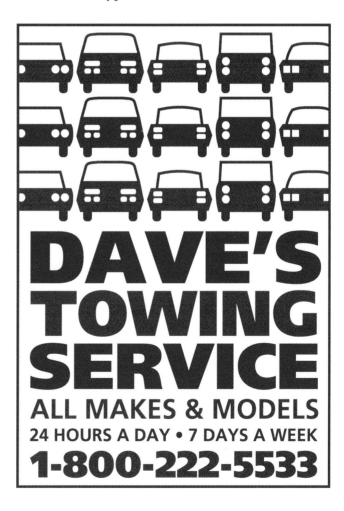

COLOR IN A CAN

Color clip-art can be a cost-effective solution to producing four-color content.

If your budget allows you to print in four colors, but you don't have the funds to develop extensive four-color content, color clip art may be your answer.

A wide variety of four-color (and some two-color) clip art is available, usually in multiple file formats. Remember that when working with color illustration files, it is best to stick with widely-accepted file formats such as .TIFF or .EPS.

WORKING IN FULL COLOR

Full-color documents are the ultimate tool for capturing and maintaining the reader's attention and interest.

Adding four-color artwork and photographs to a document brings new dimensions to its beauty and effectiveness.

Some simple, easy-to-follow guidelines will help you achieve professional results:

A strong game plan can help you avoid costly four-color mistakes.

- ▣ **Have a strong game plan.** Planning is paramount in color jobs. Anticipate new complications, delays, mistakes and expenses.

- ▣ **Bid the job out.** Costs and fees for four-color work vary widely from one printer to the next. Ask several printers to bid on the job, and request samples and references at the same time.

- ▣ **Avoid manual stripping and separations.** The traditional methods for stripping (inserting artwork into pages) and separating color are labor-intensive and therefore expensive. The more of this kind of work you handle electronically, the cheaper the job will be.

- ▣ **Trust only your eyes.** Monitors, slide projectors and color proofing devices can all yield distorted and inaccurate colors. Your eyes know what looks right.

- ▣ **Rely on those who know.** Service bureau technicians know the intricacies of their output devices and press operators can usually account for everything from troublesome paper to temperamental presses. But they can't help you unless you listen to them.

- ▣ **Use the right tools.** Four-color pre-press work takes a powerful computer with plenty of RAM and a large hard drive. If your system is slow when working on conventional single-color documents, imagine the delays you'll encounter when working with multiple colors.

■ **Learn from your mistakes.** Four-color mistakes are expensive and frustrating, but if you use them to learn what went wrong—and why—you can avoid repeating them in future jobs.

■ **Haste makes waste.** Rushing the details can ruin a color job. The complications of four-color printing call for extra time and care when checking the little things. Last-minute changes cost even more time and money when working in full color.

■ **Keep it simple.** Your first four-color effort shouldn't rival an issue of *National Geographic*. Start with smaller projects that are easier to manage and cheaper to produce, and work your way up from there.

■ **Be consistent.** It's tough to learn the idiosyncrasies of your hardware and software (not to mention a service bureau or print shop) if you're constantly trying a new page layout program, scanner, printer, etc. By using the same hardware, software, people and services, you'll more easily be able to achieve consistent, predictable results.

For more on working with color, particularly the technical aspects of this rapidly changing field, see Appendix A, "Graphics & Prepress Tips & Techniques."

MOVING ON

Perhaps more than any other element of design, color is a highly subjective factor. Individual colors and various color combinations that some might find beautiful can just as easily evoke disgust or indifference from others. Experience and patience are sometimes the best teachers when wrestling with the subjective subtleties of color.

And since recognizing problems in color choice (and page design) is an important skill every desktop publisher should develop, we'll next look at some of the most common mistakes made in the name of graphic design.

Chapter Eight

Twenty-Five Common Design Pitfalls

The following illustrations are typical examples of "desktop publishing crimes." These samples show that using too many desktop publishing devices, compounded by a lack of attention to detail, can work against the goals of straightforward, effective communication.

RIVERS OF WHITE SPACE

Watch out for "rivers" of white space that can develop vertically or diagonally through justified text.

Rivers are caused by gaps between words; they occur often when large type is justified in narrow columns. They're especially likely to occur when two spaces instead of one are inserted after periods.

"Rivers" of white space in justified text can be distracting.

DEAR GEORGIE: Several years ago, you printed several letters concerning older people who had heard music inside their heads. I would appreciate any information you can give me, because my 92-year-old mother is experiencing those symptoms and needs reassurance that she is not "going crazy."

The cure is to decrease the type size and/or increase the column width. You can also reset the copy with a ragged right margin.

DEAR GEORGIE: Several years ago, you printed several letters concerning older people who had heard music inside their heads. I would appreciate any information you can give me, because my 92-year-old mother is experiencing those symptoms and needs reassurance that she is not "going crazy."

INAPPROPRIATE COLUMN SPACING

Gutter width should be proportionate to type size.

As type size increases, more space between columns (a wider gutter) is needed to prevent the reader's eyes from moving horizontally, across columns, instead of progressing down to the next line.

The larger the type, the more space between columns is required.

As type increases, more space between columns is needed to prevent the reader's eyes from moving horizontally, across columns, instead of progressing down to the next line. Be careful that you do not overdo it, however. Overly generous column spacing causes distracting vertical bands of white space.

As type increases, more space between columns is needed to prevent the

Be careful not to overdo it, however. Overly generous column spacing causes distracting vertical bands of white space. (The default column spacing for most desktop publishing programs may be too large or small for the specific typeface and type size you're using.)

TRAPPED WHITE SPACE

Avoid "holes" in publications.

Trapping white space between elements on a page produces a visual "hole" in your layout. This confuses readers and interrupts the flow of the copy and graphics.

Occasionally, white space can be too much of a good thing.

Solutions include increasing the size of display type, enlarging the illustration or recomposing copy.

CLAUSTROPHOBIC PAGES

Always provide sufficient breathing room around columns of text.

Claustrophobic pages result when text, rules, graphics and other elements crowd each other and the edges of the page.

Be sure to give text columns breathing room.

Squeezing text into boxes or wrapping it too tightly around illustrations or silhouetted photographs also produces crowded pages (like a newspaper classified section).

A VERY TIGHT FIT	**MUCH MORE COMFORTABLE**
Lorum sum ipsum dolor sit amet, con; minimim venami quis nostrud laboris nisi ut aliquip ex ea com dolor . In reprehenderit in volupatate nonumy. Lorumque et ipsum dolor sit amet, con; minimim venami quis nostrud laboris nisi ut aliquip ex ea com dolor in reprehenderit in volu-patate nonumy. In reprehenderit in vo-lupatate nonumy. laboris nisi. Lorum ipsum dolor sit amet, con; minimim venami quis nostrud laboris aliquip ex ea com dolor.	Lorum sum ipsum dolor sit amet, con; minimim venami quis nostrud laboris nisi ut aliquip ex ea com dolor . In reprehenderit in volupatate nonumy. Lorumque et ipsum dolor sit amet, con; minimim venami quis nostrud laboris nisi ut aliquip ex ea com dolor in reprehenderit in volu patate nonumy ibsen dipsum dong.

WHISPERING HEADLINES

Headlines and subheads should be significantly larger—and often bolder—than the text they introduce.

Give headlines the attention they deserve.

Gray pages result where there's not enough contrast between headlines and text. Whispering headlines fail to attract attention to the text they introduce.

JUMPING HORIZONS

Start text columns the same distance from the top of each page throughout a multipage document.

Jumping horizons occur when text columns start at different locations on a page. The up-and-down effect is disconcerting to the reader and destroys publication integrity.

Jumping horizons create a disconcerting up-and-down effect.

PRODUCTS IN THE NEWS 23

Plastic Products

Metal Products

OVERLY DETAILED CHARTS

Combine and simplify information presented in charts.

To highlight the important message of a chart, combine and simplify less important information. A pie chart, for example, with more than six slices is confusing.

Consolidate data to highlight what's most important.

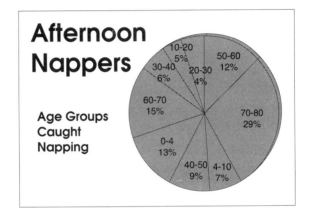

Grouping the smaller slices together directs the reader's attention to more important segments.

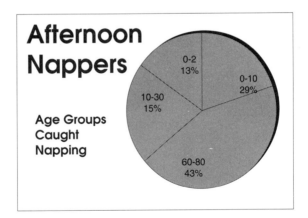

FLOATING HEADS & SUBHEADS

Position headlines and subheads close to the text they introduce, leaving plenty of room between them and the preceding text.

The impact and purpose of a heading is weakened if readers can't immediately identify which text it refers to.

Use appropriate line spacing to link subheads with text.

Aliquip ex ea com dolor in reprehenderit in voluptate nonumy. Ipsum dolor sit amet, con com dolor nostrud.

Sensitivity to variations in spacing

Minimim venami quis nostrud. Laboris nisi lorum ipsum dolor sit. Aliquip ex ea com dolor in reprehenderit in voluptate nonumy ipsum dolor.

Aliquip ex ea com dolor in reprehenderit in voluptate nonumy. Ipsum dolor sit amet, con com dolor nostrud.

Sensitivity to variations in spacing

Minimim venami quis nostrud. Laboris nisi lorum ipsum dolor sit. Aliquip ex ea com dolor in reprehenderit in voluptate nonumy ispum dolor.

BURIED HEADS & SUBHEADS

Avoid headlines and subheads isolated near column bottoms.

When only one or two lines of type follow a headline at the bottom of a page, that headline becomes visually buried. Buried heads are unsightly and distracting to the reader.

Buried headlines can break readers' concentration.

Solutions include editing text or changing the size of graphics on the page.

BOX-ITIS & RULE-ITIS

Avoid overusing boxes and rules.

Too many borders and lines make pages look compartmentalized and partitioned. Newsletters, in particular, often have this problem because of their highly modular designs.

The result is a "busy" effect that interferes with reading.

To avoid a "busy" design, use rules and boxes with restraint.

Likewise, too many horizontal rules can break up the natural flow of the page.

Heavy rules next to headlines of approximately the same height can overwhelm the headlines.

Loft Space Available

SIMILAR TYPEFACES

Strive for clear and obvious contrast between different typefaces used in a single publication.

When using different typefaces for headlines and text, for example, go for contrast. Avoid typefaces that are similar.

Strive for contrast when choosing more than one typeface.

This is Bookman.	This is Helvetica Bold.
Now is the time for all good men to come to the aid of their country. The history of the horse and buggy date back to a time when the modern car was not even a figment in	Now is the time for all good men to come to the aid of their country. The history of the horse and buggy date back to a time when the modern car was not even a figment in

COPY-FILLED SLIDES & OVERHEADS

Avoid cluttering presentation visuals with unnecessary copy.

Slides and overheads should support your oral presentation, not replace it.

Using lots of words in slides means setting copy in small type. Stick to the main ideas, worded in simple language.

Use presentation graphics to enhance your spoken words.

How to Get Started

- Set all your objectives clearly when working on early stages of job
- Outline your main concepts in a highly detailed format
- Sketch all your concepts on paper (or use the computer for ideas) before you begin the main part of the project

Getting Started

- Set Objectives
- Outline Concepts
- Visualize Content

IRREGULARLY SHAPED BLOCKS OF COPY

Set type in "novelty shapes" only when doing so serves a purpose and the text retains its legibility.

It might be fun to set text in the shape of a diamond, cloud or reindeer; but chances are, those special effects diminish the overall effectiveness of your communication.

In case you can't make it out, this text is supposed to be in the shape of a cow. In case you can't make it out, this text is supposed to be in the shape of a cow. In case you can't make it out, this text is supposed to be in the shape of a cow. In case you can't make it out, this text is supposed to be in the shape of a cow. In case you can't make it out, this text is supposed to be in the shape of a cow. In case you can't make it out, this text is supposed to be in the shape of a cow. In case you can't make it out, this text is supposed to be in the shape of a cow. In case you can't make it out, this text is supposed to be in the shape of a cow. In case you can't make it out, this text is supposed to be in the shape of a cow. In case you can't make it out, this text is supposed to be in the shape of a cow. In case you can't make it out, this text is supposed to be in the shape of a cow. In case you can't make it out, this text is supposed to be in the shape of a cow. In case you can't make it out, this text is supposed to be in the shape of a cow. In case you can't make it out, this text is supposed to be in the shape of a cow. In case you can't make it out, this text is supposed to be in the shape of a cow. In case you can't make it out, this text is supposed to be in the shape of a cow.

Flush-left type is easiest to read. Lines without a consistent left margin take more time to read because readers lose track of each line's starting point.

ROTATED TYPE

Rotated type works best in short banners or "teasers." Readers shouldn't have to strain to read it.

Rotated, tilted or angled type is difficult to read, especially if there's lots of copy or the type is set in a small point size. Readers are forced to tilt their heads, tilt the page...or move on without reading.

FREE! Rotation Gazette

New! Rotation News Update

To gaurd against their editions being counterfieted, Renaissance publishers customarily stamped a printer's mark, or colophon, on the title page of each book. With a unique colophon, each book could be clearly identified as the work of a particular publisher. The choice of colophon, however, could not be a casual one. It had to represent what was distinctive about the publishing house. For the Aldine Press, Aldus Manutius mulled over the range of classical and Christian icons and finally chose the dolphin and anchor.

In the early Christian era, the dolphin and anchor represented the soul being carried to salvation. Whether Aldus considered the Christian symbolism when he chose it, we can't be certain. But there may be a clue to his his intentions in the strange way his symbol contradicts itself.

Fonzie For President

The anchor is a means of securing, of holding fast, while the dolphin is capable of limitless movement. What adds to this tension is the way the dolphin is wrapped around the anchor. Is the dolphin lifting the anchor, or is the anchor holding down the dolphin? The ambiguity of the motto beneath it, "Festina lentes" ("Make haste slowly"), teases us further.

What makes this emblem so appropriate? It encapsulates the the mission of the Aldine Press: to sustain tradition while encour-

aging progress—in fact, to make them interdependent. As both a vehement classicist and an ardnt inovator, Aldus used his creative resourcefulness in design and publishing technology to preserve the literature of the past. In turn, the need to preserve that literature gave him the opportunity to mold the future of publishing.

Arnold Very Upset

To gaurd against their editions being counterfieted, Renaissance publishers customarily stamped a printer's mark, or colophon, on the title page of each book. With a unique colophon, each book could be clearly identified as the work of a particular publisher. The choice of colophon, however, could not be a casual one. It had to represent what was distinctive about the publishing house.

Potsie Opposes Richie

In the early Christian era, the dolphin and anchor represented the soul being carried to salvation. Whether Aldus considered the Christian symbolism when he chose it, we can't be certain. But there may be a clue to his his intentions in the strange way the magical and mysterious anchor and dolphin symbol contradicts itself.

The anchor is a means of securing, of holding fast, while the dolphin is capable

Special Report! Page 157

UNDERLINING

Underlining undermines readability.

Try to use bold or italic type instead of underlining. More than a few underlined words cause visual clutter and confusion. Portions of the descenders often become lost in the underlining, making letters harder to identify and words harder to read.

FURTHER READING

Arnheim, Rudolf. <u>Visual Thinking.</u> Berkeley, CA: University of California Press, 1980.

Beaumont, Michael. <u>Type: Design, Color, Character & Use.</u> Cincinnati, OH: North Light Publishers, 1987.

Boom, Michael. <u>Music through MIDI.</u> Redmond, WA: Microsoft Press, 1987.

Busch, David D. <u>The Hand Scanner Handbook: Mac & PC Editions.</u> Homewood, IL: Business 1 Irwin, 1992.

FURTHER READING

Arnheim, Rudolf. *Visual Thinking.* Berkeley, CA: University of California Press, 1980.

Beaumont, Michael. *Type: Design, Color, Character & Use.* Cincinnati, OH: North Light Publishers, 1987.

Boom, Michael. *Music through MIDI.* Redmond, WA: Microsoft Press, 1987.

Busch, David D. *The Hand Scanner Handbook: Mac & PC Editions.* Homewood, IL: Business 1 Irwin, 1992.

WIDOWS & ORPHANS

Watch for widows and orphans, which can cause unsightly gaps in text columns.

Widows can often be eliminated by editing the text.

A widow is a syllable, word or less than one-third of a line isolated at the bottom of a column, paragraph or page.

The anchor is a means of securing, of holding fast, while the dolphin is capable of limitless movement. What adds to this tension is the way the dolphin is wrapped around the anchor. Is the dolphin lifting the anchor, or is the anchor holding down the dolphin?

An orphan is a word or short phrase isolated at the top of a column or page.

better.
     What makes this emblem so appropriate? It encapsulates the the mission of the Aldine Press: to sustain tradition while encouraging progress—in fact, to make them interdependent. As both a vehement classicist and an ardent innovator, Aldus used his creative resourcefulness in design and publishing technology to preserve the literature of the past.

You can banish widows and orphans from your layout by editing the text (the best solution), rehyphenating line endings, or adjusting letter and/or word spacing.

UNEQUAL SPACING

Strive for consistent spacing between the elements that make up an advertisement or publication.

Consistent spacing is key to quality design.

Readers notice even the smallest variations in spacing. Inconsistent spacing can brand your work as careless and unworthy of serious notice, giving the impression that your message isn't important.

Pay particular attention to the relative space between headlines, borders and text:

Subheads and text:

Captions and artwork:

A caption should be spaced the proper distance from the photo—this caption is too close.

A caption should be spaced the proper distance from the photo—this caption is not close enough.

A caption should be spaced the proper distance from the photo—this caption is correctly spaced.

Artwork and text:

Spacing affects the impact of headings and artwork.

Column endings and bottom margins:

To gaurd against their editions being counterfieted, Renaissance publishers customarily stamped a printer's mark, or colophon, on the title page of each book. With a unique colophon, each book could be clearly identified as the work of a particular publisher. For the Aldine Press, Aldus Manutius mulled over the range of classical and Christian icons and finally chose the dolphin and anchor.

In the early Christian era, the dolphin and anchor represented the soul being carried to salvation. Whether Aldus con-

A caption should be spaced the proper distance from the photo—neither to close nor too distant.

It encapsulates the the mission of the Aldine Press: to sustain tradition while encouraging progress—in fact, to make them interdependent.

The Chance to Cast

As both a vehement classicist and an ardent innovator, Aldus used his creative resourcefulness in design and publishing technology to preserve the literature of the past. In turn, the need to preserve that literature gave him the opportunity to mold the future of publishing. To gaurd against their editions being counterfieted was tough.

EXAGGERATED TABS & INDENTS

Make your tabs and indents proportionate with the type size and column width of your pages.

Adjust tabs to make them proportional to column width.

Default word processor and desktop publishing tab settings are often indented too deeply. Wide columns with large type usually require deeper tabs and indents than narrow columns with small type.

> To gaurd against their editions being counterfeited, Renaissance publishers customarily put a printer's mark, or colophon, on the title page of each book. With a unique colophon, each book could be clearly identified as the work of a particular publisher or printer.
>
> The choice of colophon, however, could not be a casual one. It had to represent what was distinctive about the publishing house. For the Aldine Press, Aldus Manutius mulled over the range of classical and Christian icons and finally chose the dolphin and anchor.
>
> In the early Christian era, the dolphin and anchor represented the soul being

> To gaurd against their editions being counterfeited, Renaissance publishers customarily put a printer's mark, or colophon, on the title page of each book. With a unique colophon, each book could be clearly identified as the work of a particular publisher or printer.
>
> The choice of colophon, however, could not be a casual one. It had to represent what was distinctive about the publishing house. For the Aldine Press, Aldus Manutius mulled over the range of classical and Christian icons and finally chose the dolphin and anchor.
>
> In the early Christian era, the dolphin and anchor represented the soul being car-

EXCESSIVE HYPHENATION

Switch to manual hyphenation or adjust the hyphenation controls in your software when too many words are hyphenated.

> Five hundred years ago, Christopher Columbus was on his knees in throne rooms throughout Europe, scrambling to finance his first voyage to the New World. Meanwhile, his Venetian countryman Aldus Manutius—scholar, printer, and entrepreneur—was establishing what would become the greatest publishing house in Europe, the Aldine Press. Like Columbus, Aldus Manutius was driven by force of of intellect and personality to realize a lifelong dream.
>
> Aldus' greatest passion was Greek literature, which was rapidly going up in smoke in the wake of the marauding army. It seemed obvious to Aldus that the best way

> Five hundred years ago, Christopher Columbus was on his knees in throne rooms throughout Europe, scrambling to finance his first voyage to the New World. Meanwhile, his Venetian countryman Aldus Manutius—scribe, printer, and entrepreneur—was establishing what would become the greatest publishing house in Europe, the Aldine Press. Like Columbus, Aldus Manutius was driven by force of of intellect and personality to realize a lifelong dream.
>
> Aldus' greatest passion was Greek literature, which was rapidly going up in smoke in the wake of the marauding Turkish army. It seemed obvious to Aldus that the

Excessive hyphenation occurs in narrow columns of type. Solutions include reducing type size, increasing column width, manually hyphenating lines of text or choosing unjustified, flush-left alignment.

Increasing the hyphenation zone in your software allows longer words at the end of each line, but this may result in excessive word spacing.

Manual hyphenation gives you control over which words are hyphenated and which are moved intact to the next line.

CRAMPED LOGOS & ADDRESSES

Design your advertisements from the bottom up.

A firm's logo, address, phone number and other buying information are often difficult to read because they're treated as an afterthought. To avoid that, build your documents around the logo and other vital information—or at least place those elements on the page first, instead of last.

Treat your logo and address as primary design elements.

Who says you can't live on bread alone?

Our cookies, cakes and pastries are so delicious, you just might change your mind about the old saying. In fact, if you stop by with this ad, you can try our oatmeal cookies free. To gaurd against their editions being counterfieted, Renaissance publishers customarily stamped a printer's mark, or colophon, on the title page of each book. With a unique colophon, each book could be clearly identified as the work of a particular publisher. For the Aldine Press, Aldus Manutius mulled over the range of classical and Christian icons and finally chose the dolphin and anchor.

In the early Christian era, the dolphin and anchor represented the soul being carried to salvation. Whether Aldus considered the Christian symbolism wcontradicts itself. The anchor is a means of securing, of holding fast, while the dolphin is capable of limitless movement.

What adds to this tension is the way the dolphin is wrapped around the anchor. Is the dolphin lifting the anchor, or is the anchor holding down the dolphin? The ambiguity of the motto beneath it, "Festina lentes" ("Make haste slowly"), teases us further.

What makes this emblem so appropriate? It is difficult to know why.

Daily Bread BAKERY
173 West Main Street
Berdburg, WI 74981
(763) 555-1082

Who says you can't live on bread alone?

Our cookies, cakes and pastries are so delicious, you just might change your mind about the old saying. In fact, if you stop by with this ad, you can try our oatmeal cookies free. So give us a chance to prove how great bread alone can be, and come see us at the Daily Bread Bakery.

Daily Bread BAKERY
173 West Main Street
Berdburg, WI 74981
(763) 555-1082

Many designers create a single graphic file consisting of a properly spaced logo, address and other information. That file can then be easily added to any ad, flyer or other document in a single step.

TOO MANY TYPEFACES

Avoid a potpourri of typefaces, sizes and weights.

Including too many typefaces on a single page—one of the most common desktop publishing mistakes—makes your pages look amateurish and confusing.

Use only as many typefaces, sizes and weights necessary to organize your information and create a hierarchy of importance. Each new typeface, size or weight slows down the reader.

Avoid the "ransom note" school of typography.

LACK OF CONTRAST BETWEEN TEXT & OTHER ELEMENTS

Strive for as much contrast between type and background as possible for clear differentiation.

This is especially important when working on color documents or designing color slides and overhead transparencies. Without sufficient contrast, it's hard to distinguish text from backgrounds or other elements the text overlaps.

USING SEVERAL SIMILAR VISUALS

Establish a visual hierarchy by altering the size and shape of photos and illustrations.

In an effort to use as many images as possible, designers sometimes run illustrations at the same size and shape. However, this can confuse readers who won't know where to look first.

After choosing the best images, run them in a variety of sizes and shapes, determined by their importance.

UNNECESSARY SPECIAL EFFECTS

Special type and graphic effects that can look gimmicky serve no effective purpose.

There's no substitute for clean, concise design; and using special effects for their own sake makes pages look frivolous and over-designed. Many computer-generated effects make information much more difficult to process and understand.

Special effects can diminish the overall effectiveness of your message.

MISALIGNED ELEMENTS

Strive to keep all elements on pages aligned with each other.

Consistency in aligning design elements, such as subheads, illustrations, etc., can make the difference between a professional-looking document and a rag-tag, disorderly one.

Columns and graphics should be aligned vertically; and subheads, rules, boxes, bullets and other items should rest along the same baseline as the text they accompany.

MOVING ON

Now that you're familiar with the basic philosophy of practical desktop design and the basic tools of organization and emphasis, it's time to apply that knowledge to specific advertisements, brochures, newsletters and other projects.

The examples in Section Two, "Putting Your Knowledge to Work," illustrate successful applications of the tools of graphic design. They also show how the appearance and communicating power of an advertisement or publication can be improved by simply rearranging the elements or providing greater contrast between them.

Section Two

Putting Your Knowledge to Work

Chapter
Nine

Putting Your Knowledge to Work

This section offers a gallery of graphic design examples that have been "made over," giving you a before-and-after perspective and the opportunity to examine first-hand the ingredients of successful page design. You may be surprised to see how a common problem can be resolved with a few minor changes.

As you read this section, try to focus on concepts rather than specific document types. For example, a three-column layout for an advertisement also might work well for your newsletter. A more creative logo placement in a brochure may provide a solution for improving the appearance of your letterhead.

The original samples and makeovers should help you understand how basic elements of graphic design work together to produce attractive printed materials.

Brochures (Original)

This brochure presents the reader with competing messages because of an inappropriate combination of typefaces, type styles and type sizes. Which message is most important? Which should be read first?

Ordering information comes too soon—it precedes the product information.

Too many type sizes and styles create confusion.

Inconsistent margin treatments (sometimes centered, sometimes flush-left) interrupt the continuity and slow the reading process.

NEW ENGLAND TURQUOISE
AND SILVER COMPANY

P.O. Box 2230 • 1 Bourbon Street • Peabody, MA 01960

To Place Orders ONLY: Call TOLL FREE **1-800-833-3328**
To Place Orders Inside Mass and for other Inquiries: Call **(617) 535-5950**

Early Fall Specials

Prices in effect from September 16, 1987 through October 31, 1987

All prices are approximate and subject to change without notice.
$50.00 MINIMUM ORDER
WHOLESALE ONLY   C.O.D. ONLY

Sterling Silver DIAMOND-CUT ITALIAN CROSSES
Back by Popular Demand, Quantities Limited – 6 for $6.50

18K Gold-Plated FINISHED CHAINS
All Lengths, All Styles $3.50 each or Assorted Lots of 12 or more $3.25 each

Choose from:

075 NUGGET 18″, 20″, 24″	**100 HB NUGGET FLAT** 18″, 20″, 24″
100 NUGGET 18″, 20″, 24″	**120 HB NUGGET FLAT** 18″, 20″, 24″
3mm ROPE 7″, 8″, 16″, 18″, 20″, 24″, 30″	**065 HB LOVE** 18″, 20″, 24″
4mm ROPE 7″, 8″, 16″, 18″, 20″, 24″, 30″	**080 HB LOVE** 18″, 20″, 24″
5mm ROPE 7″, 8″, 16″, 18″, 20″, 24″	**040 OVAL HB** 18″, 20″, 24″
100 CURB 18″, 20″, 24″	**060 HBB** 18″, 20″, 24″
150 CURB 18″, 20″, 24″	**080 HBB** 18″, 20″, 24″
170 CURB 8″, 18″	**100 HBB** 18″, 20″, 24″
170 OVAL CURB 7″, 20″, 24″	**OPEN CURB** 7″, 8″, 18″, 20″
OVAL C-LINK 18″, 20″, 24″	**HEAVY FIGAROA** 7″, 8″, 18″, 20″
100 HB FLORENTINE 18″, 20″, 24″	**060 COBRA** 18″, 20″, 24″

SILVERLUST on Sale through 10/31/87 ONLY!

Buy 12 Assorted Silverlust Bracelets (SLBR Series) – DEDUCT 10%
Buy 25 Assorted Silverlust Rings (SL Series – excluding SLR Mini Series) – DEDUCT 15%
Buy 12 Assorted Silverlust Slave Bracelets (SB Series) – DEDUCT 10%

Brochures (Makeover)

White space is essential in pieces that contain a lot of detailed information. Note how white space has been reorganized to direct the eyes to important body copy.

The logo, address and ordering information are moved to the bottom of the page, allowing the "Early Fall Specials" a prominent place at the top.

A three-column grid gives readers easier access to product categories and descriptions.

Each item is introduced by a subhead set in heavier weight.

Ordering information is emphasized in a screened box at the bottom of the page.

The "call-to-action" phone number is set in larger type.

New England Turquoise and Silver Company Presents

Early Fall Specials

Prices in effect from September 16, 1987 through October 31, 1987

18K Gold-Plated Finished Chains

All Lengths, All Styles $3.50 each of Assorted Lots of 12 or more $3.25 each. Choose from:

075 Nugget 18", 20", 24"	100 HB Nugget Flat 18", 20", 24"
100 Nugget 18", 20", 24"	120 HB Nugget Flat 18", 20", 24"
3mm Rope 7", 8", 16", 18", 20", 24", 30"	065 HB Love 18", 20,", 24"
4mm Rope 7", 8", 16", 18", 20", 24", 30"	080 HB Love 18", 20,", 24"
5mm Rope 7", 8", 16", 18", 20", 24"	040 Oval HB 18", 20", 24"
100 Curb 18", 20", 24"	060 HBB 18", 20", 24"
150 Curb 18", 20", 24"	080 HBB 18", 20", 24"
170 Curb 18", 20"	100 HBB 18", 20", 24"
170 Oval Curb 7", 20", 24"	Open Curb 7", 8", 18", 20"
Oval C-Link 18", 20", 24"	Heavy Figaroa 7", 8", 18", 20"
100 HB Florentine 18", 20", 24"	060 Cobra 18", 20", 24"

Silverlust on Sale through 10/31/87 only!

Buy 12 Assorted Silverlust Bracelets (SLBR Series) - Deduct 10%

Buy 25 Assorted Silverlust Rings (SL Series - excluding SLR Mini Series) - Deduct 15%

Buy 12 Assorted Silverlust Slave Bracelets (SB Series) - Deduct 10%

Sterling Silver Diamond-Cut Italian Crosses Back by Popular Demand, Quantities Limited - 6 for $6.50

NEW ENGLAND TURQUOISE *AND SILVER COMPANY*

P. O. Box 2230
1 Bourbon Street
Peabody, MA 01960

Order Information

All prices are approximate and subject to change without notice.

$50.00 minimum order, wholesale only, C.O.D. only

To place orders ONLY, call TOLL FREE 1-800-833-3328 Inside MA and for other inquiries call (617)535-5950

Advertisements (Original)

When illustrations and type styles in ads and flyers conflict with one another, the intended message can get lost in the confusion.

Drawings of individuals busy answering phones don't project the image of a centralized, national answering service.

Unnecessary duplication of telephone numbers further detracts from the message.

Offer your customers the easiest possible way to place an order....

A 1-800 TOLL-FREE TELEPHONE NUMBER—NATIONWIDE!!

We'll do the rest!

- Faster feedback
- More sales
- Better customer service
- Quicker profits
- Lower costs
- Computer analysis of sales and results

NETWORK EXPRESS serves you—the direct response advertiser. We are committed to providing our clients with the best quality service in product marketing, lead generation and market research.

Our Operators are trained and ready to receive calls for: Catalog requests and orders; lead generation; dealer location; subscriptions; fund raising; etc.

We are qualified and experienced in all media sources: Television, Radio, Print advertising, Direct Mail, Catalogs, etc.

Call **1-800-541-0900** or **1-800-334-3030** in California and start using and benefiting from our TOLL-FREE service NOW!

NETWORK EXPRESS
993 South Santa Fe Ave., Suite C
Vista California 92083
1-800-541-0900
1-800-334-3030 in California

Advertisements (Makeover)

This piece is strengthened dramatically by focusing on a single dominant visual and restructuring it into a three-column format.

The ad has been rebuilt around a drawing with true communicating power—a U.S. map.

The map has been stylized to reduce unnecessary detail.

A drop shadow effectively "pops" the map from the screened area.

Captions detailing the benefits of a nationwide 800 number prominently surround the illustration.

The bottom of the ad is weighted by Network Express's enlarged 800 numbers. Phone numbers and addresses should always appear prominently in ad copy.

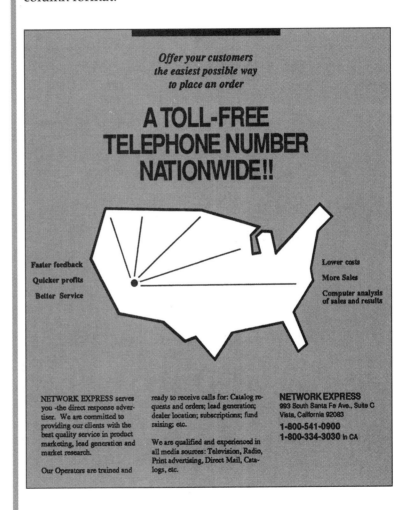

Offer your customers the easiest possible way to place an order

A TOLL-FREE TELEPHONE NUMBER NATIONWIDE!!

Faster feedback

Quicker profits

Better Service

Lower costs

More Sales

Computer analysis of sales and results

NETWORK EXPRESS serves you -the direct response advertiser. We are committed to providing our clients with the best quality service in product marketing, lead generation and market research.

Our Operators are trained and

ready to receive calls for: Catalog requests and orders; lead generation; dealer location; subscriptions; fund raising; etc.

We are qualified and experienced in all media sources: Television, Radio, Print advertising, Direct Mail, Catalogs, etc.

NETWORK EXPRESS
993 South Santa Fe Ave., Suite C
Vista, California 92083
1-800-541-0900
1-800-334-3030 In CA

Advertisement (Original)

All the text is treated with equal strength. As a result, no concept or benefit clearly emerges.

> **WANT TO SAVE**
> # MONEY
> **ON YOUR LONG DISTANCE**
> # PHONE BILL?
> # 013/434-1278
> **North Central Communications**
> **Jack Winter**

The rhetorical question the copy begins with will probably turn off all but the most determined reader.

The page border lacks definition and character.

(Makeover)

Reducing the border and extending the keypad visual to break out of the box above and below make the ad appear larger.

The most important word has been significantly increased in size and shadowed, giving a three-dimensional effect.

Important words and the phone number, the call to action, are significantly larger than subordinate information.

Text alignment reflecting the diagonal shape of the graphic integrates text and visual.

Advertisement (Original)

The image of a house being struck by lightning may cause a negative reaction, making this advertisement more a hindrance than a help to this business.

A potpourri of type styles and sizes creates confusion in this small ad.

The small, underlined headline looks like the most insignificant line of copy in the ad.

(Makeover)

Simple graphic accents and a typographic overhaul create a more cohesive, appealing effect.

Similar type sizes link the headline and phone number, the most important items in the ad.

Screens of different values in the lightning image create interesting effects.

Catalogs (Original)

Catalogs and price lists without illustrations present a unique set of design challenges. Type must be handled skillfully to avoid visual monotony.

Often, a symmetrical type treatment provides too little contrast to fully engage the reader.

Note how undifferentiated spacing creates a run-on effect, further discouraging readers.

NORMAN ROCKWELL
323 MAGAZINE COVERS
By Finch. 456 pages. Huge 12 X 15 1/4. This magnificent, large-format, full color volume spans the artist's long and prolific career, reproducing 323 of his cover paintings for the SATURDAY EVENING POST, LADIES HOME JOURNAL and other magazines. Published at $85.00. Only $45.00

GREAT MAGAZINE COVERS OF THE WORLD
By Kery. 184 pages. 9 1/4 X 12. A panorama of more than 500 great magazine covers (most reproduced in full color) from 20 countries, spanning a century and a half of magazine publishing around the world. Including examples from 200 19th and 20th century magazines. Published at $65. Only $$5.00

VASARELY
150 pages. 9 1/4 X 13. 180 illustrations, including 64 full color plates. Masterful reproductions and a text by the artist combine to form an authoritative yet personal study of one of the major figures of modern art. Published at $60.00. Only $35.00

CHAGALL BY CHAGALL
Sorlier. 262 pages. 11 1/4 X 12. 285 illustrations, including 83 full color plates. Illustrated autobiography. Published at $50.00. Only $40.00.

MALFIELD PARRISH
By Ludwig. 223 pages. 9 X 12. 184 illustrations, 64 in full color Published at $25.00. Only $18.00.

THE GREAT BOOK OF FRENCH IMPRESSIONISM
By Kelder. 448 pages. 12 X 14 1/4. Over 200 illustrations, including 200 full color plates and 16 spectacular full color fold-outs. Huge, exquisitely produced treasury of French Impressionist art, packed with full-page reproductions. Examines the lives and works of all the major Impressionists and Post-Impressionists. Published at $100.00. Now $59.00

CARL FABERGE: GOLDSMITH TO THE IMPERIAL COURT OF RUSSIA
By Snowman. 100 pages. 8 1/4 X 10 1/2. Over 185 photos, 111 in full color. Originally published at $35.00. Only $22.00

CONTEMPORARY PAINTING
By Vogt. 135 pages. 7 1/2 X 10 1/2. Over 50 in full color. Penetrating analysis of World War II European and American art. Including paintings by Jaspar Johns, Andy Warhol, Roy Lichtenstein, Jackson Pollock, others. $19.95. Now $14.95

TWENTIETH CENTURY MASTERS OF EROTIC ART
By Smith. 212 pages. 9 X 12. 190 full color plates presents erotic works by such top-ranking artists as Picasso, Segal, Dali, Ernst, Rauschenberg, Rivers, Warhol, Schiele and others, many of which have never been displayed in public exhibitions. $30.00. Now $20.00

LEONARDO DA VINCI
538 pages. 11 X 14 1/2. Huge. 1,635 illustrations, including many large full color plates. Originally published in Italy by the Instituto Geografico De Agostini, this new edition is the most lavish, authoritative ever produced. Published at $60. Now $50.00.

REMBRANT PAINTINGS
By Gerson. 527 pages. 11 X 14 1/2. Huge. Over 730 illustrations, including many large full color plates. Complete, authoritative and beautiful presentation of the great master's work. Written by one of the world's foremost Rembrandt authorities. The book was thirty years in the making in Amsterdam, and is lavishly illustrated with spectacular reproductions. Published at $60.00. Only $50.00

ENGLISH CAMEO GLASS
By Grover. 480 pages. 8 X 11. A wealth of rare firsthand material and over 1,000 color and black and white plates makes this book an invaluable reference. Published at $50.00. Now $25.00.

20,000 YEARS OF WORLD PAINTING
By Jaffe. 416 pages. 9 X 13. Historical survey from early to modern art. 1,000 reproductions in full color. Was $50.00. Now $20.00.

STAINED GLASS
By Seddon & Stephens. 205 pages. 473 full color photos. 11 X 14. Covers stained glass from the beginning to the present. Was $39.95. Now $19.95.

THE COMPLETE BOOK OF EROTIC ART
By Kronhausen. 781 black and white plates. Extraordinary collection of the world's erotic art from Japan, China, India, Renaissance masters and modern greats. Originally published in 2 Volumes at $50.00. New, Complete 1 Volume Edition only $25.00.

COLLECTING POLITICAL AMERICANA
By Sullivan 1980. 250 pages. 8 X 11. 400 illustrations. Packed with reading. Out of print. $15.95. Now $10.00.

Diamonds
Myth, magic and reality. Revised edition. Over 420 full color illustrations. Beautiful and informative look at the worlds most magnificent and mysterious stone. Tells how to recognize and appreciate quality stones, more. 288 pages. Large. 10 1/4 X 12/ Originally published at $50.00. Only $29.00.

THE GREAT BOOK OF JEWELS
By Heninger. 206 full color plates. 94 black and white photos. The most spectacular, lavishly illustrated, comprehensive volume ever published on jewels and jewelry. Nearly 300 photos specially made for this volume, many gems now available for public inspection before. Includes bibliography, table of gemstones: much more. Huge. 11 1/4 X 13 3/4. Published at $69.50. Now $29.95.

10

Catalogs (Makeover)

Subtle changes in spacing and typeface create contrast and promote readability.

The two-columned format is retained, but body copy is set ragged-right (instead of justified) to add contrast and break up type.

Titles now appear in sans-serif type, which provides more contrast to body copy.

The "Reference Art Books" logo (taken from the front cover) has been reversed and repeated on each page.

The firm's toll-free phone number is repeated on each page, creating a consistent response mechanism.

NORMAN ROCKWELL
323 Magazine Covers
By Finch. 456 pages. Huge 12 X 15 1/4. This magnificent, large-format, full color volume spans the artist's long and prolific career, reproducing 323 of his cover paintings for the SATURDAY EVENING POST, LADIES HOME JOURNAL and other magazines. Published at $85.00. Only $45.00

GREAT MAGAZINE COVERS OF THE WORLD
By Kery. 184 pages. 9 1/4 X 12. A panorama of more than 500 great magazine covers (most reproduced in full color) from 20 countries, spanning a century and a half of magazine publishing around the world. Including examples from 200 19th and 20th century magazines. Published at $65. Only $$5.00

VASARELY
150 pages. 9 1/4 X 13. 180 illustrations, including 64 full color plates. Masterful reproductions and a text by the artist combine to form an authoritative yet personal study of one of the major figures of modern art. Published at $60,00. Only $35.00

CHAGALL BY CHAGALL
Sorlier. 262 pages. 11 1/4 X 12. 285 illustrations, including 83 full color plates. Illustrated autobiography. Published at $50.00. Only $40.00.

MALFIELD PARRISH
By Ludwig. 223 pages. 9 X 12. 184 illustrations, 64 in full color. Published at $25.00. Only $18.00.

THE GREAT BOOK OF FRENCH IMPRESSIONISM
By Kelder. 448 pages. 12 X 14 1/4. Over 200 illustrations, including 200 full color plates and 16 spectacular full color fold-outs. Huge, exquisitely produced treasury of French Impressionist art, packed with full-page reproductions. Examines the lives and works of all the major Impressionists and Post-Impressionists. Published at $100.00. Now $59.00

CARL FABERGE: GOLDSMITH TO THE IMPERIAL COURT OF RUSSIA
By Snowman. 100 pages. 8 1/4 X 10 1/2. Over 185 photos, 111 in full color. Originally published at $35.00. Only $22.00

CONTEMPORARY PAINTING
By Vogt. 135 pages. 7 1/2 X 10 1/2. Over 50 in full color. Penetrating analysis of World War II European and American art. Including paintings by Jaspar Johns, Andy Warhol, Roy Lichtenstein, Jackson Pollock, others. $19.95. Now $14.95

TWENTIETH CENTURY MASTERS OF EROTIC ART
By Smith. 212 pages. 9 X 12. 190 full color plates presents erotic works by such top-ranking artists as Picasso, Segal, Dali, Ernst, Rauschenberg, Rivers, Warhol, Schiele and others, many of which have never been displayed in public exhibitions. $30.00. Now $20.00

LEONARDO DA VINCI
538 pages. 11 X 14 1/2. Huge. 1,635 illustrations, including many large full color plates. Originally published in Italy by the Instituto Geografico De Agostini, this new edition is the most lavish, authoritative ever produced. Published at $60. Now $50.00.

REMBRANT PAINTINGS
By Gerson. 527 pages. 11 X 14 1/2. Huge. Over 730 illustrations, including many large full color plates. Complete, authoritative and beautiful presentation of the great master's work. Written by one of the world's foremost Rembrandt authorities. The book was thirty years in the making in Amsterdam, and is lavishly illustrated with spectacular reproductions. Published at $60.00. Only $50.00

ENGLISH CAMEO GLASS
By Grover. 480 pages. 8 X 11. A wealth of rare firsthand material and over 1,000 color and black and white plates makes this book an invaluable reference. Published at $50.00. Now $25.00.

20,000 YEARS OF WORLD PAINTING
By Jaffe. 416 pages. 9 X 13. Historical survey from early to modern art. 1,000 reproductions in full color. Was $50.00. Now $20.00.

STAINED GLASS
By Seddon & Stephens. 205 pages. 473 full color photos. 11 X 14. Covers stained glass from the beginning to the present. Was $39.95. Now $19.95.

THE COMPLETE BOOK OF EROTIC ART
By Kronhausen. 781 black and white plates. Extraordinary collection of the world's erotic art from Japan, China, India, Renaissance masters and modern greats. Originally published in 2 Volumes at $50.00. New, Complete 1 Volume Edition only $25.00.

COLLECTING POLITICAL AMERICANA
By Sullivan 1980. 250 pages. 8 X 11. 400 illustrations. Packed with reading. Out of print. $15.95. Now $10.00.

DIAMONDS
Myth, magic and reality. Revised edition. Over 420 full color illustrations. Beautiful and informative look at the worlds most magnificent and mysterious stone. Tells how to recognize and appreciate quality stones, more. 288 pages. Large. 10 1/4 X 12/ Originally published at $50.00. Only $29.00.

THE GREAT BOOK OF JEWELS
By Heninger. 206 full color plates. 94 black and white photos. The most spectacular, lavishly illustrated, comprehensive volume ever published on jewels and jewelry. Nearly 300 photos specially made for this volume, many gems neve available for public inspection before. Includes bibliography, table of gemstones: much more. Huge. 11 1/4 X 13 3/4. Published at $69.50. Now $29.95.

Reference Art Books   PHONE TOLL-FREE / 1-800-238-8288

Correspondence *(Original)*

Letters produced on a typewriter lack the professional appearance of desktop-typeset output.

There are too many words on the page. Margins are minuscule.

Indented items are indistinct from each other and from body copy.

The uniform type size throughout lacks color and dynamics.

THE WOODEN BOAT SHOW

The Wooden Boat Show in Newport, Rhode Island is the largest show of its kind in the country. Ten thousand qualified showgoers and hundreds of exhibitors attend this show each year. Undoubtedly, it is one of the most important events of the wooden boat industry.

The Wooden Boat Show is the ideal chance for you to reach your audience and to increase your sales. The 1987 show, August 27 - 30, will be our biggest and best one yet. The following are some of the changes we have made to ensure this:

o   Layout

    We have added a small boatbuilder's section located near the main gate with excellent visibility to Newport's America's Cup Avenue. Please note that the cost for exhibiting in this section will be based on <u>only</u> the amount of space utilized and not on designated 10 X 20 or 20 X 20 blocks.

o   Exhibitor's Breakfast with a presentation by Jon Wilson, Editor & Publisher of <u>WoodenBoat Magazine.</u>

    On Friday August 28, at 8am, Jon will be speaking to all interested exhibitors on the market outlook for wooden boats. There will also be a question/answer period immediately following the discussion. Further information about the presentation will be mailed later.

o   Advertising/Public Relations

    We will be increasing our advertising and publicity campaign in order to broaden our pre-show coverage while still attracting the very unique wooden boat attendee.

The enclosed package contains all the necessary information pertaining to exhibiting in this year's show. Please take the time to review the materials and return them as soon as possible. If you have any questions on the forms or the show itself, please don't hesitate to call.

I look forward to working with you on a quality and successful Wooden Boat Show.

Best regards,

Abby Murphy
Show Manager

P.O. BOX 549, NEWPORT, RHODE ISLAND 02840   (401) 846-1600

Correspondence (Makeover)

Even the simplest desktop publishing techniques can greatly improve letters to selected recipients.

To unify the letterhead, the illustration has been moved to the left and integrated with the address.

A salutation engages the reader.

A highly readable Times Roman serif typeface condenses the message.

Boldface type contrasts subheads with text.

The copy for indented sections is set smaller, with reduced leading.

The letter ends by returning to a single wide column that matches the first paragraph.

THE WOODEN BOAT SHOW

P.O. BOX 549, NEWPORT, RHODE ISLAND 02840 (401) 846-1600

Dear Wooden Boat Enthusiast,

The Wooden Boat Show in Newport, Rhode Island is the largest show of its kind in the country. Ten thousand qualified showgoers and hundreds of exhibitors attend this show each year. Undoubtedly, it is one of the most important events of the wooden boat industry.

The Wooden Boat Show is the ideal chance for you to reach your audience and to increase your sales. The 1987 show, August 27 - 30, will be our biggest and best one yet. The following are some of the changes we have made to ensure this:

Layout

We have added a small boatbuilder's section located near the main gate with excellent visibility to Newport's America's Cup Avenue. Please note that the cost for exhibiting in this section will be based on *only* the amount of space utilized and not on designated 10 x 20 or 20 x 20 blocks.

Exhibitor's Breakfast

On Friday August 28, at 8am, Jon Wilson, Editor & Publishers of *Wooden Boat Magazine*, will be speaking to all interested exhibitors on the market outlook for wooden boats. There will also be a question/answer period immediately following the discussion. Further information about the presentation will be mailed later.

Advertising/Public Relations

We will be increasing our advertising and publicity campaign in order to broaden our pre-show coverage while still attracting the very unique wooden boat attendee.

The enclosed package contains all the necessary information pertaining to exhibiting in this year's show. Please take the time to review the materials and return them as soon as possible. If you have any questions on the forms or the show itself, please don't hesitate to call.

I look forward to working with you on a successful Wooden Boat Show.

Best regards,

Abby Murphy
Show Manager

Flyers (Original)

On this and the next three pages, two similar "question-and-answer" motifs are manipulated to produce different but effective results.

The question marks are redundant because the headline and the content clearly communicate the Q&A format.

The text and visuals are crowded.

Answers beginning with a single, boldface word (e.g., "Yes!") look as if they might belong with the preceding boldface question.

**Answers to Questions
Frequently Asked About
Tri-Steel Homes**

1. What is the Tri-Steel concept and why is it different from conventional wood frame construction?
   The Tri-Steel concept is based upon the utilization and superior quality and strength of steel to form the frame or shell of the home. This allows the home to be stick built on site, but with steel instead of wood and bolts and fasteners instead of nails and staples.
   The superior strength of steel means that the frame spacing can be on 6-foot and 8-foot centers instead of 16-inch and 24-inch centers. Plus, we can utilize 9 inches of insulation on the sides and also provide consistent quality, less maintenance, and much greater strength than is possible with conventional construction. In addition, this gives you much greater flexibility inside the home since none of the walls need to be load bearing. **Also important, the entire shell can often be dried-in within 4 to 5 days by an inexperienced crew.**

2. How are Tri-Steel homes unique?
   Our homes utilize an engineered and computer designed steel structural system. You can choose from a wide selection of contemporary slant wall designs which stand out among conventional wooded structures or numerous conventional-looking straight wall designs ranging from conservatively gabled roof lines to ultra-modern units allowing clerestory window placement.

3. What are some of the advantages of Tri-Steel homes?
   Tri-Steel homes can cost less to erect and can go up much faster. They are exceptionally energy efficient, require almost no exterior maintenance, and are tremendously flexible in their design. In addition to these areas of savings, they offer the strength and durability of steel to withstand extreme weather conditions, termites and fire. The quality of steel is consistently high. Pre-engineered framing components ensure your home goes up one way - the right way! Special snow or wind loads are possible with very little extra cost. The also meet Seismic 4 earthquake specifications - the highest rating possible.

4. Have these homes been tried and proven?
   Absolutely! In terms of the history of home building, Tri-Steel homes are a new and unique concept; however, these homes have been in use throughout the South for over ten years. Tri-Steel has thousands of structures all across the nation and we are constantly receiving letters from satisfied homeowners attesting to the beauty, strength and energy savings of Tri-Steel structures.

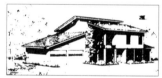 

5. Can I put up one of these homes myself and is construction assistance available?
   Yes! The home is actually designed to be constructed independently by the buyer. No heavy lifting equipment or special tools are required. The steel beams are designed to bolt together - A to B, B to C - with prepunched holes so you are basically working with a giant erector set. No cutting or welding is required on the job site and complete instructions and drawings are included in the package. Tri-Steel can provide your choice of construction assistance. As part of the assistance available, we can consult with you over the phone, have your shell erected, or provide on-site supervision on a daily or weekly basis.

6. How much flexibility do I have choosing a home size?
   Infinite! A virtually unlimited variety of home sizes are offered from 800 square feet on up. Our homes come in one, two of three level designs with slant of straight walls. We have hundreds of plans drawn and available for immediate mailing and we can also draw custom designs to meet virtually any floor plan or size requirements.

7. Can I add to the home at a later date?
   Yes! Additional space may be added in the future at low cost and relative ease allowing you to enlarge your home economically

Tri-Steel Structures

Flyers (Makeover)

This informative "magazine style" format uses creative type treatments to lure the reader into the piece.

Question marks and illustrations have been omitted to allow larger type and more white space.

Numbers in drop-cap style create further contrast and visual attention that attract attention.

Answers now appear in a different typeface, which helps distinguish them from the questions.

The Tri-Steel logo feature is now larger and more readable.

1. *What is the Tri-Steel concept and why is it different from conventional wood frame construction?*

    The Tri-Steel concept is based upon the utilization and superior quality and strength of steel to form the frame or shell of the home. This allows the home to be stick built on site, but with steel instead of wood and bolts and fasteners instead of nails and staples.

    The superior strength of steel means that the frame spacing can be on 6-foot and 8-foot centers instead of 16-inch and 24-inch centers. Plus, we can utilize 9 inches of insulation on the sides and also provide consistent quality, less maintenance, and much greater strength than is possible with conventional construction. In addition, this gives you much greater flexibility inside the home since none of the walls need to be load bearing. **Also important, the entire shell can often be dried-in within 4 to 5 days by an inexperienced crew.**

2. *How are Tri-Steel homes unique?*

    Our homes utilize an engineered and computer designed steel structural system. You can choose from a wide selection of contemporary slant wall designs which stand out among conventional wooded structures or numerous conventional-looking straight wall designs ranging from conservatively gabled roof lines to ultra-modern units allowing clerestory window placement.

3. *What are some of the advantages of Tri-Steel homes?*

    Tri-Steel homes can cost less to erect and can go up much faster. They are exceptionally energy efficient, require almost no exterior maintenance, and are tremendously flexible in their design. In addition to these areas of savings, they offer the strength and durability of steel to withstand extreme weather conditions, termites and fire. The quality of steel is consistently high. Pre-engineered framing components ensure your home goes up one way - the right way! Special snow or wind loads are possible with very little extra cost. The also meet Seismic 4 earthquake specifications - the highest rating required.

4. *Have these homes been tried and proven?*

    Absolutely! In terms of the history of home building, Tri-Steel homes are a new and unique concept; however, these homes have been in use throughout the South for over ten years. Tri-Steel has thousands of structures all across the nation and we are constantly receiving letters from satisfied homeowners attesting to the beauty, strength and energy savings of Tri-Steel structures.

5. *Can I put up one of these homes myself and is construction assistance available?*

    Yes! The home is actually designed to be constructed independently by the buyer. No heavy lifting equipment or special tools are required. The steel beams are designed to bolt together - A to B, B to C - with prepunched holes so you are basically working with a giant erector set. No cutting or welding is required on the job site and complete instructions and drawings are included with the package. Tri-Steel can provide your choice of construction assistance. As part of the assistance available, we can consult with you over the phone, have your shell erected, or provide on-site supervision on a daily or weekly basis.

6. *How much flexibility do I have choosing a home size?*

    Infinite! A virtually unlimited variety of home sizes are offered from 800 square feet on up. Our homes come in one, two of three level designs with slant of straight walls. We have hundreds of plans drawn and available for immediate mailing and we can also draw custom designs to meet virtually any floor plan or size requirements.

7. *Can I add to the home at a later date?*

    Yes! Additional space may be added in the future at low cost and relative ease allowing you to enlarge your home economically as your needs and income requires.

Tri-Steel
Structures

5800 Campus Circle, Irving, TX 75063
Telephone (214) 580-3400
© 1987, All Rights Reserved
™

Flyers (Original)

Too much copy crammed into a small space creates a "dark" look that discourages reading.

The company name, SPORT IT, disappears into the headline.

Questions set in bold, uppercase type are hard to read.

Answers are also difficult to read because the type size is too small in proportion to the line length.

Justified type creates exaggerated word spacing and often produces widows.

THE MOST FREQUENTLY ASKED QUESTIONS ABOUT A SPORT IT DEALERSHIP

1. **WHAT IS THE INITIAL INVESTMENT FOR A SPORT IT DEALERSHIP?**

   $1,500.

2. **IS THERE A ROYALTY OR SERVICE FEE?**

   There is no royalty fee, however, there is a minimal $25.00 service fee to cover the following: monthly newsletters, toll free consultation service and on-going research for obtaining new suppliers. This $25.00 service fee is due the 10th of each month and can not fluctuate during the five year term of the Sport It Dealer Agreement.

3. **ARE THERE ANY OTHER FEES OR CHARGES?**

   Yes. There is a $100.00 renewal fee at the end of the five year term of the Agreement which will renew the Agreement for an additional five year period. Also, if you elect to sell your dealership or transfer to a new location a $100.00 transfer fee is needed to cover the cost of changes and modifications to our records, files, et cetera.

4. **WHAT QUALIFICATIONS ARE NEEDED TO BECOME A SPORT IT DEALER?**

   The Sport It Home Office receives over 1,600 inquiries per month. From these inquiries nearly 400 applications are received. The evaluation committee selects approximately 40 applicants that will become Sport It Dealers. These applicants must have a good credit standing, positive references and have potential to represent Sport It as professional dealers.

5. **WHAT DO I RECEIVE FOR MY INITIAL INVESTMENT OF $1,500?**

   The initial $1,500 investment provides you with a business opportunity allowing immediate access to brand name merchandise at very competitive prices which would not be available to you as an independent dealer. The Sport It Dealership puts you in business immediately. You will receive catalogs, price lists, purchase order forms, an Operations Manual and miscellaneous samples in your initial box of materials.

6. **WHAT IS THE TERM OF THE SPORT IT DEALERSHIP AGREEMENT?**

   Five years.

7. **MAY I HAVE A PARTNER OR PARTNERS WITH MY SPORT IT DEALERSHIP?**

   Yes. You may have as many partners as you wish.

8. **ARE THERE ANY TAX ADVANTAGES WITH MY SPORT IT DEALERSHIP?**

   There are many tax advantages available for your home operated business. A portion of your rent, house payment, electricity, heat, insurance, taxes, et cetera, can be used as deductions. In addition, automobile expenses and depreciation may be deducted according to the percentage that your vehicle is used for business.

9. **CAN I FINANCE MY INITIAL INVESTMENT OF $1,500?**

   The initial $1,500 investment can be charged to your MasterCard or Visa credit card enabling you to make monthly payments for your Sport it Dealership.

10. **CAN I SELL MY SPORT IT DEALERSHIP?**

    Yes. Some Dealers, due to unforeseen circumstances, have had to sell their Dealership. Most Dealers who have sold their Dealership have done so at a substantial profit.

Flyers (Makeover)

A three-column format clearly separates questions and answers, letting readers pick and choose according to their specific interests.

The company name is reversed and enlarged for greater impact and recognition.

A "friendlier" typeface and flush-left/ragged-right alignment have been used for all text.

A three-column format, with questions appearing in the narrow left-hand column, provides better organization and more white space.

Shorter lines set in narrower columns make the answers more readable.

SPORT IT

The Most Frequently Asked Questions About a Sport It Dealership

1. **WHAT IS THE INITIAL INVESTMENT FOR A SPORT IT DEALERSHIP?**

   $1,500

2. **IS THERE A ROYALTY OR SERVICE FEE?**

   There is no royalty fee, however, there is a minimal $25.00 service fee to cover the following: monthly newsletters, toll free consultation service and on-going research for obtaining new suppliers. This $25.00 service fee is due the 10th of each month and can not fluctuate during the five term of the Sport I dealer agreement.

3. **ARE THERE ANY OTHER FEES OR CHARGES?**

   Yes. There is a $100.00 renewal fee at the end of the five year term of the agreement which will renew the agreement for an additional five year period. Also, if you elect to sell your dealership of transfer to a new location a $100.00 transfer fee is needed to cover the cost of changes and modifications to our records, files, et cetera.

4. **WHAT QUALIFICATIONS ARE NEEDED TO BECOME A SPORT IT DEALER?**

   The Sport It home office receives over 1,600 inquiries per month. From these inquiries nearly 400 applications are received. The evaluation committee selects approximately 40 applicants that will become Sport It dealers. These applicants must have a good credit standing, positive references and have potential to represent Sport It as professional dealers.

5. **WHAT DO I RECEIVE FOR MY INITIAL INVESTMENT OF $1,500?**

   The initial $1,500 investment provides you with a business opportunity allowing immediate access to brand name merchandise at very competitive prices which would not be available to you as an independent dealer. The Sport It dealership puts you in business immediately. You will receive catalogs, price lists, purchase order forms, Operations Manual and miscellaneous sample merchandise in you initial box of materials.

6. **WHAT IS THE TERM OF THE SPORT IT DEALERSHIP AGREEMENT?**

   Five years.

7. **MAY I HAVE A PARTNER OR PARTNERS WITH MY SPORT IT DEALERSHIP?**

   Yes. You may have as many partners as you wish.

8. **ARE THERE ANY TAX ADVANTAGES WITH MY SPORT IT DEALERSHIP?**

   There are many tax advantages available for you home operated business. A portion of your rent, house payment, electricity, heat, insurance, taxes, etc., can be used as deductions. In addition, automobile expenses and depreciation may be deducted according to the percentage that your vehicle is used for business.

9. **CAN I FINANCE MY INITIAL INVESTMENT OF $1,500?**

   The initial $1,500 investment can be charged to your MasterCard of Visa credit card enabling you to make monthly payments for your Sport It dealership.

10. **CAN I SELL MY SPORT IT DEALERSHIP?**

    Yes. Some Dealers, due to unforeseen circumstances, have had to sell their dealership. Most dealers who have sold their Dealership have done so at a substantial profit.

User Manuals (Original)

Because of their practical and simple design, user guides, reference manuals and technical documents are ideal formats for desktop publishing.

The copy begins unceremoniously with "READ AND SAVE THESE INSTRUCTIONS."

The "UL" symbol is an unnecessary visual distraction. It is irrelevant by the time the customer gets to the instructions.

ıe code number (T-1), primarily an internal document tracking number, is given too much prominence. (Such identifiers should be placed in small type on the last page of the document.)

Code # T-1

CREST

READ AND SAVE THESE INSTRUCTIONS

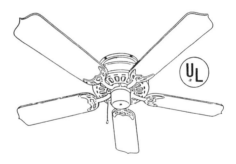

These instructions are intended for use with the following U.L. Listed Crest models.

SERIES:	MODELS:
4000	*04-002 Through 04-498
4500	*04-502 Through 04-698

*Includes only those models which end in <u>even</u> numbers.

We thank you for selecting one of our products to make your house a home. We dedicate considerable time to insure that our products provide high quality and the highest level of customer satisfaction. If, however, problems should arise, please keep your bill of sale as proof of purchase.

24.

User Manuals (Makeover)

Note how a few modifications have made this document more inviting *and* more informative. The page is now usefully organized so that each element—body copy, illustration, table of contents, etc.—is distinguished by its own appropriate format.

The heading is now friendlier and not as intimidating.

The illustration has been touched up and screened, strengthening its impact.

Series and model numbers are set closer together at the upper tight-hand corner, where the purchaser can quickly find them.

The Crest logo is moved to a bottom corner, where readers are accustomed to finding such information.

A small but complete table of contents balances the introductory paragraph and acts as a quick reference.

HOW TO INSTALL YOUR NEW CREST FAN

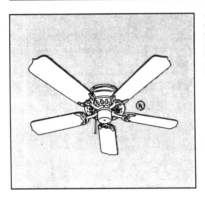

These instructions are intended for use with the following U.L. Listed Crest models. Save this manual for future reference.

Series: **4000**
Models: **04-001** through **04-499**

Series: **4500**
Models: **04-501** through **40-699**

TABLE OF CONTENTS:

We thank you for selecting one of our porducts to make your house a home. We dedicate considerable time to insure that our products provide high quality and the highest level of customer satisfaction. If, however, problems should arise, please keep your bill of sale as proof of purchase.

CREST

User Manuals (Original)

On the inside pages, formatting changes are in order, to improve the readability and appeal of the piece.

The wide column of type is gray and monotonous.

The illustration is buried, unconnected to the text.

■■■■■■■ GENERAL ■■■■■■■

1. To ensure the success of the installation, be sure to read the instructions and review the diagrams throughly before beginning. Review and follow only the instructions that are applicable for your fan.

2. All electrical connections must be in accordance with local codes, ordinances, or National Electrical Code. If you are unfamiliar with methods of installing electrical wiring, secure the services of a qualified electrician.

3. Make sure that your installation site will not allow rotating fan blades to come in contact with any object. A minimum clearance of 7 feet from the floor to the trailing edge of the blade is required.

4. If you are installing more than one ceiling fan, make sure that you do not mix fan blade sets.

5. If the fan will be mounted on a ceiling outlet box, a 4" x 2¼" deep metal octagon outlet box is required. The outlet box must be directly supported by the building structure. The outlet box and its support must be able to support the moving weight of the fan (at' least 50 lbs.) The outlet box must not twist or work loose. Do not use plastic outlet boxes! The mounting bracket must be attached using the hardware supplied with the ceiling outlet box.

6. If mounting fan to a joist, the joist must be able to support the moving weight of the fan (at least 50 lbs.)

7. Installation to a concrete ceiling should be performed by a qualified electrician.

8. Before beginning, disconnect power by removing fuse or turning off circuit breaker.

9. After the fan is completely installed, make sure that all connections are secure to prevent fan from falling.

10. Do not insert anything into fan blades while ceiling fan is operating.

11. Fan must be turned off and stopped before reversing fan direction.

NOTE: The important safeguards and instructions appearing in this manual are not meant to cover all possible conditions and situations that may occur. It must be understood that common sense, caution and care are factors which cannot be built into any product. These factors must be supplied by the person(s) caring for and operating the unit.

┌─ TOOLS AND MATERIALS REQUIRED ─┐

- Philips screw driver
- Blade screw driver
- Adjustable wrench
- Step ladder
- Wire cutters
- Wiring supplies as required by electrical code

CAUTION: Before assembling your ceiling fan, refer to sections titled MOUNTING OPTIONS and ELECTRICAL CONNECTIONS. If you feel you do not have electrical wiring knowledge or experience, refer to a do-it-yourself wiring handbook or have your fan installed by a licensed electrician.

User Manuals (Makeover)

With text, illustrations and caution notes organized into appropriate formats, the user instructions are easier to read and follow.

Subheads are now set flush-left (flush-right on right-hand pages) so readers can quickly spot major information categories.

The illustration has been moved to the top and screened to call immediate attention to required items.

Horizontal rules have been thickened to match the type size of the headings.

Skillful layout of text and illustrations allows more information on each page.

GENERAL

1. To ensure the success of the installation, be sure to read the instructions and review the diagrams thoroughly before beginning. Review and follow only the instructions that are applicable for your fan.
2. All electrical connections must be in accordance with local codes, ordinances, or National Electrical Code. If you are unfamiliar with methods of installing electrical wiring, secure the services of a qualified electrician.
3. Make sure that your installation site will not allow rotating fan blades to come in contact with any object. A minimum clearance of 7 feet from the floor to the trailing edge of the blade is required.
4. If you are installing more than one ceiling fan, make sure that you do not mix fan blade sets.
5. If the fan will be mounted on a ceiling outlet box, a 4" x 2 1/8" deep metal octagon outlet box is required. The outlet box must be directly supported by the building structure. The outlet box and its support must be able to support the moving weight of the fan (at least 50 lbs.) The outlet box must not twist or work loose. Do not use plastic outlet boxes! The mounting bracket must be attached using the hardware supplied with the ceiling outlet box.
6. If mounting fan to a joist, the joist must be able to support the moving weight of the fan (at least 50 lbs.).
7. Installation to a concrete ceiling should be performed by a qualified electrician.
8. Before beginning, disconnect power by removing fuse or turning off circuit breaker.
9. After the fan is completely installed, make sure that all connections are secure to prevent fan from falling.
10. Do not insert anything into fan blades while ceiling fan is operating.
11. Fan must be turned off and stopped before reversing fan direction.
12. This fan is not intended to be supported by single threaded J-Hook supports.

NOTE: The important safe guards and instructions appearing in this manual are not meant to cover all possible conditions and situations that may occur. It must be understood that common sense, caution and care are factors which cannot be built into any product. These factors must be supplied by the person(s) caring for and operating the unit.

TOOLS AND MATERIALS REQUIRED

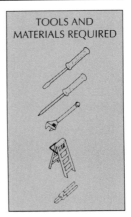

CAUTION: Before assembling your ceiling fan refer to sections titled MOUNTING OPTIONS and ELECTRICAL CONNECTIONS. If you feel you do not have electrical wiring knowledge or experience, refer to a do-it-yourself wiring handbook or have your fan installed by a licensed electrician.

UNPACKING THE FAN

Unpack the fan and check contents: You should receive:
☐ Fan motor assembly
☐ Downrod assembly
☐ Canopy
☐ Blade set
☐ Blade attachment flange
☐ Package of hardware for mounting blades
☐ Mounting bracket and hardware
☐ Wire nuts for electrical connection
☐ Wooden tassel

• Some models have these parts factory assembled

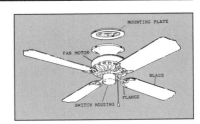

Advertisements (Original)

Repetition can easily lead to confusion. In this page design, continuity and coherence are sacrificed.

Three repeating head-lines waste valuable space and segment the ad unnecessarily.

Phone numbers and hotel information are required throughout the piece, creating visual "clutter."

Love Yosemite in summer? It *sparkles* in the winter.

Savor the magnificence of Yosemite at our special Vintners' Holidays.

Indulge your senses in one of America's most beautiful places while attending seminars on wine with some of California's most prestigious vintners. Including those from Jordan, Chateau St. Jean, Schramsburg, Charles Shaw, Calera, and Fetzer.

Stay at either the Ahwahnee Hotel or Yosemite Lodge. And

wine and dine with your favorite winemakers at our gourmet Vintners' Dinner in the grand Ahwahnee dining room.

Eight sessions of the Vintners' Holidays are scheduled Nov. 13 through Dec. 17 For more information or reservations, call our Holiday Hotline at (209) 252-2700.

There's no more refreshing way to get away from it all.

YOSEMITE
VINTNERS' HOLIDAYS

Love Yosemite in summer? It *cooks* in the winter.

Get a taste of Yosemite at our special Chefs' Holidays.

Attend gourmet cooking classes led by famous American chefs amid America's famous breathtaking scenery.

Each chef will teach a class featuring his or her own American regional cooking style. Among those who participated last January are Ken Frank of La Toque in Los Angeles, Bradley Ogden of Campton Place in San Francisco, and Marcel Desaulniers of The Trellis in Williamsburg, Virginia.

Stay at the Ahwahnee Hotel or Yosemite Lodge. And at the end of your holiday, enjoy a gala dinner created especially by your chef.

Six sessions of the Chefs' Holidays are scheduled Jan. 5-23. For more information or reservations, call our Holiday Hotline

at (209) 252-2700. You just can't find a tastier vacation.

YOSEMITE
CHEFS' HOLIDAYS

Love Yosemite in summer? It *sings* in the winter.

With Yosemite as the stage, you'll have a great seat for our Musicians' Holidays. Enjoy arias from Handel to the present, highlights of Bizet's "Carmen," and Cimerosa's "The Secret Marriage." Or revel in a

Richard Rodgers revue and a concert performance of "West Side Story."

This festival will feature two sessions on opera and two on Broadway musicals, all hosted by leading composers, singers and directors.

Choose your lodging, the Ahwahnee Hotel or Yosemite Lodge. And enjoy a grand dinner, followed by a show.

The Musicians' Holidays are scheduled Jan. 26 through Feb. 6. For more information or reservations, call our Holiday Hotline at (209) 252-2700.

And find harmony with nature.

YOSEMITE
MUSICIANS' HOLIDAYS

Yosemite Park and Curry Co., an MCA Company, is a concessioner authorized by the U.S. Department of the Interior, National Park Service.
©1985 Yosemite Park and Curry Co.

Advertisements (Makeover)

The ad is strengthened and unified considerably by the large headline and the more natural vertical orientation of the columns of body copy.

A single "master headline" now dominates the page.

The headlines from the original ad are retained but used as subheads within the copy.

The original illustrations are reduced and repositioned.

Runaround type effectively ties body copy to illustrations.

The bottom of the ad has been cleaned up and the response vehicle—Yosemite's Holiday Hotline phone number—is now a dominant visual element.

Newsletters (Original)

This piece demonstrates how design principles applied inappropriately can result in a poorly designed document.

The rules in the body copy fight with the illustration box and rules in the nameplate.

Nonproportional type-faces create uneven word spacing.

Indention within narrow columns often causes awkward blocks of white space.

Technology Today

LOUISIANA TRANSPORTATION RESEARCH CENTER

Vol. 3 No. 1   January 1987

RESEARCH PROFILES

NEW METHOD STUDIED FOR BRIDGE REPAIRS

One of the most common forms of damage to the superstructure of steel bridges results from vehicle impact. This damage rarely causes a bridge to collapse, but results in the serious weakening of the structure as such damage accumulates. Member replacement is an expensive repair, and thus a more economical alternative has been needed.

Heat straightening offers the potential for quick and effective repairs for bent steel members. LSU has just completed the first phase of a research project on heat straightening under the sponsorship of LTRC. The process of heat straightening consists of heating the bent member at appropriate locations such that during the cooling process the unequal shrinkage will induce thermal stresses that straighten the member. The few experts who currently employ this technique base the process on experience. The research project will develop a rational methodology for determining the type, number and location of heat application points required to straighten damaged members. The specific objectives of this research project are:

Phase 1 : Analytical and experimental evaluation of heat straightening techniques in the laboratory.

Phase 2 : Field evaluation of heat straightening techniques and development of an interactive program for automated design of the repair scheme.

Phase 3 : Documentation and training sessions for La. DOTD personnel.

The information obtained in phase one of this project is available upon request from LTRC.

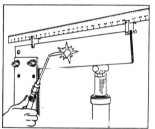

HEATING LABORATORY SAMPLE

STUDY UNDERWAY ON EMBANKMENT FAILURES

An in-house study on slope rehabilitation is moving forward in an effort to find an economical solution to a problem that has troubled the department for more than a decade--failing slopes on man-made embankments, particularly along the Interstate system.

Five failed slopes are being rehabilitated under the project, using three different methods: injection of lime and lime-fly ash; rebuilding with lime-

Newsletters (Makeover)

Contrasting typefaces and rules give the piece a contemporary feel appropriate to a technology newsletter.

The nameplate has been completely reworked.

A highly readable Times Roman typeface contrasts text with the sans-serif headline.

The caption is moved inside the illustration for better balance.

A 20 percent screen behind the illustration adds contrast and balances the nameplate with the text.

TECHNOLOGY

TODAY

A quarterly publication of the Louisiana Transportation Research Center

Summer 1987   Vol. 3, No. 3   **LTRC**

Research Profiles

New Method Studied for Bridge Repairs

One of the most common forms of damage to the superstructure of steel bridges results from vehicle impact. This damage rarely causes a bridge to collapse, but results in the serious weakening of the structure as such damage accumulates. Member replacement is an expensive repair, and thus a more economical alternative has been needed.

Heat straightening offers the potential for quick and effective repairs for bent steel members. LSU has just completed the first phase of a research project on heat straightening under the sponsorship of LTRC. The process of heat straightening consists of heating the bent member at appropriate locations such that during the cooling process the unequal shrinkage will induce thermal stresses that straighten the member. The few experts who currently employ this technique base the process on experience. The research project will develop a rational methodology for determining the type, number and location of heat application points required to straighten damaged members. The specific objectives of this research project are:

Phase 1: Analytical and experimental evaluation of heat straightening techniques in the laboratory.

Phase 2: Field evaluation of heat straightening techniques and development of an interactive

program for automated design of the repair scheme.

Phase 3: Documentation and training sessions for La. DOTD personnel.

The information obtained in phase one of this project is available upon request from LTRC.

Study Underway on Embankment Failures

An in-house study on slope rehabilitation is moving forward in an effort to find an economical solution

to a problem that has troubled the department for more than a decade—failing slopes on man-made embankments, particularly along the Interstate system.

Five failed slopes are being rehabilitated under the project, using three different methods: injection of lime and lime-fly ash; rebuilding with lime treated, compacted lifts; and reinforcement with geogrid. Construction is essentially complete on three study slopes on I-20 district 04 (Monroe), and a fourth slope is underway on I-210 in district 07 (Lake Charles). A fifth slope on I-20 in district 04 is still to be let to

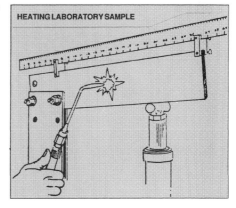

HEATING LABORATORY SAMPLE

Newsletters (Original)

In-house newsletters and other time-sensitive documents often can be made more appealing at no additional cost.

Headlines "butt" each other at the top, creating too much uniformity and symmetry.

A lack of indention sets up a uniformity that leads to boredom when the readers' eyes aren't challenged by contrast.

Matching type styles in headlines and text create a "gray" look.

Similarly, the lack of contrast caused by large square blocks of text and excessive leading between paragraphs causes readers to lose interest.

Computer Center
FACULTY BULLETIN

CALIFORNIA STATE UNIVERSITY, NORTHRIDGE   OCTOBER 1985

WHATEVER HAPPENED TO
COMPUTER AIDED INSTRUCTION
by Kurt Webb

Computer Aided Instruction (CAI) had its moments in the sun several years ago and has since seemed to have faded from the academic computing scene. However, there are now indications that a resurgence in CAI is occurring. This renaissance may be due to two factors; (1) The increased availability of authoring systems on micros and mainframe computers; and (2) The increased awareness and utilization of computing among educators.

An authoring system is a software product that allows the educator: (1) to organize the subject material, to be presented to the student, in a systematic way; (2) to query the student taking the computerized lessons on their comprehension of the study material: (3) to review the material previously presented or continue on with new material depending on how the student responded to the queries; and (4) to analyze student response to the lesson as a whole to help determine the next step in the learning process. Once such a CAI lesson has been prepared by using an authoring system, it can be presented to any number of students with each student taking the lesson at their convenience and at their own pace.

The Computer Center has recently purchased two authoring systems for the IBM PC. These are TENCORE and the McGraw-Hill Authoring System. These Two systems do require that the author as well as students have access to IBM PC computers. A third authoring, Instructional Workbench, is available on the AT&T 385 mainframe computers. These computers can be accessed from virtually any terminal on campus.

More on CAO and authoring systems will be forth coming. In the Meantime, If you are interested in any of these products contact Kurt Webb at Extension 3966.

MICROCOMPUTER JOURNAL FOR
INSTRUCTIONAL USERS
By J.S. Fleming

Collegiate Microcomputer is "a quarterly journal devoted to all aspects of microcomputers in the higher education curricula." A sample copy received by the Computer Center included articles such as "The Use of Microcomputers in the Teaching of Calculus," "An Introductory Course in System Dynamics," "Using Microcomputers to Store and Evaluate Exam Items" and "Computer Literacy for Undergraduate Humanities and Social Majors."

If interested, this journal is published by Collegiate Microcomputer, Rose-Hulman Institute of Technology, Terre Haute, IN 48703. Individual subscriptions are $28.00. A sample copy may be reviewed at the Computer Center, Engineering 121.

MICROCOMPUTER GRAPHICS
BEGIN TO GROW UP
By Dave Crawford

Do you remember what life was like before computer graphics?

If you are old enough to be reading this you probably do, since computer graphics for popular consumption have been with us for only a few years. But computer-generated pictures have become so common in movies and on television that most of us no longer marvel at them. We accept them unthinkingly, as if they had always been with us.

We watch science fiction movies in which vivid alien landscapes have been created in a computer's memory without using models of any kind. We are perfectly accustomed to music videos in

Newsletters (Makeover)

Creative use of white space, indention and leading helps make the piece more readable.

A simple, appealing nameplate often is the best way to improve a newsletter or tabloid.

Rules between columns and in the margins tie the nameplate to the text.

Exaggerated indents at beginnings of paragraphs add contrast without the intricacies of drop caps.

A "rag bottom" format provides design flexibility and saves production time.

Faculty
B U L L E T I N

COMPUTER CENTER / CALIFORNIA STATE UNIVERSITY / NORTHRIDGE CAMPUS / SEPTEMBER 1985

WHAT HAPPENED TO COMPUTER AIDED INSTRUCTION

Computer Aided Instruction (CAI) had its moments in the sun several years ago and has since seemed to have faded from the academic computing scene. However, there are now indications that a resurgence in CAI is occurring. This renaissance may be due to two factors: (1) The increased availability of authoring systems on micros and mainframe computers; and (2) The increased awareness and utilization of computing among educators.

An authoring system is a software product that allows the educator: (1) to organize the subject material, to be presented to the student, in a systematic way; (2) to query the student taking the computerized lessons on their comprehension of the study material; (3) to review the material previously presented or continue on with new material depending on how the student responded to the queries; and (4) to analyze student response to the lesson as a whole to help determine the next step in the learning process. Once such a CAI lesson has been prepared by using an authoring system, it can be presented to any number of students with each student taking the lesson at their convenience and at their own pace.

The Computer Center has recently purchased two authoring systems for the IBM PC. These are TENCORE and the McGraw-Hill Authoring System. These Two systems do require that the author as well as students have access to IBM PC computers. A third authoring, Instructional Workbench, is available on the AT&T 385 mainframe computers. These computers can be accessed from virtually any terminal on campus.

More on CAO and authoring systems will be forth coming. In the Meantime, If you are interested in any of these products contact Kurt Webb at Extension 3966.

MICROCOMPUTER JOURNAL FOR INSTRUCTIONAL USERS

Collegiate Microcomputer is "a quarterly journal devoted to all aspects of microcomputers in the higher education curricula." A sample copy received by the Computer Center included articles such as "The Use of Microcomputers in the Teaching of Calculus," "An Introductory Course in System Dynamics," "Using Microcomputers to Store and Evaluate Exam Items" and "Computer Literacy for Undergraduate Humanities and Social Majors."

If interested, this journal is published by Collegiate Microcomputer, Rose-Hulman Institute of Technology, Terre Haute, IN 48703. Individual subscriptions are $28.00. A sample copy may be reviewed at the Northridge Campus Computer Center, Engineering 121.

MICROCOMPUTER GRAPHICS BEGIN TO GROW UP

Do you remember what life was like before computer graphics?

If you are old enough to be reading this you probably do, since computer graphics for popular consumption have been with us for only a few years. But computer-generated pictures have become so common in movies and on television that most of us no longer marvel at them. We accept them unthinkingly, as if they had always been with us.

We watch science fiction movies in which vivid alien landscapes have been created in a computer's memory without using models of any kind. We are perfectly accustomed to music videos in which computer-generated scenery and characters leap across the screen in rapid succession. Even Lynn Benton, CSU's top computer-graphics expert, admits to being a bit jaded by some of the current crop of animation clips.

Newsletters (Original)

Lack of type size and typeface variety, and too much horizontal movement make for an undistinguished cover.

The nameplate lacks impact: the type size is too small, and it's set in a hard-to-read typeface. "Newsletter," set in a different typeface, clashes with the title.

The four parallel lines next to an undersized globe logo clutter the visual. The arrow icon is isolated rather than being integrated into the nameplate.

The type is too small for the width.

Reduced hyphenation in justified text causes disconcerting gaps between words.

The photograph "floats" on the page, and its centered, italicized caption seems weak.

Flight Safety Foundation Newsletter

Please Route To

FLIGHT SAFETY FOUNDATION, INC.   5510 Columbia Pike, Arlington, VA 22204 USA

VOL. 27 NO. 1 (10)   JANUARY 1986

39th IASS CALL FOR PAPERS

FLIGHT SAFETY FOUNDATION has issued a Call for Papers to be presented at the 39th annual FSF INTERNATIONAL AIR SAFETY SEMINAR (IASS) to be held Oct. 6-9 at the Westin Bayshore Hotel in Vancouver, British Columbia, Canada.

The 39th IASS will be devoted to the theme of "IMPROVING SAFETY IN A CHANGING AVIATION SYSTEM."

In announcing the Call for Papers, the FSF noted that the term, "Aviation System," encompasses all aspects of the aviation industry's requirements, including airframe, engine and component designers and manufacturers, as well as users of the aircraft, airports, support equipment and the air traffic control system.

"Perhaps of most importance," the announcement said, "is the effective utilization of the skills, knowledge and judgement of the people involved in designing, developing, producing, operating, maintaining and regulating this complex 'Aviation System.'"

Continued on Page 2

BRUCE N. WHITMAN NEW FSF GOVERNOR

Bruce N. Whitman, executive vice president of FlightSafety International, was elected to the FSF Board of Governors at the Dec. 5 meeting of the Board's Executive Committee.

Whitman joined FlightSafety International in 1961 with the title of Assistant to the President after two years as senior executive assistant with the U.S. National Business Aircraft Association. He was elected to the post of vice president and to the company's board of directors later in the same year.

He was elected executive vice president in 1962 and also serves as a member of the FlightSafety International Board of Directors Executive Committee.

Following graduation from Trinity College in 1955, Whitman was commissioned a lieutenant in the U.S. Air Force and earned the triple rating of pilot, navigator and bombardier while serving with the Strategic Air Command.

After active duty, he attended George Washington University Law School in Washington, D.C., flew as a captain with East Coast Flying

Bruce N. Whitman

Service and was a flight instructor in the U.S. Air Force Reserve.

He and his wife and three sons live in Greenwich, Conn., where he is The Commodore and a member of the board of directors of the Belle Haven Club.

Newsletters (Makeover)

A vertical screen, rearranged elements and varied type sizes provide pleasing contrast and spotlight the name of the sponsoring organization.

The title gains character and impact set in a large, "safe" sans-serif type with tightly spaced letters.

A narrow, screened vertical column gives balance to the page and provides space for the logo, date, issue and contents listing.

The reversed type in the screened area adds balance and interest to the page design.

Column widths have been reduced, and text size increased, allowing for a more comfortable relationship between type size and line length.

A frame helps anchor the photo and relate it to the text; a small aviation icon reversed out of a bullet enhances the boldface caption.

Flight Safety Foundation
N e w s l e t t e r

January 1990
Volume 27 Number 1 (19)

In this Issue
- Plans for Future IASS, OASS Sessions
- Deadlines for Seminar Submissions

Flight Safety Foundation, Inc.
5510 Columbia Pike
Arlington, VA 22204 USA

Bruce N. Whitman New FSF Governor

Bruce N. Whitman, executive vice president of FlightSafety International, was elected to the FSF Board of Governors at the Dec. 5 meeting of the Board's Executive Committee.

Whitman joined FlightSafety International in 1961 with the title of Assistant to the President after two years as senior executive assistant with the U.S. National Business Aircraft Association. He was elected to the post of vice president and to the company's board of directors later in the same year.

He was elected executive vice president in 1962 and also serves as a member of the FlightSafety International Board of Directors Executive Committee.

Following graduation from Trinity College in 1955, Whitman was commissioned a lieutenant in the U.S. Air Force and earned the triple rating of pilot, navigator and bombardier while serving with the Strategic Air Command.

After active duty, he attended George Washington University Law School in Washington, D.C., flew as a captain with East Coast Flying Service and was a flight instructor in the U.S. Air Force Reserve.

He and his wife and three sons live in Greenwich, Conn., where he is The Commodore and a member of the board of directors of the Belle Haven Club.

● Bruce N. Whitman

39th International Air Safety Seminar: Call for Papers

Flight Safety Foundation has issued a Call for Papers to be presented at the 39th annual FSF International Air Safety Seminar (IASS) to be held Oct. 6-9 at the Westin Bayshore Hotel in Vancouver, British Columbia, Canada.

The 39th International Air Safety Seminar will be devoted to the theme of *"Improving Safety in a Changing Aviation System."*

In announcing the Call for Papers, the FSF noted that the term, "Aviation System," encompasses all aspects of the aviation industry's requirements, including airframe, engine and component designers and manufacturers, as well as users of the aircraft, airports, support equipment and the air traffic control system.

"Perhaps of most importance," the announcement said, "is the effective utilization of the skills, knowledge and judgement of the people involved in designing, developing, producing, operating, maintaining and regulating this complex 'Aviation System.'"

It also noted that, with the currently changing environments and concepts in all segments

● See IASS Call for Papers on Page 2

Newsletters (Original)

Failure to organize white space and prioritize copy results in a smorgasbord effect.

Again, the text is not easy to read because of the small type set justified with almost no hyphenation. The unnaturally wide space between the two columns creates a distracting "landing strip."

Indention for paragraphs and listed information is too deep for the type size used.

Headlines "whisper" because they don't contrast enough with text.

Headlines and subheads aren't linked with their appropriate spacing above and below.

It also noted that, with the currently changing environments and concepts in all segments of aviation and the even greater changes anticipated for the future, the persons involved "will experience changing roles and responsibilities for making the Aviation System function with greater efficiency and improved margins of safety."

DISCUSSION AREAS

The seminar will consider ideas, concepts and methods for increasing the levels of safety in a changing aviation-system environment, including the potential impact of current and future technological developments in such areas as:

- Powerplants
- Structures
- Performance
- Communications
- Navigation
- Airway Traffic Control
- Airports
- Support Equipment

The roll of the human in the man/machine environment also will be considered at the seminar, including its impact upon:

- Safety Management
- Human Factors
- Training
- Communications

The Foundation encourages persons from all segments of the aviation industry, worldwide, to share their knowledge and experiences in these areas through active participation in the 39th IASS.

MARCH 15 DEADLINE

Authors/speakers wishing to present papers at the seminar should submit an abstract, proposed title and the name(s) of the author(s) and organization by March 15 to:

FLIGHT SAFETY FOUNDATION
Attn: L. Homer Mouden
Vice President-Technical Affairs
5510 Columbia Pike
Arlington, VA 22204-3194 USA
Telex: 901176 FSF INC AGTN

PLANS DRAFTED FOR FUTURE IASS, CASS SESSIONS

Detailed planning was conducted during the November 38th annual FSF INTERNATIONAL AIR SAFETY SEMINAR (IASS) in Boston, Mass., for the 1986, 1987 and 1988 international seminars and the Foundation's 1986 and 1987 CORPORATE AVIATION SAFETY SEMINARs (CASS).

During a meeting on Nov. 4, the FSF International Advisory Committee (IAC) completed plans for the 1986 IASS to be held Oct. 6-9,

Members of the FSF International Advisory Committee met in Boston during the 38th IASS to discuss plans for future Foundation International Air Safety Seminars.

FSF NEWSLETTER, JANUARY 1986

1986, at the Westin Bayshore Hotel in Vancouver, British Columbia, with the theme of "IMPROVING SAFETY IN A CHANGING AVIATION SYSTEM;" the 40th annual seminar to be held in late October of 1987 in Tokyo, Japan, and the 41st IASS to be held Oct. 4-7, 1988, in Sydney, Australia.

Following the IAC meeting, FSF President John H. Enders and Foundation Administrative Officer and Treasurer Luciana P. Frost discussed detailed planning for the Sydney seminar with Robert H. Naylor, of Ansett Airlines, and Capt. Trevor Jensen, of Qantas Airways, representing the 41st IASS host, the Australasian Airline Flight Safety Council.

Meeting on the same day, the FSF Corporate Advisory Committee (CAC) reviewed plans for the 31st annual CORPORATE AVIATION SAFETY SEMINAR to be held April 14-16, 1986, at the Omni Netherlands Hotel in Cincinnati, Ohio, and decided upon the St. Francis Hotel in San Francisco, Calif., as the site for the 32nd CASS in the spring of 1987.

At the conclusion of the session, Mrs. Frost met with 31st CASS Co-Chairman Robert Gray, chief pilot of Procter and Gamble Co., to discuss final planning for that seminar, whose theme will be "SAFETY IN OUR ENVIRONMENT."

Newsletters (Makeover)

The long, narrow, left-hand column is used again, reinforcing the newsletter's visual identity established on the front cover. This feature also serves as a convenient receptacle for the photograph's caption.

Larger headlines in the text typeface attract attention, while sans-serif subheads provide comfortable contrast.

Shallower indents and lighter spacing of list items remove excessive white space.

Airplane symbols used as bullets reinforce the aviation theme.

Important mailing address information, now set in boldface type, is easily located.

Publication information is relegated to the bottom of the page.

Plans Drafted for Future IASS, CASS Sessions

Detailed planning was conducted during the November 38th annual FSF International Air Safety Seminar (IASS) in Boston, Mass., for the 1986, 1987 and 1988 international seminars and the Foundation's 1986 and 1987 Corporate Aviation Safety Seminars (CASS).

During a meeting on Nov. 4, the FSF International Advisory Committee (IAC) completed

▶ Members of the FSF International Advisory Committee met in Boston during the 38th IASS to discuss plans for future Foundation International Air Safety Seminars.

plans for the 1986 IASS to be held Oct. 6-9, 1986, at the Westin Bayshore Hotel in Vancouver, British Columbia, with the theme of *"Improving Safety in a Changing Aviation System"*; the 40th annual seminar to be held in late October of 1987 in Tokyo, Japan; and the 41st IASS to be held Oct. 4-7, 1988, in Sydney, Australia.

Following the IAC meeting, FSF President John H. Enders and Foundation Administrative Officer and Treasurer Luciana P. Frost discussed detailed planning for the Sydney seminar with Robert H. Naylor, of Ansett Airlines, and Capt. Trevor Jensen, of Qantas Airways, representing the 41st IASS host, the Australasian Airline Flight Safety Council.

Meeting on the same day, the FSF Corporate Advisory Committee (CAC) reviewed plans for the 31st annual Corporate Aviation Safety Seminar to be held April 14-16, 1986, at the Omni Netherlands Hotel in Cincinnati, Ohio, and decided upon the St. Francis Hotel in San Francisco, Calif., as the site for the 32nd CASS in the spring of 1987.

At the conclusion of the session, Mrs. Frost met with 31st CASS Co-Chairman Robert Gray, chief pilot of Procter and Gamble Co., to discuss final planning for that seminar, whose theme will be *"Safety in Our Environment."*

IASS Call for Papers
Continued from page 1

of aviation and the even greater changes anticipated for the future, the persons involved "will experience changing roles and responsibilities for making the Aviation System function with greater efficiency and improved margins of safety."

Discussion Areas

The seminar will consider ideas, concepts and methods for increasing the levels of safety in a changing aviation-system environment, including the potential impact of current and future technological developments in such areas as:

- ✈ Power plants
- ✈ Structures
- ✈ Performance
- ✈ Communications
- ✈ Navigation
- ✈ Airway traffic control
- ✈ Airports
- ✈ Support equipment

The role of the human in the man/machine environment also will be considered at the seminar, including its impact upon:

- ✈ Safety management
- ✈ Human factors
- ✈ Training
- ✈ Communications

The Foundation encourages persons from all segments of the aviation industry, worldwide, to share their knowledge and experiences in these areas through active participation in the 39th IASS.

March 15 Deadline

Authors/speakers wishing to present papers at the seminar should submit an abstract, proposed title and the name(s) of the author(s) and organization by March 15 to:

FLIGHT SAFETY FOUNDATION
Attn: L. Homer Mouden
Vice President-Technical Affairs
5510 Columbia Pike
Arlington, VA 22204-3194 USA
Telex: 901176 FSF INC AGIN

Newsletters (Original)

The original *Executive* presents a confusing mixture of typefaces and graphic elements, all vying for the reader's immediate attention.

Heavy horizontal rules separating articles in the second and third columns compete with the nameplate, headlines, drop caps and article lead-ins.

In the nameplate, the type for the words "The Executive" is too flamboyant for a corporate image.

Underlining the "Shirtsleeve Seminar March 7" kicker makes it difficult to read.

Default line spacing for "Turning Your Ideas..." wastes vertical space. The dollar sign is too cute—again, inappropriate for executives.

The boxes at the ends of articles are overly prominent.

The box around the dinner meeting announcement separates it from the article it relates to.

The Executive

MARCH '88
VOL. 1 NO. 3

Sales & Marketing Executives: "1988—A Positive Vision Towards Accomplishment"

"How To Get A Watermelon From A Seed"

Turning Your Ideas Into Million$ — An Eight-Step Process

Robert C. Boint, executive director of PLUS Business, Inc., in Huntington Beach, and a member of the National Speakers Association, will be the guest speaker at the Monday, March 7, 1988 dinner meeting of Sales & Marketing.

Boint has served as the national sales leader for several major corporations, including Bell & Howell, Brunswick, G.A.F. and Sylvania.

Boint's presentation is entitled: "How To Get A Watermelon From A Seed — Turning Your Ideas Into Millions, An Eight-Step Process." He will address the ways to channel your creative energy in regards to your company's products or service to penetrate competitive markets and increase sales.

The PLUS Business Strategy identifies more than 117 areas of potential increased sales and how these can be analyzed as a check list for greater business performance. With Boint's system, you will see how to

create and develop your own plans to aid you in a better understanding of the marketing tasks and field selling strategies ahead of you.

Boint's style of presentation, and the information made available, will make this a dinner meeting you don't want to miss.

The meeting at the Long Beach Airport Marriott begins with no-host cocktails at 6 p.m., with dinner served at 7:15 p.m. □

Thank You For Prizes

Special thank you to the Ramada Renaissance Hotel, Long Beach Airport Marriott, and the SME Board of Directors for providing prizes for the February 1 dinner meeting.

If your firm would like to donate prizes for our monthly raffle drawings, please call John Craig at 213/988-1239. □

Robert C. Boint
Executive Director
PLUS Business, Inc.

Dinner Meeting

Date: Monday, March 7, 1988
Time: Cocktails 6 p.m.
Dinner 7:15 p.m.
Place: Long Beach Airport Marriott
4700 Airport Plaza Drive
Cost: Members $18 Guests $25

Shirtsleeve Seminar March 7

Money Management And Tax Planning

Our first SHIRTSLEEVE SEMINAR will be held Monday, March 7, prior to our monthly dinner meeting. "Money Management and Tax Planning" will be presented by Max and Linda DeZemplen of Preferred Financial Advisory Corp.

The shirtsleever runs from 4:45 to 6 p.m.and is free to members. There is a $20 cost to non-members and guests.

The DeZemplen's will emphasize retirement, tax and estate plans, protection and

savings, and investment strategies. Please make reservations in advance by calling 213/988-1239.

This will be one of several forums during the year for discussion and input on issues of concern to you, the member. These shirtsleevers, led by recognized experts in their fields, will provide information that can be put to immediate use ... another member benefit. □

A NEW MEMBER BENEFIT!

As a new SME member, you receive a "free" table top display for your products or services...to be used at the next dinner meeting following your approval for membership.

Newsletters (Makeover)

The nameplate's condensed typeface and superimposed triangle now appropriately express the "positive vision" focus of the newsletter.

The subtitle emerges clear and strong. The four-column format, with headlines set in the left-hand column, opens up the layout and lets readers skim the titles.

Using fewer typefaces and type sizes contributes to consistency.

The Dinner Meeting information is now properly seen as part of the article.

The caption is now more informative and relates the photograph to the adjacent article.

Thick horizontal bars extending from the thin rules between articles help define the left-hand column. They also strengthen the headlines.

VOLUME 1 NUMBER 3   MARCH 1988

SALES AND MARKETING EXECUTIVES
1988: A POSITIVE VISION TOWARDS ACCOMPLISHMENT

How to Get a Watermelon from a Seed

Robert C. Boint, executive director of PLUS Business, Inc., in Huntington Beach, and a member of the National Speakers Association, will be the guest speaker at the Monday, March 7, 1988 dinner/meeting of Sales & Marketing.

Boint has served as the national sales leader for several major corporations, including Bell & Howell, Brunswick, G.A.F. and Sylvania.

Boint's presentation is entitled: "How To Get A Watermelon From A Seed—Turning Your Ideas Into Millions, An Eight-Step Process." He will address the ways to channel your creative energy in regards to your company's products or service to penetrate competitive markets and increase sales.

The PLUS Business Strategy identifies more than 117 areas of potential increased sales and how these can be analyzed as a check list for greater business performance. With Boint's system, you will see how to create and develop your own plans to aid you in a better understanding of the marketing tasks and field selling strategies ahead of you.

Boint's style of presentation, and the information made available, will make this a dinner meeting you don't want to miss.

The meeting at the Long Beach Airport Marriott begins with no-host cocktails at 6 p.m., with dinner served at 7:15 p.m.

Robert C. Boint, Executive Director, PLUS Business, Inc., will share his strategies for success on March 7.

Dinner Meeting

Date:	Monday, March 7, 1988
Time:	Cocktails 6 p.m. Dinner 7:15 p.m.
Place:	Long Beach Airport Marriott 4700 Airport Plaza Drive
Cost:	Members $18 Guests $25

Money Management and Tax Planning

Shirtsleeve Seminar March 7

Our first **shirtsleeve seminar** will be held Monday, March 7, prior to our monthly dinner meeting. "Money Management and Tax Planning" will be presented by Max and Linda DeZemplen of Preferred Financial Advisory Corporation.

The shirtsleever runs from 4:45 to 6 p.m. and is free to members. There is a $20 cost to non-members and guests.

The DeZemplens will emphasize retirement, tax and estate plans, protection and savings, and investment strategies. Please make reservations in advance by calling 213/988-1239.

This will be one of several forums during the year for discussion and input on issues of concern to you, the member. These shirt-sleevers, led by recognized experts in their fields, will provide information that can be put to immediate use... another member benefit.

Upcoming Meetings

March 7
Dinner/Meeting

May 16
Distinguished Sales Awards Banquet

June 6
Dinner/Meeting

July 11
Luau!

Nameplates

The four illustrations on this spread show how nameplates can be reworked to set the proper tone for a newsletter's content.
(Original)

The map of Louisiana is too complex; it detracts from the message.

The outdated typeface doesn't effectively communicate "technology."

Technology Today

LOUISIANA TRANSPORTATION RESEARCH CENTER

Vol. 3 No. 1   January 1987

RESEARCH PROFILES

NEW METHOD STUDIED FOR BRIDGE REPAIRS

One of the most common forms of damage to the superstructure of steel bridges results from vehicle impact. This damage rarely causes a bridge to

Phase 3 : Documentation and training sessions for La. DOTD personnel.

The information obtained in phase one of this project is available upon request from LTRC.

(Makeover)

An upbeat typeface, contrasted with the bold sans-serif "Today," creates a high-tech flavor.

Hairline rules are used sparingly but effectively to link headlines with publication information and logo.

TECHNOLOGY
TODAY

A quarterly publication of the Louisiana Transportation Research Center

Summer 1987   Vol. 3, No. 3   **LTRC**

Research Profiles

New Method Studied for Bridge Repairs

One of the most common forms of damage to the superstructure of steel bridges results from vehicle impact.

program for automated design of the repair scheme.

Phase 3: Documentation and training sessions for La. DOTD personnel.

The information obtained in phase one of this project is available upon

to a problem that has troubled the department for more than a decade—failing slopes on man-made embankments, particularly along the Interstate system.

Five failed slopes are being rehabilitated under the project, using three different methods: injection of

Nameplates

Creating a good nameplate is often the best way to improve the look of a newsletter or tabloid.
(Original)

Excessively heavy type set against thin horizontal lines is distracting.

The subhead is far too large and contributes little to the message.

(Makeover)

Simple nameplates are best; slender, condensed, lowercase type creates valuable white space, punctuated by a thick rule above and thin rule below the name.

The subhead has been eliminated and replaced by the less obtrusive "Restaurant Technology" slugline.

Business Reports (Original)

The low-contrast, "gray" tone of business reports and memos often neutralizes the positive effects of good writing, persuasive argument and strong evidence.

Because busy managers have often a short time to read a lot of material, a page full of typewritten copy can be very unappealing.

Although critical to the report, long blocks of supporting evidence tend to discourage readers.

Awkward spacing of data interrupts the flow of reading.

---

the average late riser, this product will revolutionize his or her sleeping habits.

CURRENT SNOOZE ALARM SALES

As stated previously, we believe that a high number of present users of snooze alarm technology will want to own TardiSnooz. Current sales of snooze alarms have never been higher, as the figures below show:

YEAR	# UNITS SOLD	$ RETAIL
1965	1,000	$ 12,000
1970	65,000	430,000
1975	220,000	2,800,000
1980	673,000	5,900,000
1985	1,220,000	11,760,000

A corresponding trend of employee tardiness has become evident, particularly in the last ten years. In fact, some researchers believe that snooze alarms have indeed played a large part in causing employee tardiness. According to Real Life Information in Palo Alto, California, "Snooze alarm technology is largely responsible for the dramatic rise in employee tardiness and late calls. Further, the admonishment thrust upon the average employee, compounded by the guilt, feelings of inadequacy and consequent resentment, creates an unresolved authority-figure conflict, resulting in sharply decreased productivity.... One solution to this problem is a mechanism whereby the employee can at least call in late with a feeling of efficiency and accomplishment, instead of languishing in a commuter-frustrated dissonance on his or her way to work."

Clearly, the above findings indicate the need for added features to snooze technology. This, coupled with the fall in wholesale modem chip prices, could make TardiSnooz our sale item of the decade.

PROJECTED TARDISNOOZ SALES

Based on a 1,000-piece consumer survey mailed last month (see attached data), we found consumers receptive, and indeed eager, to pay the slightly higher price that TardiSnooze would command. Below are projected sales figures, based on out survey:

PROJECTED TARDISNOOZ SALES

YEAR	# UNITS PROJECTED	$ RETAIL
1990	34,000	$ 430,000
1991	81,000	970,000
1992	239,000 (Break-even)	2,400,000
1993	310,000	3,700,000
1994	228,000 (Recession Projected)	2,200,000
1995	426,000	4,450,000

When you examine the above figures, and consider that all we have to do is add a $.93 modem chip to our present alarms, the conclusion is inescapable to all but the most ardent critics that our company should move forward with plans to implement our new

Business Reports (Makeover)

Even the most basic layout software allows you to substitute interesting, informative charts, diagrams and other visuals for text-based data.

Charts and diagrams present information in easy-to-understand, interesting forms.

Diagonal lines in the bar chart add needed contrast to the page.

Research information is broken into several paragraphs and indented left and right for additional emphasis.

the average late riser, this product will revolutionize his or her sleeping habits.

CURRENT SNOOZE ALARM SALES

As stated previously, we believe that a high number of present users of snooze alarm technology will want to own TardiSnooz. Current sales of snooze alarms have never been higher, as the figures below show:

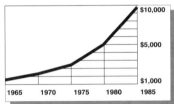

Snooze Alarm Sales 1965 — 1985

A corresponding trend of employee tardiness has become evident, particularly in the last ten years. In fact, some researchers believe that snooze alarms indeed played a large part in causing employee tardiness. According to Real Life Information in Palo Alto, California,

> "Snooze alarm technology is largely responsible for the dramatic rise in employee tardiness and late calls. Further, the admonishment thrust upon the average by the guilt, feelings of inadequacy and consequent resentment, creates an unresolved authority figure conflict resulting in sharply decreased productivity.... One solution to this problem is a mechanism whereby the employee can at least call in late with feeling of efficiency and accomplishment, instead of languishing in commuter frustrated dissonance on his or her way to work."

"Clearly, the above findings indicate the need for added features to snooze technology. This, coupled with the fall in wholesale modem chip prices, could make TardiSnooz our sale item of the decade.

Based on a 1000- piece consumer survey mailed last month (see attached data), we found consumers receptive, and indeed eager to pay the slightly higher price that TardiSnooz would command. Below are projected sales figures, based on our survey:

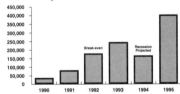

Projected TardiSnooze Sales

When you examine the above figures, and consider that all we have to do is add a $.93 modem chip to our present alarms, the conclusion is inescapable to all but the most ardent critics that our company should move forward with

Charts & Diagrams

Quantitative information can be comprehended quicker and more thoroughly with visual representations. The illustrations below show four ways the same information can be presented to make data more appealing.

A three-dimensional effect enhances a basic line chart.

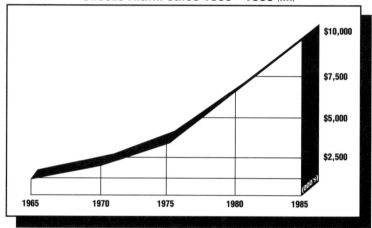

Snooze Alarm Sales 1965 - 1985 (000's)

Illustrations within a presentation graphic can add humor and further identify the content.

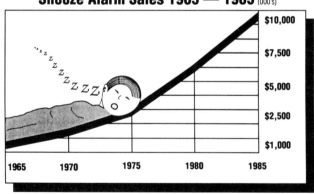

Snooze Alarm Sales 1965 — 1985 (000's)

Charts & Diagrams

You can use your layout software to make revisions and embellishments to charts and diagrams.

Rules, screens and drop shadows can make a simple bar chart more compelling.

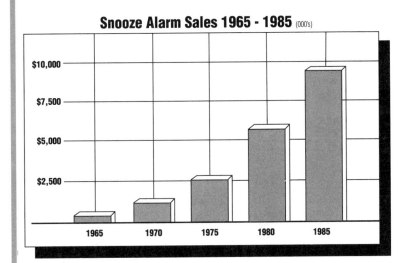

Images that relate to the subject matter can form a chart or diagram's most important visual.

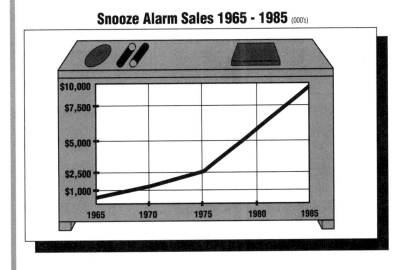

The combination of small, light type and wide columns reduces readability.

Distracting white space is created by the wide gap between columns of unhyphenated text set in small type, the extra space after periods and the two returns between paragraphs.

The three upper diagrams conflict with the two-column layout, and especially with the two diagrams at the bottom of the page.

The charts are hard to understand without legends or unit labels.

Lack of a jumpline at the end of the second column leaves the reader suspended in midsentence with no direction for continuation of the text.

Business Reports (Original)

A conservative image does not dictate visual uniformity.

McKenzie Management, Inc.
MARKET LETTER

VOLUME 2 - NUMBER 17   AUGUST 20, 1986

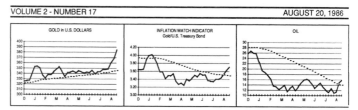

Gold broke out of its long term trading range on August 8th. It achieved the $380 objective and then some before settling down this week in the 370s. Oil started moving higher earlier that week in response to the OPEC production cut agreement.

However, the most common reason cited for the action in gold was the prospective sanctions against South Africa by Western governments. Since that's not exactly a new item on the investment scene, I suspect that the balance between buying and selling over the past six months, which had resulted in a narrow trading range, had shifted to a position of net buying. In other words, technically, the gold market was ready to break out.

U.S. investors are naturally concerned with the price of gold in dollars. For a major bull market to evolve in gold, however, it is equally important for the price of the metal to be in uptrends in other major currencies.

As evidenced in the charts below, gold remains in long-term downtrends both in D-marks and yen. It does appear to be bottoming out against the West German currency and, on its recent strength, the current price

rose above the 30-week moving average.

Japan has bought 220 tons of gold since the beginning of the year. Much of that buying was done in order to mint a new coin celebrating Emperor Hirohito's 60 years reign.

Business Week in its August 25th issue reported that Zurich's Bank Julius Bär & Co. shifted 5% of its clients portfolios into gold. And also noted that Middle Eastern clients are flocking back.

Overall, sentiment regarding gold seems rather passive. There was some increase in public buying of gold-oriented mutual funds immediately after the move, but interest quickly subsided. This lack of enthusiasm tends to strengthen the technical outlook for the price of gold. It suggests that the uptrend will have to be further along before attracting a surge of buying interest.

The rise in gold prices had a big impact on the Inflation Watch Indicator. The indicator is a ratio of gold to Treasury bonds. The middle chart above shows that gold has been outperforming bonds since late April of this year. The indicator is now in a long-term uptrend

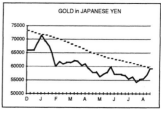

Business Reports (Makeover)

Four narrower columns and smaller, heavier type increase information density and readability.

The most important word in the nameplate, "McKenzie," projects more strength and character when set in a significantly larger, more stylized serif type, in contrast to the smaller, more conservative treatment of "Management." The "i" has been dotted with a stylized logo.

Reversed headlines and subheads provide contrast and organization. Enlarged initial caps lead the reader from the headlines into the articles.

Charts are placed in a "contrast" column, defined at the top by the issue date. Shading makes the charts' trend lines easy to follow.

McKenzie

MANAGEMENT

Gold/U.S. Dollars

Gold/West German Marks

Gold/Japanese Yen

Gold/U.S. Treasury Bonds

GOLD
This Week

Gold broke out of its long term trading range on August 8th. It achieved the $380 objective and then some before settling down this week in the 370s. Oil started moving higher earlier that week in response to the OPEC production cut agreement.

However, the most common reason cited for the action in gold was the prospective sanctions against South Africa by Western governments. Since that's not exactly a new item on the investment scene, I suspect that the balance between buying and selling over the past six months, which had resulted in a narrow trading range,

had shifted to a position of net buying. In other words, technically, the gold market was ready to break out.

U.S. investors are naturally concerned with the price of gold in dollars. For a major bull market to evolve in gold, however, it is equally important for the price of the metal to be in uptrends in other major currencies.

As evidenced in the charts, gold remains in long-term downtrends both in D-marks and yen. It does appear to be bottoming out against the West German currency and, on its recent strength, the current price rose above the 30-week moving average.

Japan has bought 220 tons of gold since the beginning of the year. Much of that buying was done in order to mint a

new coin celebrating Emperor Hirohito's 60-year reign.

Business Week in its August 25th issue reported that Zurich's Bank Julius Bar & Co. shifted 5% of its clients' portfolios into gold. And also noted that Middle Eastern clients are flocking back.

Overall, sentiment regarding gold seems rather passive. There was some increase in public buying of gold-oriented mutual funds immediately after the move, but interest quickly subsided. This lack of enthusiasm tends to strengthen the technical outlook for the price of gold. It suggests that the uptrend will have to be further along before attracting a surge of buying interest.

INFLATION
Watch Indicator

The rise in gold prices had a big impact on the Inflation Watch Indicator. The indicator is a ratio of gold to Treasury bonds. The chart to the left shows that gold had been outperforming bonds since late April of this year. The indicator is now in a long-term uptrend indicating a shift in investor expectations from deflation to inflation.

Or is it? Conventional wisdom ties investor preference

of gold to an inflationary environment. But another possibility, given the sluggish U.S. economy and the persistent trade and budget deficits, may be a flight from the dollar. Gold may be in demand because the dollar is not. The Japanese, among other foreign investors, are awash in dollars and they have to invest in something. Perhaps we should turn the Inflation Watch Indicator upside down and call it "Interest in the Dollar"—a rising trend would indicate a favorable outlook for the dollar, a

declining trend would be adverse.

The other side of the equation is the bond market. It has remained near its high in anticipation of another discount rate cut by the Federal Reserve Board. If the Central Banks of Japan and West Germany go along with the prospective U.S. cut, the bond market would probably go to new highs bringing long-term rates lower. If the foreign banks resist stimulating their economies, the U.S. bond market would probably sell off.

Business Reports (Original)

Inconsistent spacing, sizing and organization create barriers to continuity.

The wide gutter collides with the "Buy Recommendations" box.

Headlines and subheads float, without clear linkage to the text they introduce.

The chart, expanded to match the column width, seems unnaturally large.

In the box, continuity is inhibited by column heads of undifferentiated weight and size.

---

indicating a shift in investor expectations from deflation to inflation.

Or is it? Conventional wisdom ties investor preference of gold to an inflationary environment. But another possibility, given the sluggish U.S. economy and the persistent trade and budget deficits, may be a flight from the dollar. Gold may be in demand because the dollar is not. The Japanese, among other foreign investors, are awash in dollars and they have to invest in something. Perhaps we should turn the Inflation Watch Indicator upside down and call it "Interest in the Dollar"- a rising trend would indicate a favorable outlook for the dollar, a declining trend would be adverse.

The other side of the equation is the bond market. It has remained near its high in anticipation of another discount rate cut by the Federal Reserve Board. If the Central Banks of Japan and West Germany go along with the prospective U.S. cut, the bond market would probably go to new highs bringing long-term rates lower. If the foreign banks resist stimulating their economies, the U.S. bond market would probably sell off.

The Stock Market

Prices

Prices improved on a broad front during the past two weeks. The Utility Average went to a new high reflecting lower interest rates. Short term price trends have reversed to the upside.

Volume

Volume has picked up slightly. This level of activity is fairly typical of August. Volume remains neutral.

Breadth

The breadth indicators have swung into line with the Averages. This set of indicators has been upgraded from negative to positive.

Sentiment

The sentiment indicators remain neutral.

Money and Interest Rates

Short term rates continue to ease to new lows in anticipation of a cut in the discount rate. The bond market remains near its high; i.e. long term rates are at their lowest levels in years. This indicator remains bullish.

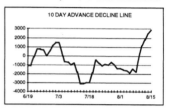

Momentum

A successful test of the selling wave in mid-July did take place in early August. In the previous issue, I suggested that it might be happening, but that it was too early to confirm it. The 10-Day Advance Decline Line above clearly shows that the greater selling pressure occurred in July even though the DJIA hit bottom on August 4th (the closing low was on Friday, August 1st). Momentum is upgraded to positive.

Summary of Stock Market Indicators

Long Term: Bullish
Intermediate Term: Bullish

The indicators have all improved during the past two weeks. The selling pressure of July has clearly subsided. We appear to be in a normal August environment of low volume. Post Labor Day activity will provide us with a better clue as to the potential power of this move.

Investment Strategy

Retain 12%-15% in cash reserves. Gold Mining and International Oils are among the best performing issues on this rally.

Buy Recommendations

Industry	Company	Symbol	Exchange	Recent Price	Buying Range	Date & Price Recomended		Sell if Price Closes Below
Computers	Evans & Sutherland	ESCC	OTC	22.2	21-23	8-6-86	22.0	19
Drugs	Johnson & Johnson	JNJ	NYSE	70.8	Hold	1-2-85	36.0	62
	Merck	MRK	"	116	"	"	47.0	96
Mining	Echo Bay Mines Ltd.	ECO	AMEX	18.5	17-20	7-23-86	15.5	14
Oil	Mobil	MOB	NYSE	34.5	31-34	7-23-86	31.0	29
Wood Products	Scott Paper	SPP	"	57.6	Hold	1-2-85	34.0	52

2

Business Reports (Makeover)

An illusion of spaciousness is created without sacrificing any information.

Reversed headlines, the prominent bar across the top of the box and generous white space around the charts add color, contrast and organizational value to the page.

A "drop" of white space at the top of the page framing the logo reinforces the publication's corporate identity.

Redistribution of white space above and below subheads and the addition of underline rules clearly relate each subhead to its text.

"Buy Recommendations" are now easier to read, with increased vertical spacing and added contrast between column heads and text.

McKenzie
MANAGEMENT

STOCK
Market

Prices

Prices improved on a broad front during the past two weeks. The Utility Average went to a new high reflecting lower interest rates. Short term price trends have reversed to the upside.

Volume

Volume has picked up slightly. This level of activity is fairly typical of August. Volume remains neutral.

Breadth

The breadth indicators have swung into line with the Averages. This set of indicators has been upgraded from negative to positive.

Oil

10 Day/Advance Decline line

Sentiment

The sentiment indicators remain neutral.

Money and Interest Rates

Short term rates continue to ease to new lows in anticipation of a cut in the discount rate. The bond market remains near its high; i.e. long term rates are at their lowest levels in years. This indicator remains bullish.

Momentum

A successful test of the selling wave in mid-July did take place in early August. In the previous issue, I suggested that it might be happening, but that it was too early to confirm it. The 10-Day Advance Decline Line above clearly shows that the greater selling pressure occurred in

July even though the DJIA hit bottom on August 4th (the closing low was on Friday, August 1st). Momentum is upgraded to positive.

Summary of Stock Market Indicators
Long Term: Bullish
Intermediate Term: Bullish

The indicators have all improved during the past two weeks. The selling pressure of July has clearly subsided. We appear to be in a normal August environment of low volume. Post Labor Day activity will provide us with a better clue as to the potential power of this move.

INVESTMENT
Strategy

Retain 12%-15% in cash reserves. Gold Mining and International Oils are among the best performing issues on this rally.

BUY RECOMMENDATIONS

Industry	Company	Symbol	Exchange	Recent Price	Buying Range	Date & Price Recommended		Sell If Price Closes Below
Computers	Evans & Sutherland	ESSCC	OTC	22.2	21–23	8–6–86	22.0	19
Drugs	Johnson & Johnson	JNJ	NYSE	70.8	Hold	1–2–85	36.0	62
	Merck	MRK	"	116	"	"	47.0	96
Mining	Echo Bay Mines Ltd.	ECO	AMEX	18.5	17–20	7–23–86	15.5	14
Oil	Mobile	MOB	NYSE	34.5	31–34	7–23–86	31.0	29
Wood Products	Scott Paper	SPP	"	57.6	Hold	1–2–85	34.0	52

August 20, 1986   McKenzie Management Business Report   Page 2

Consistency Versus Correctness

Rules are made to be broken.

You may be a bit concerned that the "before-and-after" examples featured in this section break many of the conventions presented in Section One. As mentioned before, there are no absolute rules in graphic design; solutions that work in some situations simply aren't appropriate in others.

The goal in Section Two and throughout this book is not to place restrictions but to increase your awareness of appropriate and inappropriate ways of applying design principles to your desktop publishing efforts. Although fundamentals of good design should never be ignored, many decisions are largely intuitive. The more responsive you become to your own design sense and intuition, the more you'll develop your own abilities.

Many design principles are largely intuitive.

By now, you should be more comfortable with the basic concepts outlined in Section One, after seeing how they can be applied in actual examples. But instead of passively accepting these makeovers as the definitive design solutions, you may feel motivated to do even better.

Take the time now to review those examples and create your own makeovers! You may even want to stop reading at this point, boot up your computer and develop alternative ways of solving the design problems presented in the previous pages.

A Note on Style

Style doesn't emerge overnight; it evolves gradually through discipline, hard work and persistence.

As you become increasingly familiar with the capabilities—and limitations—of your desktop publishing hardware and software, your unique style will develop as you explore various ways of solving design problems.

Remember, with desktop publishing you have unprecedented creative capabilities at your fingertips—more than any previous generation of graphic designers!

Style evolves as you find ways to solve design problems.

In the past, it would have been unthinkably extravagant for a graphic artist to set type and paste up a large document simply for learning purposes. Desktop publishing allows you to go through the same learning process at no charge—on the screen of your computer! And if you have access to a laser printer, you can have the tangible results of your efforts for pennies per copy.

MOVING ON

Now that you're acquainted with the basics of graphic design and know how those elements work together to produce successful design solutions, you'll want to begin work on a project. Section Three covers several major design categories and presents valuable tips and tricks for producing different kinds of documents.

Section Three

Getting Down to Business

Chapter Ten

Designing Effective Newsletters

Newsletters are major beneficiaries of the desktop publishing revolution. Highly specialized newsletters that once were impractical because of high typesetting and paste-up costs can now be produced using the most basic desktop publishing and word processing software.

Desktop-published newsletters also provide associations, retail and service establishments with a cost-effective advertising medium.

Although they may appear simple, newsletters are surprisingly complex. The typical newsletter contains numerous elements that must be successfully integrated—often under last-minute deadline pressure.

Here are some things to look for when examining a newsletter or planning your own:

REPEATING ELEMENTS

Successful newsletters are built around a number of elements that appear in every issue.

Repeating elements can be hallmarks of good design.

While the content changes, these features are always included: nameplate, logo, publication information, department heads, kickers, headlines, lead-ins, text, teasers, artwork, captions, jumplines, credits and mailing area.

Nameplate

Your nameplate should provide immediate visual identification and communicate your newsletter's purpose.

A great deal of thought should be devoted to the design of the nameplate and logo. They're the most noticeable and essential features for promoting identification and continuity.

Newsletter nameplates usually are placed at the top of the first page and often extend across the full width of the page.

Nameplates should create a good first impression.

However, equally effective nameplates can be placed centered, flush-left or flush-right.

Although most nameplates are at the top of the page, they can be placed approximately a third of the way down from the top. This location leaves room for a feature headline and article to appear above it.

Vertical orientation, though less common, can draw more attention to an important headline.

A short motto may be incorporated into the nameplate to amplify the nameplate's meaning or target the newsletter's intended audience.

Grids

Creative column size and placement can breathe life into even the most text-heavy newsletters.

Many newsletters look prosaic and dull because they're set up with two or three columns of equal width. Two-column formats can be particularly static, because of their formal left-right balance.

Vary column widths to add motion and color to the page.

One way of avoiding monotony is to reduce the width of the columns slightly and run a vertical band of white space along the left-hand side of each page. This white space can be used for a table of contents and publication data…

"Empty" left-hand columns can showcase display text.

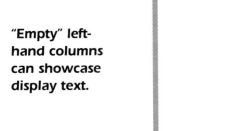

visuals…

...or short elements such as sidebars and pull-quotes.

Vertical white space can enhance sidebars and illustrations.

When using an asymmetrical column layout, be consistent on each page.

There's nothing as disappointing as a newsletter with an attractive front cover based on an asymmetrical grid...

If you use an assymetrical layout, carry it throughout your publication.

...that turns into a conventional, balanced, two-column grid when you turn the page.

Headlines

The number and length of articles included in each issue should be considered when designing the headlines.

If you plan to feature a single in-depth article plus a few shorter pieces in each issue of your newsletter, you will need a single, dominant headline.

Design the front page with head- lines in mind.

On the other hand, if you feature several short articles, the front page must be designed to accommodate more than one significant headline.

Headlines typically are placed above the articles they introduce. However, you might consider placing the headline next to the article as well.

Headlines don't necessarily have to be placed above the text.

Teasers

Use teasers to invite readers inside your newsletter.

A short table of contents on the front cover can draw attention to articles and features inside or on the back cover.

Make your newsletter's table of contents a focal point by placing it in a small shaded box…

The table of contents can beckon readers to look inside.

…in a narrow column adjacent to the text columns…

...next to the nameplate...

Place teasers where they'll draw the most attention.

...or centered below the body copy.

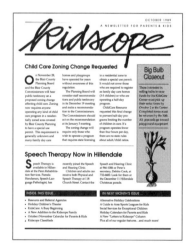

The entire front cover of your newsletter can serve as the table of contents.

Instead of merely consisting of titles and page numbers, your table of contents can include a frieze of photographs along the bottom of the cover page that relate to articles inside. The photo captions will lead the readers to the articles to find out more.

Your table of contents can include a frieze of photos.

Because most newsletters appear in the reader's mailbox address label up, you may want to place the table of contents next to the mailing label area where it can't be overlooked.

Artwork & Captions

The availability of illustrations and photographs greatly influences your newsletter's design.

If the content of your newsletter is mostly factual or technical and you plan to add supporting illustrations, be sure to leave space for them. Also allow space for a caption to accompany each illustration.

Use artwork to strengthen your message.

On the other hand, if your newsletter articles are predominantly generic commentary and photographs aren't readily available, you can safely do without artwork or use illustrations without captions to strengthen your message.

Publication Information

Readers should be able to identify the source of the newsletter quickly and easily.

Don't hesitate to tell readers who you are.

Be sure to leave space for your organization's logo, as well as your address and phone number.

In most cases, the logo appears on the front cover. It should be large enough to be noticed but not large enough to compete with or overwhelm the nameplate.

Your logo also can be placed within the nameplate.

You can place the logo at the bottom of the front cover, relegate it to the back cover or totally eliminate it, as long as your organization is identified in some way.

The volume and issue numbers and date should be prominently featured if readers are likely to save and refer to your newsletter in the future.

Include issue numbers and dates if your newsletter will be used later as a resource.

Lead-Ins

Use subheads and short summaries to provide transition between headlines and body copy. (For example, this sentence is a lead-in to this subsection.)

Lead-ins can be placed between the headline and text.

Lead-ins take different forms but provide good reader cues.

Frequently, lead-ins span more than one column.

The lead-in is often placed within the text, set off by horizontal rules or some other device.

A lead-in also can take the form of a pull-quote.

Text

Your newsletter design must take into account the length of the articles likely to be included in each issue.

If long feature articles will be used, choose small type set in multiple narrow columns.

The appearance of multicolumn newsletters can be improved by placing thin vertical rules between the columns.

However, if shorter features are the rule, choose wider columns and larger type.

The vertical rules improve the looks of multicolumn publications.

Credits

If your newsletter is designed to provide your employees with opportunities to express themselves, then identify authors by name, department and division or position.

If possible, personalize your newsletter by including a photograph or drawing of the author.

Mailing Information

If your newsletter is a self-mailer, be sure to provide sufficient space for a mailing label and other mailing information.

A newsletter's mailing area normally appears at the bottom of the back page.

The mailing label area lets readers know where you are.

Be sure to include your organization's return address next to the mailing label. (Of course, if fulfillment—or mailing list maintenance and addressing—is handled by an outside firm, put that firm's return address in the mailing area.)

The mailing area should clearly indicate whether your newsletter is First- or Third-Class mail. In either case, include your firm's postal permit number to avoid licking stamps.

Adding "Address Correction Requested" above the mailing label area helps you keep your customer or prospect mailing list up-to-date. If you include "Address Correction Requested" in the mailing area of your newsletter, you'll be informed of the new address when a recipient moves.

Many newsletter mailers choose to include "Address Correction Requested" only once or twice a year.

SIZE

Although smaller formats are possible, the standard newsletter is created by folding an 11- by 17-inch sheet of paper, called a signature, into four 8 1/2- by 11-inch pages.

Newsletters with 8, 12, 16 or so pages are assembled by using additional 11- by 17-inch sheets.

DISTRIBUTION

Distribution methods should be taken into account when you design your newsletter.

Design your newsletter with distribution methods in mind.

Newsletters can be mailed full size or folded; they can be self-mailers or stuffed into envelopes.

Decisions about distribution should be made early in your planning process. Self-mailers avoid the cost of envelopes but also keep in mind that valuable editorial or selling space must be sacrificed to leave room for the address area.

A multiple-fold newsletter is inexpensive to mail, but the nameplate and headlines aren't visible until the folds are opened. In addition, the advantage of presenting the recipient with the "billboard effect" of a full-size 8 1/2- by 11-inch newsletter is lost.

EVALUATION CHECKLIST

By answering the following questions, you can check to see whether you've incorporated all the elements necessary for a successful newsletter.

1. Is your newsletter built around a distinctive nameplate that identifies subject matter and editorial focus?

2. Is the nameplate amplified by a phrase or motto that identifies its focus or intended audience?

3. Are volume and issue numbers and dates prominently and clearly identified?

4. Do headlines compete with the nameplate or with each other?

5. Is the source of your newsletter clearly identified by a logo, address and telephone information?

6. Are there "teasers" or a table of contents on the front cover to direct the reader's attention inside?

7. Are articles clearly separated from each other?

8. Have you paid equal attention to both the front and back covers?

9. Is there enough consistency between each issue of your newsletter to maintain its identity, yet enough variety to set each issue apart and maintain interest?

10. Are all photos accompanied by captions that enhance their impact?

Chapter Eleven

Tabloids & Newspapers

Designing tabloid-sized newsletters, newspapers and other publications is a logical progression from 8 1/2- by 11-inch newsletters.

Many of the same principles involved in designing successful newsletters apply to tabloids and newspapers, particularly the need to maintain issue-to-issue consistency while accommodating a constantly changing mix of text and visuals.

For example, all three formats need high-impact headlines that don't compete with the nameplate or with each other.

And it's also important to organize photographs of varying size as effectively as possible.

TABLOIDS

Similar to newspapers, tabloids feature a larger page size, allowing more design flexibility.

The typical tabloid page is 11 by 17 inches, although those dimensions vary from newspaper to newspaper and printer to printer. Some tabloids, for example, are 11 by 14 inches.

Tabloids often are printed on a web press, which feeds the paper to the press off a large roll. As a result, the actual image area of the tabloid is slightly smaller than the page size of 11 by 17 inches.

Tabloids' large size allows more design flexibility.

Laser printers can be used to prepare tabloids, since the coarse newsprint paper most tabloids are printed on absorbs ink and consequently reduces the high-resolution sharpness normally achieved in phototypeset images. In addition, desktop publishing allows revisions to be made until deadline time.

Most desktop publishing software programs let you create tabloid pages. Most laser printers, however, are not designed to handle paper sizes larger than 8 1/2 by 11 inches. (Tabloid-sized laser printers are available, although uncommon.)

To get around that limitation, desktop publishing programs offer a tiling feature that automatically overlaps, or tiles, a series of 8 1/2- by 11-inch pages that can then be pasted together to create one large tabloid page.

Front Cover

The tabloid page size can accommodate large, bold headlines and large photographs.

Larger page sizes allow a bolder treatment for photos and display type.

You can let one large photograph dominate the front cover of a tabloid.

Or, you can combine a large photo with a grid of smaller photos.

The front page can feature text or visuals.

In some cases, the front cover consists mostly of headline type.

Inside Pages

Choose a consistent format for the inside pages of your tabloid.

Design your tabloid as a series of two-page spreads. Include your organization's logo at least once on every spread. Ideally, nameplate or firm name and tabloid title or theme are repeated in each spread. An ideal place for such items is in a drop (a deep top border).

Design your tab-loid for two-page spreads.

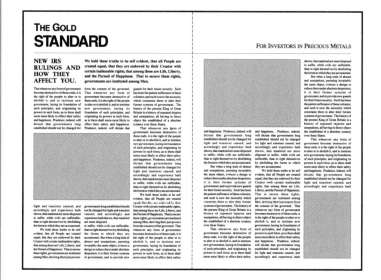

Choosing a three-column format lets you use a variety of photograph sizes.

The wider columns of a three-column format are more suitable for tabloids than for newsletters.

A five-column grid creates even more design flexibility, just as it does with newsletters.

Wider columns are better suited for tabloids than for newsletters.

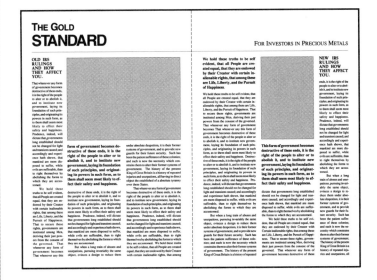

Content

Because of their size, tabloids let you creatively mix editorial and selling space.

Tabloids creatively mix editorial and selling space.

You can mix information and advertising in your tabloid to enhance your firm's credibility and image; pre-sell prospective customers on your firm's competence and professionalism; and expand the market for your products by answering basic questions first-time buyers might have.

You can highlight editorial information in several ways: Between parallel rules on the top half of each page…

Rules and white space can provide a framework for your message.

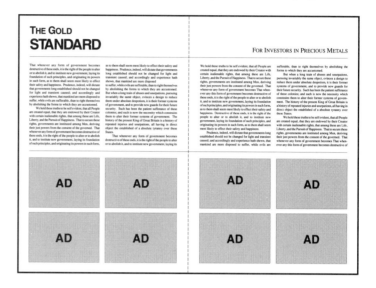

In vertical columns adjacent to the selling area…

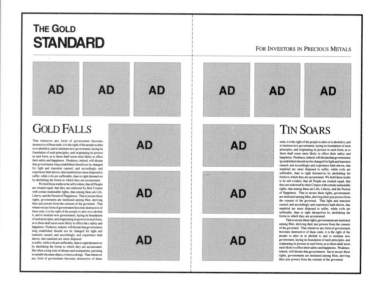

Between the selling areas…

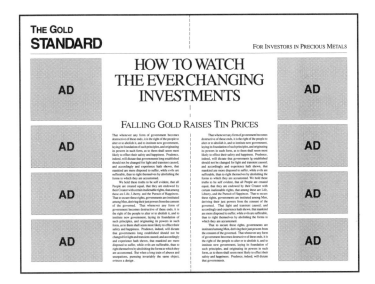

At the bottom of each page…

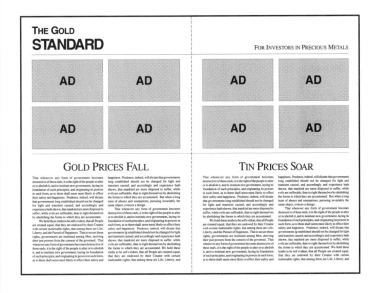

With a screen to integrate the editorial material into one unit...

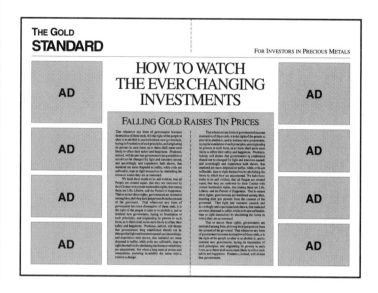

Screens can unify blocks of editorial material.

Back Cover

Pay as much attention to the back cover as you do to the front.

Many readers see the back of a newspaper before the front. Therefore, you should use the back as well as the front to promote your theme. One way is to summarize important points contained in the front-cover articles.

Use the back cover as well as the front to promote your theme.

Another way is to repeat your best ads and promotions on the back cover, including special financing incentives and limited-time offers.

Previewing Your Tabloid

You can preview your finished tabloid by printing reduced-size pages.

To preview full pages of your tabloid, print them at 65 percent of actual size. You'll be able to see an entire 11- by 17-inch tabloid page on an 8 1/2- by 11-inch sheet of paper.

NEWSPAPERS

Once you're comfortable producing tabloid-size newsletters, you'll find it an easy step up to newspaper design.

One of the key differences between the two formats is the number of columns. Tabloids are usually set up on fewer, wider text columns.

Newspaper pages, however, are divided into many—often six or more—narrow text columns. The resulting shorter line lengths require smaller type sizes and more attention to hyphenation and letter and word spacing.

More columns mean smaller type sizes.

Headlines

An important challenge that faces newspaper designers is working out a hierarchical order among the various articles that will appear on the same page.

Confusion will reign if all articles are introduced by the same size headline.

The most important articles need larger headlines.

And if larger headlines are placed too low on the page, the result is an unbalanced, bottom-heavy layout.

Let the top of the page carry most of the weight.

The solution is to arrange headlines in a way that clearly identifies their importance without allowing them to over-power subordinate articles.

Photographs

Newspapers must accommodate a wide variety of photographs of differing size and degree of importance.

In a typical newspaper, the front page alone often contains more photos than are found in an entire newsletter issue.

When arranging multiple photographs, each should be placed appropriately in relation to the others and to the page design as a whole.

the
Newspaper

We Hold These Truths

We hold these truths to be self-evident, that all People are created equal, that they are endowed by their Creator with certain unalienable rights, that among these are Life, Liberty, and the Pursuit of Happiness. That to secure these rights, governments are instituted among Men and Women.

We hold these truths to be self-evident, that all People are created equal, that they are endowed by their Creator with cer-

tain unalienable rights, that among these are Life, Liberty, and the Pursuit of Happiness. That to secure these rights, governments are instituted among Men and Women. We hold these truths to be self-evident, that all People are created equal, that they are endowed by their Creator with certain unalienable rights, that among these are Life, Liberty, and the Pursuit of Happiness. That to secure these

rights, governments are instituted among Men and Women.

We hold these truths to be self-evident, that all People are created equal, that they are

endowed by their Creator with certain unalienable rights, that among these are Life, Liberty, and the Pursuit of Happiness. That to secure these rights, governments are insti-

tuted among Men and Women.

We hold these truths to be self-evident, that all People are created equal, that they are endowed by their Creator with.

To Be Self

We hold these truths to be self-evident, that all People are created equal, that they are endowed by their Creator with certain unalienable rights, that among these are Life, Liberty, and the Pursuit of Happiness. That to secure these rights, governments are instituted among Men and Women.

We hold these truths to be self-evident, that all People are created equal, that they are endowed by

their Creator with certain unalienable rights, that among these are Life, Liberty, and the Pursuit.

All Men Are Created

That to secure these rights, governments are instituted among Men and Women. We hold these truths to be self-evident, that all People are created equal, that they are endowed by their Creator with certain unalienable rights, that among these

are Life, Liberty, and the Pursuit of Happiness. That to secure these rights, governments are instituted among Men and Women.

We hold these truths to be self-evident, that all People are created equal, that they are endowed by their.

Whereas many newsletter photographs are often simple head shots, newspaper photos include a variety of subjects, shapes and sizes.

Teasers

Because of a newspaper's greater size and complexity, it's even more important to provide front-page teasers to attract readers to the inside.

Attention must be drawn to special features and high-interest articles inside. Readers also want clear direction to specific items such as classified listings, a calendar of events and other sections.

Standing Elements

The front page of a newspaper usually includes repeating features, such as stock market highlights and weather and sports summaries.

Don't let repeating features compete with the news.

Repeating elements have to be accessible to the casual reader but not so prominent that they detract from the current events of the day.

All these elements have to coexist with the newspaper's nameplate and subtitle.

Article Jumplines

Another peculiarity of newspapers is the large number of articles continued on inside pages.

Long articles are often broken into several segments placed on succeeding pages. Each segment requires jumplines to help the reader locate the continuation. Jumplines present a challenge to the designer: they must be easily noticed but also easily distinguished from headlines and subheads.

Advertisements

Advertising is a necessary ingredient and, in fact, pays the bills for most newspapers!

It's often impossible to be sure of the number and sizes of advertisements you'll run until the last minute.

Advertisements must neither compete with nor be overshadowed by adjacent editorial material.

Many newspapers are adhering to Standard Advertising Units specifications to simplify page makeup (check this with your local newspaper). These include a variety of standard ad sizes that can be used as building blocks in assembling pages.

EVALUATION CHECKLIST

Use the following questions to test your tabloids and news-papers in terms of the elements discussed in this chapter.

1. Is the front page of your tabloid assembled around a single major story or idea?

2. Have you designed the front cover with elements that invite readers inside?

3. Do the inside tabloid pages contain a pleasing mixture of dominant and subordinate articles?

4. Are newspaper headlines sized and placed in a way that shows their relative status yet also lets readers quickly locate articles?

5. Can readers quickly locate article continuations on inside pages?

6. Is each photograph sized and placed to reflect its importance?

7. Have you used a single grid and consistent graphic accents throughout your newspaper or tabloid?

8. Have you reinforced your publication's image by repeating the nameplate on inside pages?

Magazine & Newspaper Advertisements

Desktop publishing is ideally suited to producing newspaper advertisements. In addition, important recent advances in desktop publishing hardware and software, including the ability to enhance color photographs on your computer screen and prepare color separations, now allow you to produce high-quality, professional-looking magazine advertisements.

Although we begin this chapter by analyzing factors that contribute to successful newspaper ads, you can use many of the same techniques to improve your magazine ads.

NEWSPAPER ADVERTISEMENTS

Design flexibility and pragmatism are important ingredients in effective newspaper advertisements.

Even with the typically short lead times you're given and the inevitability of content changes, you can produce newspaper ads quickly and cost-effectively with templates you have prepared in advance.

Making Maximum Use of Grids

The best way to design effective advertisements is to make maximum use of the grid as a planning tool.

Grids make it easy to plan for the approximate number of products and text blocks necessary for your marketing and promotional needs.

Start creating a flexible grid by dividing a vertical rectangle—the shape of many ads—into six equal vertical columns. Then divide each column into 13 equal squares.

Grids will speed up your ad production.

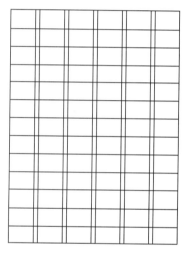

From this simple grid, a number of ways of mixing text and graphics becomes possible. For example, you can divide the space from top to bottom into four areas: a two-unit-high headline area extending across the top of the page; below that, an area for visuals also extending the width of the page; then three two-column-wide text blocks four units high; and

A grid can provide a versatile framework for your ads.

at the bottom of the page, a two-unit-high response area along the bottom of the ad. The response area would contain your firm's logo, address and perhaps a coupon.

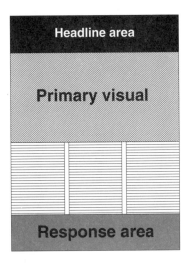

Relocating one element can give your ad a whole new look.

Without changing any of the proportions, notice how you can completely alter the appearance of the ad by relocating the headline below the visual.

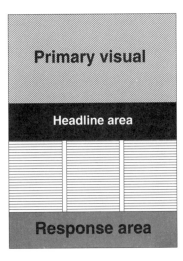

If you wanted to use a smaller amount of body copy, you could set the text in larger type and use only two parallel text blocks, each three columns wide.

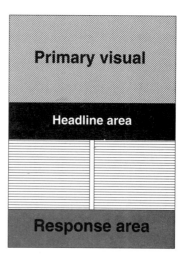

Another way to divide the space is to arrange the text in an L-shaped block wrapped around a vertical photograph. You might choose an "atmosphere" photo showing the benefits of the product or service you're advertising.

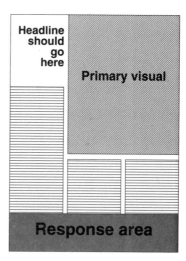

In an alternate arrangement, you could subdivide the space by using a box containing a smaller photograph accompanied by a two-column caption and a large price.

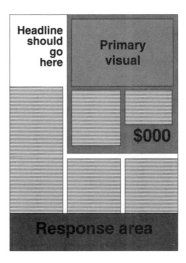

Introducing Variety   *Basing your layout on a grid makes it easy to vary the size, shape and placement of text and visual elements.*

Things get interesting when you include both dominant and subordinate visual elements: for example, the combination of a large "atmosphere"—or "premise"—photograph, a column

Dominant and subordinate visuals can create interest.

of "premise" copy, plus three boxes, each containing the photo, caption and price of a specific product.

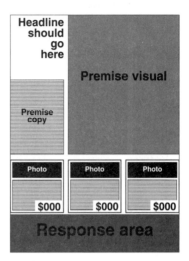

To include *more* products, you could reduce the primary photo and add another row of product photos.

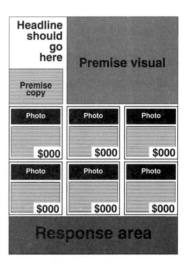

Ten products—one dominant, nine subordinate—are included in the layout example below.

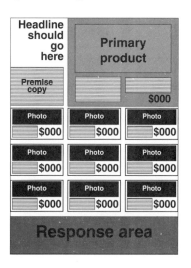

Grids don't limit but, in fact, liberate space.

As the preceding examples show, grids don't limit your creative freedom; they actually *liberate you* to utilize space in more creative and cost-effective ways!

Pyramid Ad Layouts *Choose a pyramid ad layout when you want to emphasize some products more than others.*

A multicolumn "pyramid" ad allows a hierarchical organization. Place a large photograph of your most competitive product at the top of the ad. Immediately below it, place the next two or three most competitive products. Below this, add several columns of product listings.

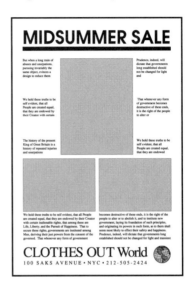

Pyramid layouts establish a hierarchy of importance.

More Grid Options *When your products are of equal importance, organize product offerings in equal-sized boxes.*

As an alternative, photos, captions and prices can be contained within a grid of equal-sized boxes. Although the boxes are the same, a great deal of flexibility is still possible.

A grid of equal-sized boxes creates a lot of flexibility.

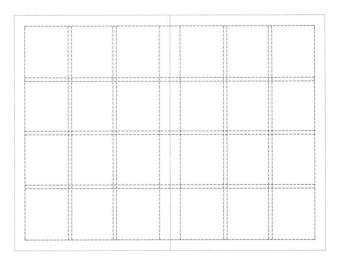

The columns and rows of your grid can be organized horizontally or vertically by reversed-out category dividers.

To break up the monotony, featured items can be placed in double-wide or double-high boxes.

Featured item boxes can also be four times normal size. This technique can be used to balance ads running on facing pages of a two-page spread.

Featured items in a two-page ad can be placed in larger boxes.

Pyramid Ad Layouts

Choose a column-based ad structure when your competition is using pyramid or grid-based ads.

Multiple products can be organized by category, using vertical columns with subheads at the top of each column.

Your ad should set you apart from the competition.

When a wider ad is designed, however, horizontal organization works just as well. Subheads can be placed in a column to the left.

Templates for Newspaper Ads

Templates can save you time and effort in designing and producing newspaper ads.

Key elements can be saved in templates for use in other ads.

For example, create and save ad templates for various sizes—full-page, half-page, one-third-page and one-quarter-page. Design them all to reflect a strong family resemblance, with consistent treatments of headlines, borders, artwork and buying information.

By letting you predetermine the number of items you can use, grids make your planning sessions easier.

Borders

Because most newspaper advertisements occupy less than a full page, pay special attention to borders and white space.

Strong borders separate your newspaper ad from the "clutter" of other page elements that surround it. The type of border you choose will often be determined by the shape of the ad.

A wide, vertically oriented ad should have strong top and bottom rules.

Strong borders make an ad stand out on the page.

Thinner side rules can make small advertisements look taller than they actually are.

A small, square advertisement should be bordered with rules of equal thickness.

White Space

Use white space to further isolate your newspaper advertisement from its surroundings.

The impact of your ad can be increased by providing sufficient "breathing room" within the ruled borders of the ad to set off artwork and text.

One way to do that is to place the borders of your ad within the space allotted. As a result, there will be white space around your borders, clearly separating your copy from its surroundings.

Leave enough "breathing room" within the borders of an ad.

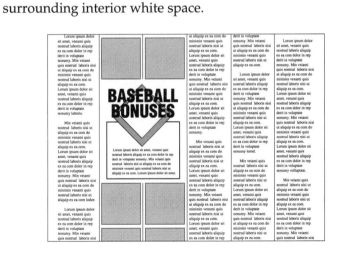

Using this technique, you can make small ads look larger by letting part of the ad break through the border into the surrounding interior white space.

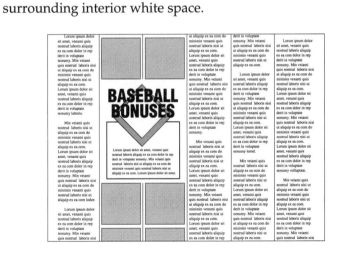

White space within ads can be created by using a multi-column grid, indenting body copy and allowing headlines to begin in the vertical band of white space to the left of the ad.

JOIN US FOR A GREAT FUTURE.

White space within small ads can be created by using a multicolumn grid, indenting body copy and allowing headlines to begin in the vertical band of white space to the left of the ad. White space within small ads can be created by using a multicolumn grid, indenting body copy and allowing headlines to begin in the vertical band of white space to the left of the ad.

Worldwide Imports   Anytown, USA

Headlines

Use the same headline treatment for all the ads in your newspaper, regardless of their sizes.

A common technique is to reverse the headline out of the upper one-fourth to one-third of the area occupied by the ad.

Avoid reversing headlines out of long, narrow boxes. This creates "frowning" ads that obscure the headline.

Another effective technique is to place a graduated dark-to-light screen behind the headline and primary photograph or illustration. This allows the headline to be reversed and the text to be set in black type against a light background.

Adding a graduated screen behind headlines can be effective.

Headlines are often centered in newspaper ads, although that doesn't have to be the case.

An alternate technique is to balance a strong flush-right headline with a smaller flush-left subhead. This draws the reader into the ad by speeding the transition from "premise" headline to "supporting" subhead.

Base your ad layout on product visuals.

Handling Artwork

In multiproduct ads, base your layout on the number of products you want to include in your advertisement.

Your ad design and layout should evolve out of the number and size of the products you want included, and should also be influenced by the appearance of your competitors' ads.

Screens

Screens add a "two-color" effect to your ads.

Screens within boxes, for example, can unify horizontal and vertical elements of the ad.

Or you can place the screens behind the whole ad, which adds contrast to the boxes because of their "whiteness."

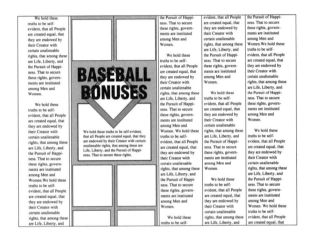

Callouts

Use callouts to draw attention to the most important selling features of your products.

A callout is a graphic arrow that connects a visual to a brief description of product features and benefits. Callouts give readers a concise "educational" message about why they should buy a particular product.

Add an educational tone to your ad by highlighting a product's key features.

New Bigger Eraser
Lasts Longer

Harder Lead
Stays Sharper

Multiple Colors
Available

Prices, Buying Information & Logos

Every ad should include all necessary purchasing information.

The logo of the firm running the ad should be prominent. This can be achieved by either size or contrast.

In this ad, the logo is relatively small, yet it's easily identified because it's surrounded by white space.

**Make it easy
for readers
to respond
to your ad.**

Clearly visible addresses, phone numbers and buying information make it easy for the reader to respond to the ad.

The type size used for captions and prices should be proportional to the size of the photograph or artwork used to illustrate the product. Set prices in large type for large photographs, in small type for small photographs.

Likewise, the size of a manufacturer's logo should be in correct proportion to the size of the visual it relates to and its surrounding information.

Consistency *Prices and manufacturer logos should always be placed in the same location.*

In grid-type ads, all logos and prices should be the same size and, whenever possible, placed in the same relative position in each box.

Not every advertised product needs to be illustrated.

Practice restraint when choosing typefaces and type sizes. Avoid using a different type size for each product. Even the most product-filled ad needs no more than a few type sizes. One size for "primary" products and a second size for secondary products may be all the variety you need.

Remember that not every product advertised needs to be illustrated. Often, the best-looking ads simply list the products with a few representative photographs or drawings.

Smaller Newspaper Ads

Desktop publishing is ideally suited for preparing newspaper ads that cover one, two or three columns.

It's often harder to produce an effective small newspaper ad than a full- or half-page ad.

Large ads attract attention simply because of their size. Smaller ads have to be designed more carefully, so they'll emerge from the many competing elements around them.

One of the most effective designs for single-column newspaper ads reverses the headline out of solid black, focuses the ad around a single product and balances the reversed-out headline and product visual with a bulleted list of product benefits, concluding with a screened logo and address at the bottom.

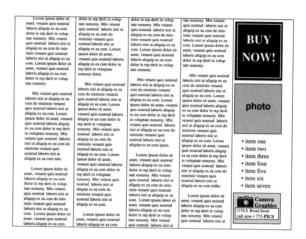

This technique provides visual interest, because the strong reversed area at the top of the ad is balanced by the screened area at the bottom. Notice how the introductory paragraph is wrapped around the visual, integrating text and illustration.

The indention and flush-left/ragged-right alignment of the bullet items create white space to the left and right of the ad, providing separation from surrounding elements.

Small ads require restraint and attention to detail. It's easy to make them complex and hard to read. Small ads gain impact to the extent they're focused—and frequently repeated.

Smaller ads require both simplicity and attention to detail.

Classified Ads

Desktop publishing can produce attractive classified ads.

Advertisers often don't realize they can submit their own camera-ready copy rather than leaving the ad preparation to the newspaper.

The addition of a strong, high-contrast headline and prominent border can make a big difference in the response you get to your "Help Wanted" ad.

laying its foundation of such principles, and originating its powers in such form, as to them shall seem most likely to effect their safety and happiness. Minimum.

DESKTOP PUBLISHING

Art/production person to help out three tired cowboys and one cowgirl who are working day and night to finish a graphic design book. Must have DTP experience, willing to work long hours, meet hot deadlines and like pizza. Must relocate to Denver, Colorado ASAP. Send resumé to *Laser Writing Inc.*, 20 W. Bond, Denver, CO 25982.

TRUTHSAYER. We hold these truths to be self evident, that all People are created equal, that they are endowed by their Creator with certain inalienable rights, that among these are Life, Liberty, and the Pursuit of Happiness.

Indenting body copy can also draw attention to your ad by incorporating a strong vertical band of white space into an otherwise gray page.

We hold these truths to be self-evident, that all People are created equal, that they are endowed by their Creator with certain unalienable rights, that among these are Life, Liberty, and the Pursuit of Happiness. That to secure these rights, governments are instituted among Men and Women.

We hold these truths to be self-evident, that all People are created equal, that they are endowed by their Creator with certain unalienable rights, that among these are Life,

Liberty, and the Pursuit of Happiness. That to secure these rights, governments are instituted among Men and Women. We hold these

SALES MANAGER
FOR EXPANDING
COMPUTER SOFTWARE
COMPANY
Supervisory or extensive
retail experience required.
CALL TODAY!
1-800-333-4444

truths to be self-evident, that all People are created equal, that they are endowed by their Creator with certain unalienable rights, that

among these are Life, Liberty, and the Pursuit of Happiness. That to secure these rights, governments are instituted among Men and Women.

We hold these truths to be self-evident, that all People are created equal, that they are endowed by their Creator with certain unalienable rights, that among these are Life, Liberty, and the Pursuit of Happiness. That to secure these rights, governments are instituted among Men and Women. We hold these truths to be self-evident.

Quality Considerations

It's entirely appropriate to prepare camera-ready newspaper ads using your laser printer.

The quality of phototypesetting is often lost on newsprint.

It's usually not necessary to go to the expense of having newspaper ads phototypeset, because the relatively coarse newsprint absorbs the ink to such a degree that the quality advantage offered by phototypesetting is lost.

Another advantage of desktop publishing is that you can build a library of scanned line-art illustrations to use in your ads, when appropriate, in place of photographs.

The new generation of 1,000-dot-per-inch plain-paper laser printers makes it even easier to prepare high-quality newspaper ads in your office.

As newspapers continue to improve their reproduction quality, the added clarity of images and type prepared with 1,000-dot-per-inch laser printers will become more apparent.

In addition, scanners and desktop publishing programs are rapidly improving in their ability to handle photographs. The quality produced on a laser printer will soon approach the quality of newspaper photo reproduction. Thus, it's entirely feasible that you'll soon be preparing complete newspaper ads, including photographs, with your desktop publishing system and laser printer.

MAGAZINE ADVERTISEMENTS

Magazine advertisements typically feature fewer products and require higher production quality.

Fewer products are included because of the long period of time between when the ad is placed and when it appears in print. The emphasis is usually on the firm's range of products and services rather than specific items and prices.

Magazine ads generally appear in a more dignified editorial atmosphere that dictates careful selection of typefaces, type sizes, type styles and line spacing.

Magazine ad sizes are limited. Most magazines are created around a three-column grid.

Options usually include the following:

- Full-page
- Two-thirds-page (two out of three columns)
- Half-page horizontal
- Half-page vertical
- One-third-page vertical (one column, full height)
- Third-square (two columns wide, one-third-page high)
- One-third-page horizontal (three columns wide, one-third-page high)

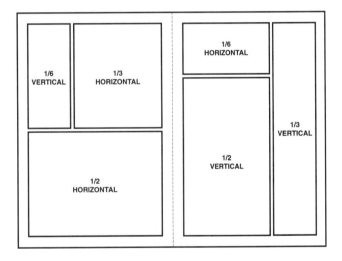

Consider high production quality in designing magazine advertisements.

You should prepare basic formats, or grids, including borders and logo placement, for the two or three sizes you're most likely to use. These will speed up planning and producing your ads.

Because most magazines are printed on high-quality coated paper, advertisements created with desktop publishing programs should be output on a phototypesetter. For this format, 300-dot-per-inch laser printing often doesn't provide the sharpness necessary for the best possible presentation of your ad.

Elements for Success

Borders, headlines and white space are crucial to the success of your magazine advertisements.

Your ad must appear as a self-contained unit, separated from surrounding material. The relatively small size of most magazine ads presents a major challenge. Typically, readers will see your ad in the context of a horizontal 17- by 11-inch spread that includes editorial material as well as other ads.

Use contrast to keep your ad from fading into the background.

You generally have no control over where your ad will appear in the magazine and no assurance that it won't be dwarfed by surrounding color ads. In this busy environment, use contrast provided by white space and type to keep your ad from fading into the background.

Effective use of asymmetrical column grids and strong headlines may be essential to the success of your ads. For example, a strong vertical band of white space on the left can add impact to the headline and focus attention on the text.

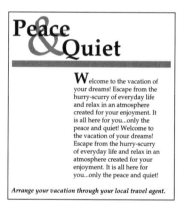

By carefully editing your copy, you can gain enough space to set the headline in larger type, surrounded by more white space or accented by horizontal rules.

One technique that can help your magazine ad emerge from its surroundings is to replace the traditional four-sided box border with horizontal rules at the top and bottom only. These rules visually reinforce the body copy and emphasize the headline by surrounding it with white space.

NEW HOMES

- carefully selected homesites in the woods overlooking the river
- seasoned architects with solar construction in mind
- your dream house is only a step away

Sunrise Builders
we *always* get an early start

Product photographs are often replaced in magazine ads by strong, bold headlines.

Because of the high costs of custom photography, magazine ads often use stock photographs—previously taken, licensed photographs that can be obtained for a fraction of the cost of a custom photograph. (Check the Yellow Pages of metropolitan phone books or the bibliographies of publications such as *Print* or *Communication Arts*. You can also purchase stock photos on CD-ROM disks.)

Stock photos can help you stretch your ad budget.

Coupons

Magazine ads often include coupons inviting prospective customers to send for further information.

Highest response will occur when the coupons are placed in the lower right corner of a right-hand page. (More time and effort are required for a reader to remove a coupon from a center column or the lower right corner of a left-hand page.)

Make coupons easy to complete and return.

Most desktop publishing programs let you create distinctive borders for your coupons. A great deal of attention should be devoted to the coupon's design. Once created, however, it can be stored as a separate file and used over and over again.

When you submit ads to several publications, you can code the coupons to identify the magazine with the response. Simply add a department designation to your address. (The next time you read a magazine, notice how frequently this is done—and how often the "Department" code matches the magazine's initials!)

Design Usable Coupons   *Avoid creating coupons with lines spaced so close together that prospective customers will have difficulty filling them out.*

Always make it as easy as possible for readers to respond to your offer.

Spaces should be large enough and long enough to accommodate the responder's name and address, written by hand.

Color

Magazine ads frequently include color.

Color can be used as a background, or spot color can highlight headlines, rules and borders.

Studies have shown that ads using color have up to 80 percent more readership than black-and-white ads. You might find that fewer, or smaller, color ads will produce more sales than black-and-white ones.

The addition of a spot color can vastly increase the readership of an ad. Color can be used as a background behind all or part of the ad or simply used to accent one or more of the rules or other graphic elements.

Four-color reproduction can be used for photographs.

Many desktop publishing programs allow you to create four-color separations. The newest color printers can produce accurate proofs of your ads right in your office.

Use spot color to draw attention to your ad.

EVALUATION CHECKLIST

Check your magazine and newspaper ads for effectiveness using the following questions.

Newspaper Ads

1. Are your ads set off from their surroundings by appropriate margins, borders and white space?

2. Is the headline large enough to attract attention without overwhelming other elements of the ad?

3. Are grids or boxes used to organize ads containing multiple products, prices and manufacturer logos?

4. Are captions and prices clearly connected to product photographs or illustrations?

5. Has all buying information—address, hours, credit terms—been clearly spelled out?

6. Is your logo prominent enough to provide a visual signature for your ad?

7. Is the design of your ad appropriate to both its content—the number and importance of products included—and the image you want to project?

8. Have you been consistent in the size and placement of repeating elements such as logos and prices?

9. Do your newspaper ads contain messages that can potentially expand your market?

10. Do you submit your own camera-ready classified ads featuring strong, distinctive headlines and attention-getting borders?

Magazine Ads

1. Is the design of your ad consistent with the long-term image you want to project?

2. Is the appearance of your ad clearly distinctive from ads run by your competitors?

3. Have you used borders, white space, screens and indents to set your ads off from surrounding elements?

4. Are coupons designed to be easily filled out?

5. Have you carefully edited headline and body copy so that only essential words remain, permitting large, easy-to-read type set off by sufficient white space?

6. Have you investigated costs, benefits and alternate ways of adding color to your ads?

Chapter Thirteen

Sales Materials

Successful sales materials require careful planning. They can be prepared in a wide variety of shapes and sizes.

Choosing the right format depends on factors such as

- The number, complexity and cost of products and services being advertised. Will the sales piece focus on a single item, or must it accommodate a variety of products and services?

- The targeted point in the purchase cycle. Will materials be designed for a wide range of potential buyers or aimed specifically at prospects who are ready to make a purchase?

- Whether to appeal to the buyer's emotions. Is the item utilitarian, or will it be perceived as an enhancement to the buyer's lifestyle or self-image?

- Production time and relative longevity of the sales piece. How much time is involved in producing it, and how long will it last?

A flyer announcing a neighborhood yard sale requires a totally different approach than an extended warranty program for a luxury automobile.

Likewise, is the brochure intended for casual browsers or is it intended to close a sale? Brochures distributed to a large audience early in the purchase cycle don't need to be as detailed—or expensively printed—as those distributed to qualified prospective buyers who are just about ready to pull out their checkbooks.

BROCHURES

There are several types of brochures: capabilities, line and product-specific brochures.

Capabilities brochures describe a firm or association's goals and products or services.

A health maintenance organization's brochures might describe its preventive medicine and long-term care plans, while a performing arts group's brochures might provide concert and instruction schedules.

Line brochures feature one category or even one item of a product line. An audio/video manufacturer might have separate brochures for compact disc players, videocassette recorders and car stereo systems.

Product-specific brochures focus on a specific purpose. A college alumni association, for example, might prepare a brochure in conjunction with a fund drive to raise money for a new building.

As for size, brochures run the gamut—from a single 8 1/2-by 11-inch sheet of paper, folded into thirds and printed in one color on both sides, to 16 four-color pages.

In addition to the various sizes and editorial approaches, brochures can also be categorized by their level of complexity. These consist of "teasers," "tell-alls" and "impressers."

Brochures are designed for a long shelf life.

Teasers

"Teasers" are brochures targeted to prospective buyers early in the decision process.

Teasers don't pretend to tell the whole story: their purpose is to direct the reader to the next level of action, such as calling a toll-free telephone number.

Teasers are printed on single sheets of paper, then folded into panels (to fit into a Number Ten business envelope). They're inexpensively produced so that they can be distributed to as many prospective buyers as possible.

Teasers are often displayed conspicuously in free-standing or counter-top racks so that any and all can feel free to take one of them.

In choosing a format, consider your brochure's level of complexity.

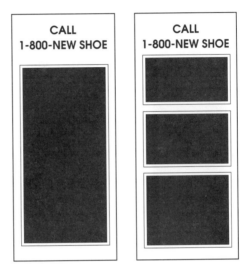

Tell-All Brochures

"Tell-all" brochures target qualified buyers.

They're designed for the next level—serious potential buyers who are closer to the moment of truth. They contain more information and often conclude with detailed specifications of the products or service being offered.

Tell-all brochures are often printed on standard 8 1/2- by 11-inch pages or on larger sheets requiring a 9- by 12-inch envelope. In fact, a great deal of flexibility is possible. The size, shape and quality of paper used for these brochures can help set your presentation of a product or service apart from competing ads. You can even use square or other nonstandard page sizes if they enhance your design.

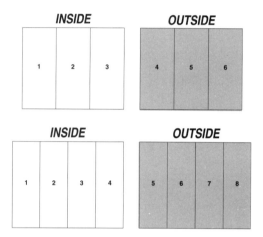

Tell-all brochures help sway serious potential buyers.

Tell-all brochures tend to be either copy- or illustration-oriented, although they can combine large and small photographs with expanded captions.

Impressers

"Impressers" approach the quality of booklets in design sophistication.

Impressers follow up and reinforce the message at the last crucial phase before purchase. They combine sophisticated graphic design with high-quality printing and paper.

The high quality of impresser brochures reflects the quality of the product.

Impressers are appropriate when the products or services are either emotionally important to the buyer or in cases where benefits can't be measured until after the purchase is made. Examples include luxury items such as expensive automobiles, complex technical products and services, and intangibles like public relations or financial services. An impresser brochure is designed to be part of the product: the high quality of the sales materials implies high quality in the product or service.

Design Considerations

When several types of brochures are used for one project, they should share a common "look," based on similar typographic and visual elements.

Although larger brochures will probably be set on more than one column, there should be as much consistency among the brochures as possible:

- The same typefaces, type sizes and type styles for headlines and body copy.

- The same primary photographs, using additional photos and larger sizes in the more focused brochures.

- Consistent margins, borders and graphic accents.

Here are other basic requirements for all brochures:

- A front-cover headline that summarizes the primary benefits of the product offered.

- All facts and figures needed to encourage a positive customer decision.

- Prominently displayed, clear reader-response instructions, including relevant names, addresses and telephone numbers.

One of the pitfalls to avoid is boxing or bordering each page, which can interfere with the reader's natural progression from panel to panel.

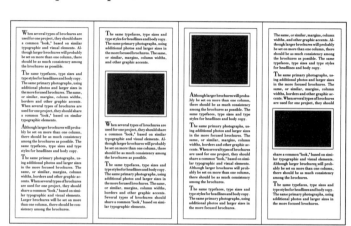

Product sheets can extend the usefulness of a brochure.

Brochures describing a standard line of products or services can be used over an extended period of time. They are typically supported by detailed product sheets (described later in this chapter), which present a more detailed look at a single product. This can save money, because individual product sheets can be revised and reprinted as products are updated, without making the full-line brochures obsolete.

CATALOGS

Catalogs are similar to brochures, except they usually contain more pages and are more product-oriented.

The challenge is to integrate numerous visual elements, captions and prices into an effective and appealing design.

Catalogs are usually produced annually or biannually. Because of their longevity, they're often printed on more expensive paper and include more color.

In many cases, particularly in the retail business, catalogs evolve from newsletters.

The volume of a catalog increases its perceived value.

However, catalogs are often smaller than newsletters. Often, page size is sacrificed for volume, which increases the perceived "reference value" of the catalog and contributes to long life. Many catalogs use a lot of color, which also increases their perceived value and selling power.

Covers

Catalog covers often are printed on a different paper stock than the inside pages.

Often, a heavier, glossy (or smooth, reflective) paper stock is used to provide higher quality photo reproduction and better color saturation.

A single photo of the company's most popular product is often used on the cover to communicate an identity and promote sales.

The cover can also feature a collage, or grouping, of photos or illustrations, calling attention to the diversity of products described inside.

Sometimes, an "atmosphere" photograph is combined with smaller shots of featured products.

Like newsletters, catalog covers often contain a nameplate, or title, that reflects the contents.

Inside Pages

Often a catalog's inside front-cover spread describes the company and its policy. Frequently there's a "Letter From the President" explaining the company's philosophy.

Inside catalog pages are generally more complex than newsletter pages. Often, pages are equally divided into sections for product photos, captions and prices.

You can use varying sizes of artwork.

Artwork can add variety to inside catalog pages.

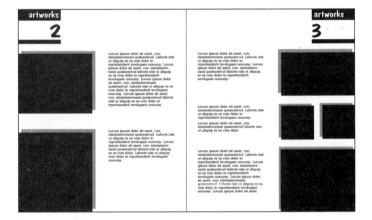

Another useful technique is to place colored or screened backgrounds behind product photos. These provide page-to-page consistency and highlight the photos.

Order Form

Ordering information and forms can be printed as part of the catalog. However, response is encouraged by providing a separate, postage-paid, self-addressed order form inserted into the middle of the catalog.

Inviting readers to respond by offering easy-to-use order forms and placing toll-free telephone numbers in the catalog can greatly increase sales.

FLYERS

Flyers contain time-sensitive information printed on one side of a single sheet of paper.

Flyers are typically used to advertise a special, limited-time promotion of a single product or service. They're ideal when a small budget and immediacy are of paramount importance. They can also be hung on walls, placed on counter-tops or used as shopping bag inserts.

Flyers are ideal for limited-time promotions and small budgets.

Flyers are appropriate vehicles for promoting a drug store's specially priced vitamins, a nightclub's upcoming performance of a popular jazz musician, an office supply dealer's sale on file folders or a music store's sale on a certain label's compact discs.

For flyers to communicate at a glance, they must include the following:

Flyers must communicate a lot of information at a glance.

- Large headlines

- A minimum of body copy

- Attention-getting visuals or graphic accents

Since the primary goal of sending out flyers is to get the message out to as many people as possible, they're usually printed inexpensively in only one or two colors on a cheaper grade of paper.

Printing your flyers on low-cost colored paper produces attention-getting two-color effects for a one-color price.

Although most flyers are printed on standard 8 1/2- by 11-inch paper, larger sizes are possible.

Tabloid-size 11- by 17-inch flyers approach posters, or miniature billboards, in terms of visual impact and amount of information communicated.

PRODUCT SHEETS

Product sheets are simpler than brochures and yet more complex than flyers.

Product sheets provide detailed information and specifications about a product or service and are usually printed on high-quality paper stock. The front cover typically contains a large photograph of the product, a paragraph or two of explanatory material (often repeating the information contained in the company's full-line brochure), plus an outline of the product features and benefits.

Specifications and details are listed in a product sheet.

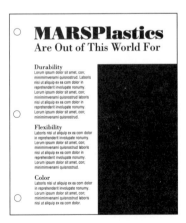

The back cover is more detailed. It often includes one or more photos of products being used, followed by specific product information and any related optional or required accessories and supplies.

Product sheets are often three-hole punched, so they can be inserted in binders or added to proposals.

Creating Consistency

A simple graphic can unify single product sheets into a series.

Consistent placement of a graphic can provide the continuity necessary to tie various product sheets together. This graphic symbol is often printed in a different color on each product sheet, to help distinguish it from others.

Consistency can also be provided by using the same sizes, styles and placement for borders, columns, visuals and logo.

MENUS

A restaurant's menu is its most important advertising medium.

Menus require special care in organizing the material and creating a design that presents an appropriate image.

A menu's design should reflect a restaurant's character.

A menu is an excellent candidate for the application of desktop publishing technology. You can create menu templates that can be easily updated as prices change or new items are added.

Indeed, many fine restaurants print new menus each day—using color printers! This allows each menu to feature the freshest produce and "catch of the day."

Design Considerations

Borders, typefaces and visuals used in the menu's design play a major role in projecting the restaurant's character.

Stylized serif typefaces and ornate borders can communicate an Old World atmosphere.

A contemporary atmosphere is suggested by sparse, angular or geometric sans-serif type.

Menus present an ideal opportunity to use clip art in establishing a mood. Clip-art publishers offer a variety of country, urban and other themes.

In creating a layout, remember that patrons must be able to quickly locate food categories. Subheads set in a contrasting typeface, type size and type style are easy to distinguish.

Avoid using dot leaders to connect food descriptions with prices.

Categories can be boxed, or separated by horizontal rules and white space.

One of the clichés of menu design is separate columns with leader dots connecting descriptions to prices. Unfortunately, the result can be a distracting horizontal pattern. Also, isolated prices place undue emphasis on the price rather than on the merits of the cuisine.

As an alternative, try centering descriptions in two or three columns across the page.

Each item can be introduced by a centered, one- or two-word identifier—perhaps in boldface italics—followed by a two- or three-line (mouth-watering) description. The price can then be discreetly tacked on at the end of the description.

This approach also focuses the reader's attention on one item at a time, instead of inviting comparisons with the other listings.

EVALUATION CHECKLIST

Use these questions to test your brochures, catalogs, flyers, product sheets and menus in terms of the important elements covered in this chapter.

Brochures

1. Have you chosen an appropriate size and format?

2. Does the front cover invite readers inside?

3. Have you maintained page-to-page consistency throughout?

4. Have you supplied all the information prospective buyers need to make favorable buying decisions?

Catalogs

1. Does your catalog begin selling on the front cover?

2. Have you paid as much attention to your catalog's nameplate as you would a newsletter nameplate?

3. Does your catalog contain information describing your company and its credentials?

4. Have you personalized your catalog by including a letter from the owner or employee photographs?

5. Have you made it easy for readers to respond by providing complete ordering information and a large, easy-to-use order form?

Flyers

1. Can readers get your flyer's message at a glance?

2. Have you edited your flyers to provide "who, what, when, where and how" information in the fewest words possible?

3. Have you avoided unnecessary clutter?

Product Sheets

1. Do your individual product sheets share a common family resemblance through consistent use of typography, photo placement and highlight color?

2. Do your product sheets maintain the "look" established by your brochures and catalogs?

Menus

1. Do type, white space and visual elements on the front cover of your menu provide an appropriate introduction to the restaurant's dining experience?

2. Can patrons quickly locate various food categories?

Chapter Fourteen

Books, Documentation & Training Materials

More and more long documents (e.g., books and technical publications such as training materials) are being produced using desktop publishing and word processing software. Designing and producing these multipage documents present both big challenges and more creative opportunities for desktop publishers.

BOOKS

Increasingly, entire books are being submitted to publishers fully designed and formatted.

Book design demands attention to page-to-page consistency.

Desktop publishing gives authors control of the graphic as well as the textual content of their books.

Desktop publishing offers another advantage. Because production costs are reduced, publishers can afford to produce more books and in a timely manner.

Book design requires constant attention to page-to-page consistency and flow.

A great deal of planning is necessary if text and artwork are to be properly balanced and integrated into an overall uniform structure.

Style Considerations

Book design should take into account the writer's style.

If the author frequently uses long paragraphs, one wide column is appropriate.

However, if shorter paragraphs are more common, a two-column format might be better.

Fiction and nonfiction require different page structures. For instance, nonfiction books frequently use subheads to introduce new topics.

Fiction requires different design considerations than nonfiction.

On the other hand, volumes of fiction rarely include subheads, making them easier to design. A single wide column often suffices.

Visuals

Visuals play an important role in book design.

A book with numerous illustrations and photographs requires a different layout than a text-oriented book. A book describing the evolution of a painter's style needs a totally different layout than a novel or an economics textbook.

In the case of books devoted to photographs or paintings, the design must accommodate numerous visuals of various shapes and sizes.

One way to organize photographs is to place them in the same location and orientation on each page. They can be placed horizontally or vertically above the first line of text or to the left of the text columns.

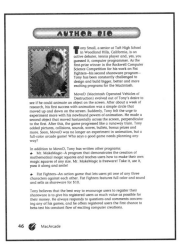

Design books with visuals in mind.

In the example below, photographs "hang" from an invisible "horizon" that spans each two-page spread. Captions are placed in the drop of white space above the photographs. This allows flexibility in using either long or short captions.

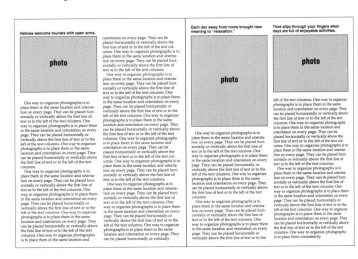

For variety, an occasional photograph can bleed to all four sides of the page. In this case, its caption is placed above the drop on the facing page.

Occasionally, photos can bleed to all four sides to add variety.

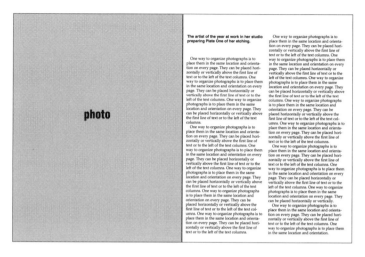

Captions

A consistent size and placement for captions must be maintained throughout the book.

A caption must be set in a contrasting typeface, type size and type style to distinguish it from the body text.

Annotations

In scholarly texts, footnote placement is very important.

Will a citation or reference appear as a footnote at the bottom of the page? Or will all references be listed together at the end of each chapter or grouped together as endnotes at the back of the book?

Organizing Elements

Attention must be paid to the design of headers and footers.

Headers let readers locate data quickly.

Readers need certain cues to keep them oriented as they progress. They must be able to see at a glance which chapter they're reading. Headers and footers on each page can provide this location information.

Headers and footers can consist of page number, chapter title and number, section title and number, and book title.

Multiple Page Layouts

Books often require several different master page layouts.

Books are divided into four major categories: front matter, back matter, chapter openings and text. Each section typically requires different page numbering, headers and footers, and column typography and placement. Therefore, layouts must accommodate specific elements yet relate visually to all the other sections of the book.

Front Matter *The first pages of a book, including the title page, table of contents and introduction, are known as front matter.*

Front matter often includes separate page layouts for copyright and publisher information, acknowledgments, preface, introduction, author's credentials and a table of contents.

Chapter openings should invite readers to go on.

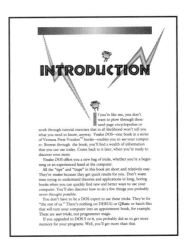

Usually, these sections are set in larger and smaller sizes of the typefaces used in the main body of the book. Copyright pages and disclaimer pages are typically set in much smaller type.

Text   *Use a consistent style to introduce new chapters and new sections.*

Chapter breaks should be significant enough to give the reader a chance to pause, reflect and begin reading again with renewed interest. Often, the chapter number is treated as a dominant visual element on the page.

Chapter breaks give readers a chance to pause.

An introductory paragraph set in italics can be used to ease the reader's transition into the text.

Chapters organized around a common theme can be subdivided into sections. These sections should be introduced by their own dividers.

Back Matter   *Information at the back of a book typically includes one or more appendices, a bibliography and an index.*

DOCUMENTATION

Training materials, such as technical documentation, introduce their own design challenges.

These publications typically include a more complex mix of graphic, textual and typographic elements than do most books. The ongoing narrative sequence is likely to be interspersed with digressions and related illustrations on specific aspects of a topic.

Training materials must often be produced within a limited time frame and budget allowance. This places extra demands on designers and desktop publishers.

The primary goal is to organize a variety of elements. Some of the special concerns in this kind of material are

- Step-by-step sequences must be clearly distinguished.

- Warnings must be highlighted.

- Cross-references must be accurate and easy to follow.

The goal is to enable readers to locate information as quickly as possible.

Technical documentation often includes more header and footer information, such as concise summaries of steps or techniques described on the page. This is especially important when specific instructions continue over several pages.

Hierarchy

The best training materials are based on a design that incorporates multiple levels of heads, subheads and indented text columns.

Take care to organize visuals before you lay out pages.

In addition, technical training materials often include a wide variety of photographs and illustrations. In the case of computer documentation, screen dumps—images from computer screens—must be included.

Confusion is certain to result unless care is taken in organizing text and visuals before page layout begins.

Subheads

Use different sizes of type to distinguish primary subheads from secondary subheads.

The most important subheads—those introducing new topics within a chapter—should be significantly larger than those introducing specific techniques. Subheads within topics should be even smaller.

Hanging indents emphasize first-level subheads. Subheads gain importance when they protrude into the white space to the left of the text column.

Consider type size and white space in setting off primary subheads.

Headers

Headers—chapter and/or section titles, page numbers, etc.—are even more important in documentation than in books.

Readers should quickly be able to locate information by referring to the headers.

EVALUATION CHECKLIST

Check your designs in relation to these questions to be sure you've covered important details.

Books

1. Is your design consistent with the author's writing style and the number and type of illustrations or photographs?

2. Are the design and typography appropriate to the content?

3. Do two-page spreads harmonize?

4. Do chapter introductions clearly invite readers into the text?

5. Are photographs consistently placed in the same location on all pages?

6. Are captions easy to locate and read?

Training Materials

1. Are the elements organized to make information easy to follow?

2. Do subhead sizes and locations clearly indicate the hierarchy of information?

3. Are warnings and cross-references easy to find?

4. Are illustrations clearly identified and set off by sufficient white space?

Chapter Fifteen

Presentation Graphics: Projecting the Right Image

Sooner or later, you'll probably try your hand at designing slides and overhead transparencies on your computer.

It's possible to use your existing desktop publishing program, but specialized presentation software can make the job easier and faster.

For example, you can easily sort or rearrange the order of slides and overheads. You can also proof your work using various "slide show" features that show your slides on the screen from the audience's point of view.

Software programs designed specifically for creating presentation materials let you prepare speaker's notes and audience handouts.

Presentation software makes it easy and fast to create slides and overheads.

CHOOSING YOUR MEDIUM

Start by choosing the appropriate presentation medium.

Options include 35mm slides, monochrome or color over-head transparencies, or computer-generated on-screen presentations.

- 35mm color slides are best for a short, formal presentation delivered to a large group in a darkened room.

- Black-and-white or color transparencies are ideal for longer, less formal presentations delivered to smaller groups, in a setting with normal or slightly subdued lighting. Overhead transparencies allow you to maintain eye contact with your audience, invite questions or discussion and eliminate or add transparencies at the last minute. (You can also write on them with a water-based, felt-tip pen.)

■ Screen presentations are ideal for small groups in normal room lighting. When the group is small, everyone can view the presentation on your computer screen. Or, you can use a projector pad on top of your transparency projector. When available, you can use big-screen monitors. Computer-based, on-screen presentations let you add fancy electronic effects—like dissolves or fancy transitions between slides—as well as quickly call up any slide. If your presentation includes charts and diagrams, you can easily update them on the basis of new information.

Concise, straight-forward visuals are essential for effective presentations.

PRESENTATION DESIGN PRINCIPLES

The same rules for making good-looking pages apply to creating good-looking slides and overheads, particularly in regard to consistency, restraint and contrast.

A few simple design tips apply to designing slides and overheads, the two most popular presentation media. Focus slides or overheads around a single point. Simple, concise visuals are essential for effective presentations. Use projected text and visuals as reinforcement, not as a replacement for your words.

Use plenty of slides, overheads or screens, but limit each one to the development of a single idea. Whenever you find yourself introducing a new concept, create a new frame.

A simple, concise design will get your point across.

Your visuals should serve only as a framework. Carefully edit your text, leaving only the key "action" words. Remember that type size must decrease each time words are added. Eliminate adjectives and adverbs; you can add those in your oral presentation in a warm, conversational manner.

Typeface Choices

Many sans-serif typefaces are ideally suited for slides and overheads.

The straightforward simplicity and lack of decoration of sans-serif type can enhance legibility. Although an entire page of sans-serif type can be boring, a slide or overhead set in a single sans-serif typeface, varying only size, placement and color, can be effective.

Consistency

Apply the same specifications, with as little variation as possible, throughout your presentation.

In creating your presentation materials, strive for consistency in the following areas:

- Typeface, type size, type style, placement and color for title, subtitle and text.

- Text formatting (e.g., margins and line spacing).

- Background color(s).

- Border size, location and color.

- Repeating elements, such as logo, show title and date.

- Graphic accents, such as shadows and bullets.

Changes that look minimal on your computer screen are likely to be greatly magnified when projected onto a large screen. Your audience will be distracted if your firm's logo or the title jumps to a different place on each slide.

Even the most informal presentation is likely to include several different formats. You're likely to use one format for single-column lists, a second for double-column lists, and a third for charts and diagrams. So be sure to integrate these various formats into a coherent presentation design by using consistent treatments of color, border effects, typographic elements and repeating features.

Adding Contrast

Add visual contrast among the various elements of your slides and overheads to prevent monotony.

The slide title should be significantly larger than the text it introduces. This is particularly true if sans-serif type is used for both.

In slides and overheads, titles should contrast strongly with each other.

In charts and diagrams, titles should be significantly larger than legends and reference values, such as percentages displayed on pie-chart slices.

In organization charts illustrating chain-of-command relationships, the top levels can be set in larger type than the subordinate levels.

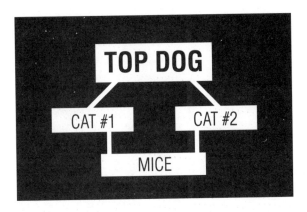

Although background colors for most of your presentation should be the same or similar, long presentations can be broken into "chapters," distinguished by different background colors to indicate different content.

WORKING WITH COLOR

Be careful in choosing colors for backgrounds and text.

Light backgrounds with dark text work best on overhead transparencies. The exact opposite (i.e., dark backgrounds with light text) is preferable for 35mm slides since they're projected in a darkened room.

Colors can have a strong effect on your audience.

Strive for as much contrast between text and background as possible. Light blue text against a dark blue background is extremely difficult to read. Yellow text against a blue background is preferable.

You can add impact to boxed titles by choosing a background color for the box that contrasts with the background in the rest of your slide.

Reactions to color appear to be biologically and emotionally based. A case in point is red, which can arouse feelings of excitement, aggression and stress. Some studies show that red increases blood pressure and pulse rate. Accountants and bankers are apt to reject proposals presented with conclusions drenched in red ink!

Blues and greens can be relaxing, while grays are often somber and depressing.

Other color properties should be considered as well. For instance, some colors "wash out" when projected. A strong yellow accent on the screen of your computer often looks too pale or actually gets lost when projected from an overhead transparency or slide.

Black & White Are Colors!

Use black and white as text colors.

Black or white text can form a strong contrast for many background colors. The text stands out against the background yet doesn't "fight" with it as many other colors do. Bullets set in a stronger color can add visual interest.

HORIZONTAL OR VERTICAL?

Choose landscape (horizontal) instead of portrait (vertical) orientation for your frames.

Although printed pages are usually formatted vertically, slides and overheads are typically prepared and projected horizontally. (Aspect ratios are 3:2 for slides and 4:3 for overhead transparencies.)

Against a color background, black or white text really stands out.

Using a vertical orientation requires small type sizes and packs too much information on each slide. You end up with frames that resemble printed outlines.

Vertical slides can end up looking like printed outlines.

WHO SLEEPS LATE?

- Those who play music in night clubs.
- Those who patrol public buildings during the night.
- People who are on vacation.
- Birds that stay up during the night.

Because fewer lines are available, horizontal orientation forces you to be more selective in the words you use on slides and overheads. So, exercise restraint in the number of points you include and in how you elaborate on them.

Late Sleepers

- **Musicians**
- **Night Watchpersons**
- **Vacationers**
- **Owls**

USING BUILDS

Builds are an effective way to pace your presentation.

Builds allow for progressive introduction of new information. Instead of revealing an entire list or chart at once, you can let the audience read ahead by presenting the material in steps:

- ■ Lists: Introduce one item or one subhead level at a time.

- ■ Pie charts: Show one pie-chart slice at a time.

- ■ Bar charts: Present sales information one quarter or one department contribution at a time.

- ■ Organization charts: Introduce management levels one by one.

- ■ Illustrations: When showing how the various parts of an item fit together, add each successive part on a separate slide or overhead.

Another technique for keeping your audience interested—especially with text-heavy slides and overheads—is to pace your presentation, using an oversized number to distinguish each frame.

Use builds to present complex material one step at a time.

1.	**2.**
Don't contract authors to design or produce your books	Don't expect too much from new publishing technologies
Resist the irresistible! • Good writing talent is hard enough to find • Most writers have no design expertise • Most writers have no DTP expertise **You lose editorial control** • Missed deadlines • Arbitrary manuscript revisions	**Expect:** • Modest dollar savings • Great time savings **Don't expect:** • Fully automated design and production **Initial start-up will cost more** • Capital expenses

Icons can be used for the same purpose. Examples include adding bricks to a building, leaves to a tree or parts to a car.

CHOOSING THE RIGHT INFORMATION GRAPHIC

Charts and diagrams interpret and display information differently.

Pie charts illustrate part-to-whole relationships, translating percentages into proportional sections.

Different types of charts can show the same data in varied ways.

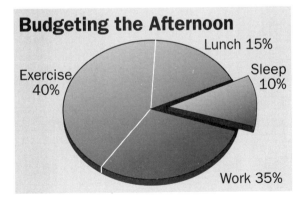

Budgeting the Afternoon
- Lunch 15%
- Sleep 10%
- Work 35%
- Exercise 40%

Bar and column charts compare information categories side by side.

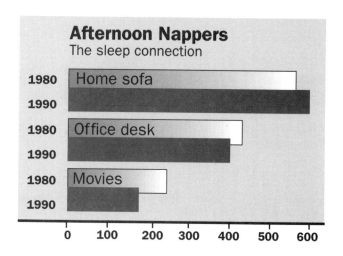

Line charts illustrate trends.

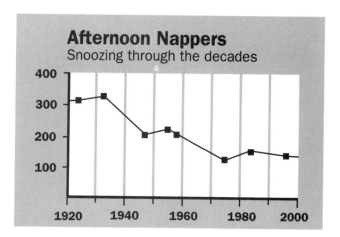

Area diagrams show trends using special comparisons.

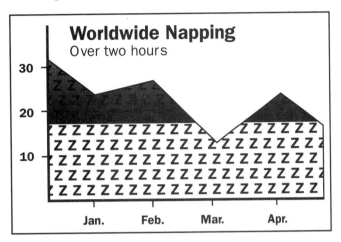

Stacked bar or column charts display the parts that contribute to the totals.

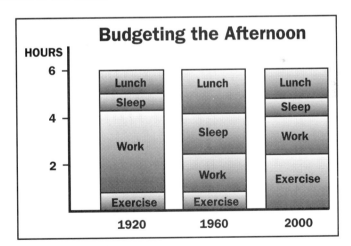

Combination charts compare two different categories of information, using a different data symbol for each category.

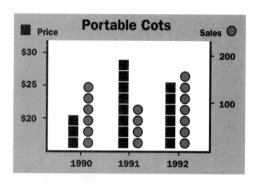

Avoid Complex Charts & Diagrams

Group small subdivisions together or create separate charts and diagrams.

Avoid pie charts with more than six sections. If your pie chart has a few large slices and numerous small ones, combine the smaller slices into a "miscellaneous" or "other" classification. If necessary, create a second pie chart.

A clear, simple design is important for black and white overheads.

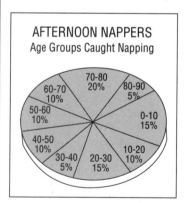

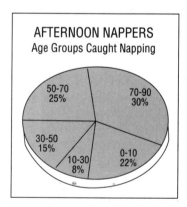

Also, avoid bar or column charts with so many segments that it's difficult to isolate the most important information and make comparisons.

Simplicity is particularly important when working with black-and-white overhead transparencies. Too many dot patterns and angled lines can quickly become distracting.

Enhancing Charts & Diagrams

You can improve a visual's communicating power by modifying the type specifications.

Often, typeface, type size and color defaults are inappropriate for a particular slide or overhead. Here are some of the ways you can selectively enhance the typography in your chart or diagram.

- Choose a different typeface and increase the type size of pie or bar chart or diagram value labels.

- Reset X and Y axis annotation in a larger type size to improve legibility.

- Make the legend more noticeable by using a larger type size and adding white space around it.

Visual Formatting

Add grid lines and tick marks as needed.

Horizontal and vertical grid lines provide a frame of reference and help the viewer's eye connect the data symbol with the reference value.

Most charts need grid lines or tick marks as a frame of reference.

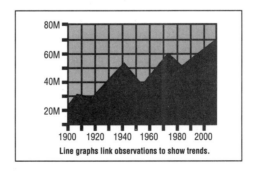

Line graphs link observations to show trends.

Too many marks produce unnecessary clutter. Be sure you use the minimum necessary to provide visual landmarks.

Charts and diagrams can be emphasized by setting them on a background color that contrasts with the color used for the slide background.

SPEAKER'S NOTES

Speaker's notes help you rehearse your presentation and focus your attention on the audience, instead of the screen behind you.

A note page can contain a miniature reproduction of a single slide or overhead, plus enough space for you to list the points you want to emphasize during your presentation.

In speaker's notes, include data not given in your projected image.

Use a large type size for your speaker's notes: 36 points is ideal—you can see them at a glance without squinting. Use only as many words as you need to provide detail while maintaining the momentum of your presentation.

In your speaker's notes, you can include details not given in your projected image, such as information sources. This data will come in handy if someone asks for it.

Audience Handouts

Most presentation software programs can produce audience handouts with reduced representations of your visuals.

These contain two, three, four or six images per page.

You can redesign these handouts by repositioning the image and adding the presentation title in large type at the top of each page, followed by the date in smaller type. You can set off the title and date with rules or boxes, if desired. You can also add page numbers at the bottom of each page.

EVALUATION CHECKLIST

Check your work against these criteria to see if you've added the right ingredients for effective visuals.

1. Did you choose the presentation format most appropriate for your message, audience and environment?

2. Are all slides, overheads and screens in your presentation assembled with the same background color, typography, borders and repeating elements?

3. Have you created visual interest by adding contrast between slide titles and supporting information?

4. Have you used builds to introduce information on a step-by-step basis?

5. Have you chosen the type of chart or diagram most appropriate for displaying your data?

6. Have you modified type specifications for chart and diagram annotation so that all information is legible?

7. Have you used grid lines and tick marks to provide visual frames of reference?

8. Can you read your speaker's notes from a comfortable distance, grasping key words and important ideas at a glance?

9. Have you designed audience handouts to include presentation title, date, logo and appropriate rules or graphic accents?

Chapter
Sixteen

Business Communications

As you develop your design sense and become more familiar with the capabilities of desktop publishing, you'll continue to discover new applications. For in-house projects, you will probably come to rely more and more on your desktop system rather than on professional service bureaus for design and production.

LETTERHEAD

A good letterhead must communicate subliminal as well as practical information at a glance.

Letterhead design is not as simple as it might seem. It's important to express something about the nature or character of your firm or association in your letterhead design, in addition to providing its name, address and phone number as response information. For instance, a district attorney requires a different letterhead style than a tanning salon.

These are the basic components of a letterhead:

Letterheads must include basic response information.

- Firm or organization name

- Logo

- Motto or statement of business philosophy

- Street address and mailing address (if different)

- Telephone number(s)

- Telex and/or facsimile number

Corporate and nonprofit letterheads often list officers or board members as well. All too often, however, that leaves little space for the actual message area and presents a real design challenge!

Logo Size & Placement

The size of your logo must be proportional to the amount of supporting information.

Logos must be large enough to be noticed, yet not so large they visually overwhelm the letterhead. In the example below, the logo detracts from the message area.

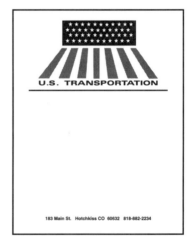

A logo shouldn't be so large that it overwhelms the message area.

Placement can be flexible. Although logos are frequently centered above the letterhead, there is no reason why they can't be placed differently, as long as you observe basic rules of good design.

For example, logos can be set flush-left or flush-right at the top of the page.

The House Specialists 244 Emerson Boulevard Wilson, NC 27846

The House Specialists
244 Emerson Boulevard
Wilson, NC 27846

The letterhead can be designed on an asymmetrical grid. This will leave a vertical band of white space along the left-hand side of the letterhead.

Designing letter-head on an asym-metrical grid increases the white space.

183 Main St.
Hotchkiss CO 60632
818-882-2234

Addresses & Phone Numbers

Be sure to include all information the letter's recipient needs in order to respond.

Insufficient address and phone information can cause problems for your correspondents.

Letterhead design becomes a bit more complicated when both telephone and facsimile numbers (and/or both street address and post office box number—sometimes with different ZIP Codes) must be included.

One common mistake is to print a telephone number without the area code. That's all right for local callers, but it puts long-distance callers at a distinct disadvantage!

Placement of telephone and address information usually depends on logo placement. When the logo is centered at the top of the letterhead, telephone and address information is often centered in a smaller type size along the page bottom .

When both telephone and fax numbers are included, as well as separate street address and post office box number, the information is often divided into thirds and placed across the bottom of the letterhead. For example, the street address can be aligned flush-left on two lines, telephone and fax numbers centered on two lines in the middle, and post office box number placed flush-right.

Don't forget to add the area code to your phone number.

| 1845 United Terrace | PHONE   987/765-5432 | P.O. Box 1659 |
| Salem, Oregon 12345 | FAX 987/765-2345 | Salem, Oregon 12345 |

When fewer items are included, they can be placed on one line and separated by white space and oversized bullets.

P.O. Box 146 ◆ Kittering, PA 15401 ◆ 900/735-8976

Another option is to indent logo and address information from the left-hand edge of the letterhead. The logo is placed at the top of the page, while address and telephone information is placed at the bottom.

The logo and address should complement each other.

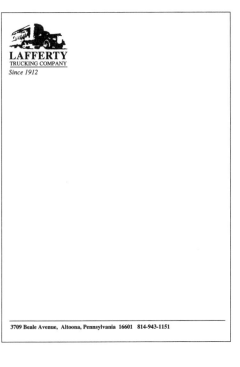

Motto

Mottos often run along the bottom of a letterhead, forming an umbrella over address and phone information.

In these cases, the motto is typically set slightly larger, and the italic version of the motto's font is used for the address and the telephone number.

"Your Professional Insurance Agency"

P.O. Box 146 ◆ Kittering, PA 15401 ◆ 900/735-8976

"Sailing Around The Clock"

P.O. Box 467 • Oriental, NC 28328 • 1-800-823-SAIL

Message Area

The final challenge is to effectively set off the letterhead elements so they don't interfere with the contents of the document.

One way to do this is to box the message area.

Or, a single rule can separate the two areas.

A screened column or panel or a second color can also be used to isolate supplementary information. This technique works well for listing board members or officers of an organization.

Screens can separate the message area from the rest of the letterhead.

Envelope Design

The letterhead design should be scaled down and repeated on the business envelope.

All sizes of an envelope family should repeat the same design.

More and more businesses are using "window" envelopes, which eliminate the need for addressing separate envelopes or labels. Care should be taken with the letterhead design to allow for properly positioning the inside address. The recipient's name and address must be placed on the page so they can be seen through the window when the letter or form is folded and inserted into the envelope.

Often a "family" of envelopes is created: a small, inexpensive envelope for sending invoices and paying bills; a Number 10 envelope, printed on the same paper stock as the letterhead, for standard correspondence; and a 9- by 12-inch envelope for formal proposals or oversize documents.

Sometimes logo and address information are rotated 90 degrees and placed vertically along the side of the envelope.

BUSINESS CARDS

Business cards are even more challenging than letterheads.

On a business card, a lot of information must be presented in a relatively small amount of space—typically 3.5 by 2 inches. Not only must address, phone and fax numbers, and a logo be included, but an individual's name and title must also be prominently displayed.

This format is an ideal candidate for the application of desktop publishing technology. Once the basic card has been designed and stored as a template, it takes just a few seconds to replace one name and/or position with another.

Establishing Priorities

Which should be larger—the individual's name or the firm's logo?

Often, the logo is so large it dwarfs all other items on the page—including the individual's name.

A "quadrant" layout can provide a framework for designing business cards.

The "quadrant" technique is one solution to this problem. The firm's logo is placed flush-left in the upper left quadrant of the card. The logo is balanced by the phone number set flush-right in the upper right quadrant. The street address is flush-left along the bottom of the card in the lower left quadrant; post office box information is flush-right in the lower right quadrant. These four elements form a framework around the individual's name and title located in the center of the card.

Another solution is to indent logo, address and phone information from the left, as on business letterhead.

FAX COVER SHEETS

Fax transmissions are an important part of today's business world.

Fax cover sheets ensure quick, complete trans- missions.

Cover sheets help ensure safe, efficient facsimile communications that are delivered quickly to the right people.

It's important for the facsimile cover sheet to indicate the total number of pages sent. This helps the recipient know that the entire transmission has been received and nothing is missing. Other important items include the following:

- Recipient's name

- Sender's name

- Date of transmission

- Subject matter or summary of contents

Some fax cover sheets include space or lines for a brief handwritten message. Or, a message can be set in a smaller type size to distinguish it from the items listed above.

In choosing type, remember that fax transmission quality varies.

Be careful when choosing typefaces for facsimile messages. Since the quality of reproduction varies, it's important to choose a face that remains legible under any circumstances.

Typefaces with thin strokes or detailed serifs tend to reproduce poorly and are not the most reliable choice for fax transmissions.

RESUMES

A resume is direct-response advertising in its purest form.

With the skillful use of typographic elements, resumes can take full advantage of desktop publishing's power to set a tone or project an aura. Also, they're an ideal format for utilizing desktop publishing's ability to organize data and establish hierarchies of importance.

Changing Trends

Today, the trend is toward less formal, more goal-oriented resumes.

Contemporary resumes focus more on what an individual has to offer a company. In past years, resumes tended to be organized chronologically, focusing on a progression through a person's education, career and activities.

In any case, white space, subheads and graphic accents should be used to separate categories of information. A prospective employer should be able to quickly locate relevant qualifications without playing detective.

Design resumes so that employers can easily find your qualifications.

Design a resume as you would an ad.

Although many desktop-published documents use a combination of sans-serif type for subheads and serif type for body copy, many resumes use the italic version of the serif type in a larger type size for subheads. This softens the contrast between subheads and body copy.

Resumes should be designed like advertisements: "selling" information should precede "supporting" or "qualifying" information. Thus, address, phone number, health and marital status should be subordinate to statements that relate to benefits the hiring firm will gain by hiring the individual.

Perhaps the best beginning for a resume is a quoted personal recommendation from an individual noted in the field, a description of a significant accomplishment or a statement of goals and objectives.

Since your resume is actually an advertisement for yourself, pay careful attention to the smallest details of letter and line spacing. At all costs, avoid errors in grammar, spelling and punctuation.

EVALUATION CHECKLIST

Check your work against these criteria to see if you've added the right ingredients for effective business communications.

Letterheads

1. Does the design of your letterhead accurately reflect your firm's philosophy and way of doing business?

2. Are your firm's logo, motto and address/phone number sized in correct proportion to the size of the message area?

3. Is the message area clearly set apart from the information area?

4. Has all necessary information been included, such as area codes, fax numbers, post office box number and street address?

5. Do envelopes repeat important information, including telephone and fax numbers? (Often, envelopes get separated from letters.)

Business Cards

1. Do business cards contain all necessary response information, as well as the individual's name and title?

2. Is background information visually distinct from the name and title?

3. Does the design of your business card reflect the design of your letterhead?

Fax Cover Sheets

1. Do your fax sheets clearly document sender, recipient, transmission date, the total number of pages sent and subject matter details?

2. Do your cover sheets include the phone number and extension of the person sending the fax, in case a transmission error is detected and the machine operator needs to be contacted?

3. Is space for a short message added directly to the fax cover sheet?

Resumes

1. Have you presented information in your resume in its order of importance to the reader?

2. Do the typeface, type size and type style send the right message about the type of person you are and the type of job you're applying for?

3. Have you used white space, subheads and graphic accents, such as rules, to organize the information in your resume?

Chapter Seventeen

Response Devices— Forms, Coupons & Surveys

The preceding chapters dealt primarily with "passive" communications—advertisements and publications designed to attract the reader's attention and communicate information.

This chapter looks at "active" communications: reader-response formats such as coupons, order forms, contracts and surveys.

Coupons are valuable for providing names and addresses of prospective customers for later follow-up. *Employment application forms* help find the right person for the job. *Price quotations* and *order forms* make it possible to sell things to people across town or around the world. *Surveys* allow customers and employees to express their opinions and make suggestions.

The success criteria for passive communications apply equally to active formats. Just as effective newsletters and ads can be easily read, successful response devices can be easily understood and used.

Regardless of specific function, coupons, forms and surveys are composed of the same basic parts. Appropriate design of these parts is essential.

Reader-response formats follow the same design principles that "passive" communications do.

TITLE

Titles should clearly identify the form's purpose. The title should be set in a typeface, type size and type style that contrast with the other type elements on the form.

Like the headline of a form or newsletter article, the title should be the dominant visual element, set significantly larger than the words that follow.

The title should contrast with other type elements.

INSTRUCTIONS

A successful response device gives clear directions for filling out and sending in the form.

Surveys should carefully explain the rating scheme used.

Coupon instructions should include payment options—prepayment, C.O.D. shipment and credit cards accepted—and to whom the check should be made out, if that payment method is used. If items are to be shipped via United Parcel Service, customers should be reminded that a post office address does not provide enough information for delivery.

Employment applications should indicate how and where the applicant can fill in education and previous employment information and references.

Surveys should carefully explain the rating scheme used—whether high numbers indicate agreement or disagreement with the statement, for instance.

Instructions are typically set in a small type size (6, 7 or 8 points) compared to other type on the page.

RESPONSE AREA

Response areas can be designed with lines to be filled in or ballot boxes or pairs of parentheses to be checked.

Forms with ballot boxes and parentheses are quick and easy to fill out. They are typically used for simple "yes" or "no" entries.

Lines accommodate names, addresses and other detailed textual information that may be required.

Category Identifiers

Categories should be clearly labeled and distinguished graphically and typographically.

Column headers identify quantity, item number, description, unit price and total price listings.

Column headers are typically centered over their listings. Other column headers might include Years, Firm or Institution, Highest Degree Earned, etc.

Labels should be carefully placed to identify the column they accompany.

There should be no question in the respondent's mind as to whether the title relates to the line above or the space below. Yet, numerous response devices resemble the example shown here:

Graphic Accents

Rules organize information by acting as horizontal and vertical dividers between items and sections.

Vertical rules, in partnership with column headers, provide directional cues and guide the respondent to ensure that all necessary information is entered in the proper locations.

Screens and rules are effective devices to set off prices.

You can also use screens for organization and emphasis. For example, you can add a light screen behind the "total price" column to draw attention to it.

Coupons are typically bordered with a dashed line. Government or institution forms are often enclosed within boxed borders.

More formal response devices, such as surveys, often use borders and the firm or association's letterhead or logo.

FUNCTIONAL ISSUES

A well-designed response device is easy to fill out.

Ballot boxes are close enough to each other so that a minimum of hand and eye movement is needed from one item to the next.

Designs that leave too much space between the ballot boxes create unattractive pools of white. This effect discourages the respondent from taking the time or effort to complete the form.

> **1. *What areas of media do you work in?***
> ☐ TELEVISION
> ☐ VIDEO PRODUCTION
> ☐ CABLE
> ☐ AUDIO/RADIO PRODUCTION

Always provide sufficient line length and space between lines. If you've ever tried to write in a long name or address on a tiny coupon, you know how frustrating it is, particularly if you must include rank, serial number and mail stop.

It's in the best interest of everyone involved to provide adequate horizontal and vertical space to permit a comfortable, readable handwriting size.

Always provide enough space for respondents to fill in a complete address.

Forms that have line spacing based on standard type-writer line spacing are always appreciated. The user can fill out the form without manually adjusting the spacing for each line.

Always provide enough address lines. Include space for five-line addresses. In addition to firm name, street and city, etc., the extra lines accommodate department or division names or numbers and suite, floor or building numbers.

Addresses for many large firms now include mail-stop information—their own internal ZIP Codes. Unless you make it easy for users to include complete delivery information, order fulfillment or return communications can be seriously delayed or may never arrive at all!

CHANGING WORLD...

As the world's economies become more interdependent, addresses become longer and more complex.

The ZIP Code portion of the address area should allow for the additional four-digit ZIP Code for carrier-route sorting. Having this information can expedite mail delivery and save your organization postage costs in the years to come.

It's also important to allow space to specify the country as well as the state.

It's always a good idea to include telephone extension numbers to avoid delays in case a follow-up call is necessary.

EVALUATION CHECKLIST

Check your work against these criteria to see if you've added the right ingredients for effective response devices.

Coupons

1. Is it clear to the respondent where he or she should send the coupon?

2. Does the coupon provide enough lines for itemizing information?

3. Is the coupon large enough to be easily filled out, yet not so large it dominates the advertisement?

Order Forms

1. Is there space to list quantity, item number, item description and total price?

2. Does the pricing area provide space for adding shipping charges and taxes?

3. Do order forms spell out the customer's payment and shipping options?

4. Does the order form include space for the respondent's telephone number, in case of problems?

5. Does the order form have sufficient space for full delivery information, including department, division, mail stop and suite number?

Employment Applications

1. Does the employment application direct the applicant through the form with typographic cues and graphic accents?

2. Does line spacing allow applicants to use a typewriter to fill out their education and employment history?

3. Have you subdivided the application form into logical, clearly defined categories?

Surveys

1. Are rating values for yes/no or agree/disagree questions clear? Are the entries closely spaced?

2. Have long surveys been subdivided into categories, avoiding the appearance of essay questions or final exams?

3. Is the appearance of the survey consistent with the organization's other print communications?

Appendix

Graphics & Prepress Tips & Techniques

The following tips and tricks are designed to help you sidestep the problems that have ensnared so many desktop publishers.

Although computers are supposed to make document creation easier, sometimes technology seems only to complicate matters. This is especially the case if you're using an untested technique, trying out new software or working with new hardware.

If you're working with color or digital photography, or if you plan to work with a service bureau for high-resolution output, the advice in this appendix will save you money and hours of frustration.

IMAGE DATABASES

Image databases help you keep track of lots of different graphics.

If you work with a lot of graphics files, you may find that keeping track of which images match which files can be a tricky process. Just as you can use a conventional database to sort and track information, you can use an image database to store a low-resolution screen image of your high-resolution digital photos and illustration files. Some image databases show thumbnail views of groups of photos according to your specific instructions.

You can also use an image database to track how frequently you use a photo or illustration, as well as in which publications and situations. While they are currently used for more high-end applications, image databases eventually will become cheaper and easier to use, giving any desktop publisher the capability to track and sort images quickly and effectively.

PICKING THE RIGHT PAPER

Paper plays a crucial role in how your documents appear.

High-end printing (especially if it involves photos or color) works best on higher-quality papers at fairly high output resolutions. Coarse papers don't hold ink well enough to create the crisp definition needed for high-resolution work. The result is muddy images that are out of registration.

Finer papers hold ink more precisely and with less bleeding, running and spreading, producing sharper images.

Also available are specially coated papers that make colors and photos "pop," or stand out even more than they would on uncoated paper.

The thickness of the paper is also important. Using paper that is too thin may cause the inks to bleed through, wreaking havoc with type or images on the other side of the page.

When planning a project, consider paper when establishing your budget. Size, thickness, coating, texture—and other factors, like availability and demand—can cause wide variations in paper prices.

Finally, don't forget that paper doesn't always have to be white. Colored paper can create a special effect technique with flyers and handbills.

You can combine the impact of colored paper (which often costs only slightly more than standard white paper) with black ink, a colored ink, or both, to grab and hold the reader's attention.

GETTING THE MOST FROM COLOR PRINTING

Four-color printing combines a number of diverse disciplines in one complex process.

Printing color documents, especially complicated four-color pieces, is a tricky process that can cost you time and money for even minor mistakes. The tips and techniques in this section will help you avoid making some of the more frustrating mistakes and will offer advice on getting more bang for your color buck.

How Four-Color Printing Works

In simplest terms, printing a color document is a matter of splitting its component colors into four different elements, or plates.

Each color is broken down as a percentage of cyan (a light blue), magenta (a pinkish purple), yellow and black (abbreviated CMYK).

These are called the *subtractive primary colors,* because combining them all gives you a full, rich black, and subtracting certain quantities of one or more colors can yield practically any other color imaginable.

At four different points in the printing process, the paper passes a spot (usually a roller) where one of the four colors (cyan, magenta, yellow and black) is applied. The final combination creates the full, vibrant colors you see in any brochure, magazine or annual report.

As you can imagine, a lot can go wrong during a large print job. Paper, printing plates and rollers can all slip out of alignment. If a single element isn't perfectly aligned with all the others, then your colors will print out of registration, ruining even the most beautiful design and artwork.

Luckily, there are a few tricks that can help your color pages print in proper registration, even covering up minor flaws in the printing process.

The Color Trap

Traditionally the realm of the prepress technician, trapping can now be controlled by the designer.

Trapping is the process of determining how much overlap or spacing to leave between color elements to ensure clean, clear printing, even if you encounter slight problems with registration.

While trapping has traditionally been handled by the printer on any given job, most desktop publishing and illustration packages provide for some means of electronic trapping control. As with most other aspects of color prepress and printing, the details of this process vary widely.

Since bad trapping can be worse than no trapping at all, it's best to consult your software manuals, service bureau and printer for the details and help you'll need.

Preparing Spot Color for Printing

Printing spot-color work is only slightly more involved than printing single-color work.

If you've planned and set up your document carefully, printing a spot color job should be no more complicated than a regular one-color document.

Printing a *separation proof* creates two pages of output for each single page in your electronic document—one page with all items in black, and another for all items in spot color.

Printing a *composite proof* gives you a single page where both colors are printed, showing you how the final product will look. (Of course, you'll have to print to a color output device for a realistic color composite.)

You can also use separation and composite proofs to check the trapping (see "The Color Trap" earlier in this appendix), alignment and registration of the items in your document.

COLOR & COMPUTER TECHNOLOGY

Computers make designing and producing color documents easier, but they aren't foolproof.

Just as advances in technology have made working with type more predictable, the disparity in color on the computer and color off the press is shrinking every day.

Part of the problem in matching color on the computer to the color of the final product lies in the media. Monitors produce colors by actually creating light as they illuminate your screen. Printed documents rely solely on reflected light.

Also, monitors use red, green and blue (or *additive color*) to create all other colors, while the printing process uses cyan, magenta and yellow (or *subtractive color*) as its palette.

Various techniques and systems have been developed to help compensate for the differences between colors on the computer and the printing press.

Color matching is the process by which the colors you choose for your computer-generated documents are matched to existing color standards. The final printed product is also checked against a set of standard colors to ensure accuracy at the final stage.

There are a number of different color matching standards, including the Pantone Matching System (PMS), in which you use a color sample book and an electronic color library to match colors with standard inks that most printers can use.

It's important to choose and stick to a single color matching system for all your color work. It's difficult (or nearly impossible) to ensure consistency and quality when constantly jumping from one standard to another. Your software package, color choices, and production and printing methods play a major role in determining which matching system (if any) you should use. Consult your software manuals and printer for advice on this matter.

Color calibration techniques involve using special software and hardware devices to compensate for the differences between computer-generated and printed colors.

Color calibration technology has not yet fully developed, and just as with color matching systems, competing vendors and platforms will struggle to develop a universally accepted standard.

Regardless of the sophistication of your color software and hardware—when printing a computer-generated color document—there's no substitute for a well-trained eye. Some colors are particularly difficult to reproduce faithfully—watch out for unrealistic flesh tones, for example.

WORKING WITH SERVICE BUREAUS

Working closely with your service bureau and printer from start to finish will help ensure consistent, predictable results.

If the last step in your desktop publishing project is printing out a final proof on a 300-dpi laser printer and having those pages photocopied or quick-printed, consider yourself lucky. But, if like a growing number of designers, you find yourself sending your work to high-resolution imagesetters or traditional print houses, there are a few simple guidelines you can follow that will ensure consistent, predictable results:

Make friends with your printer and service bureau technicians.

- Ask for help. Nobody knows everything about desktop publishing, and there's no shame in asking your service bureau or printer for advice on complex subjects like scanning photos or defining electronic color trapping parameters.

- Time is money. When large files take longer than usual to print, you'll probably have to pay a surcharge for tying up a service bureau's equipment. Rush jobs cost extra as well, so plan ahead.

- Less is more. Since time is money, don't use graphics (especially photos) digitized at a higher resolution than necessary—you'll just be wasting time processing image information you don't need.

- Run the numbers. There are plenty of equations and rules that can guide you through esoteric calculations such as how many steps to put in a graduated blend or at what resolution to scan a photo. Check with your service bureau or printer and follow their instructions.

- Keep it simple. Above all else, keep your project as simple as possible. Do not try to do something that isn't necessary, and if the traditional method is faster, cheaper and easier than the computerized way, by all means, switch off your computer and roll up your shirtsleeves.

Appendix

Photo & Clip Art Resources

If you're a budding desktop designer, you may be interested in incorporating photographs and clip art into your documents. But where do you start? Where do you find clip art? Where do you go for photographs?

This appendix offers some guidance on locating photos and canned art, and some tips on scanner manufacturers.

Professional-quality electronic clip art is widely available for any kind of desktop publishing platform. As with fonts, clip art can be bought through mail-order vendors, in retail outlets or direct from the manufacturer. It is also available on floppy and CD-ROM. Also included with the following clip-art listings are backgrounds and textures.

SOURCES FOR CLIP ART

Images With Impact

3G Graphics
114 Second Ave. South, Ste. 104
Edmonds, WA 98020
800-456-0234
A huge CD-ROM collection of excellent images ranging from cartoons to realistic, color line drawings. Images from this extensive and impressive collection can be easily edited using Adobe Illustrator. Files are stored in several formats, including black-and-white and color EPS and PICT.

Cliptures

Dream Maker Software
925 West Kenyon Ave., Ste. 16
Englewood, CO 80110
800-876-5665
A collection of EPS images, including business and sports graphics. Cliptures features an extensive collection of flags.

Artbeats

PO Box 1287
Myrtle Creek, OR 97457
800-822-0772
This package includes a number of diverse backgrounds for use in flyers, ads, brochures, on-screen presentations and other applications. The backgrounds range from natural textures to futuristic scenes, all created electronically, so the file size is smaller than with scanned backgrounds.

SOURCES FOR PHOTOGRAPHS

There are a number of inexpensive and convenient methods for locating and using good photographs.

Even if you don't have access to a staff photographer, there may be a photo resource, clip file or other backlog of images for you to choose from: amateur photographers abound, or a staff member, co-worker, family member or friend may have a portfolio of photos he or she is willing to share.

Digital Photo Sources

Perhaps of most immediate interest to desktop publishers are digital photo resources. With a digital photo, you can manipulate the images electronically and integrate them into the rest of your layout, eliminating the need for conventional photo stripping. Digital photograph sources include

- Digital cameras. Digital still cameras are being used more frequently in training materials and in database applications.

- Video capture systems. Special equipment that captures frames directly from video can be a useful if the image you need exists only on videotape.

- Photo CD. Kodak's Photo CD format allows you to shoot film in the conventional manner and then have it processed and placed on a CD-ROM disk for viewing on screen or importing into a page layout program.

- Scanners. With the price of a color flatbed scanner roughly approaching that of a PostScript laser printer, scanning prints is an increasingly viable option for the average desktop publisher.

Hewlett-Packard

PO Box 58059
MS#511L-SJ
Santa Clara, CA 95051
800-752-0900
The Hewlett-Packard ScanJet IIc is a 400 dpi color flatbed scanner that operates with both Windows and Macintosh computers. The optics of the ScanJet IIc are as good as practically any flatbed scanner on the market, and its low price makes it a performance bargain.

Light Source

17 East Sir Francis Drake Blvd., Ste. 100
Larkspur, CA 94939
415-461-8000
Ofoto scanning software is designed to calibrate your scanner to the specific monitor and output devices you use. This yields optimum results when working with continuous tone images, particularly color photos. Ofoto is compatible with a variety of scanners and runs on both Macintosh and Windows computers.

Stock Photo Services

A number of companies create and buy photos to keep on file for later sale or licensing to designers and art directors. You can request stock photos in practically any medium imaginable, including prints, slides and computer files on CD-ROM disks.

Comstock
30 Irving Pl.
New York, NY 10003
212-353-8600
Comstock is one of the larger stock photo agencies and it has released four separate CDs containing images related to business, health and fitness, travel and vacations, and people. The images vary in size and resolution, but average about 175k to 200k each.

Husom & Rose
1988 Stanford Ave.
St. Paul, MN 55105
612-699-1858
Featuring 65 images, Husom & Rose's Photographics disk contains a wide variety of general photos, including people, places, backgrounds, clouds, trees, water and other nature images. The files are available in both high-resolution 24-bit color TIFF and screen-resolution PICT formats.

Digital Gallery Limited
4422 Southwest Corbett St.
Portland, OR 97201
503-228-8105
Released each month, the Digital Gallery Limited CD is restricted to 1000 copies of each edition. With each image running around 30mb, each disk features about 20 images; and they appear only in 24-bit color TIFF format. Each image is optimized to output at 7" x 10" at a 175 line screen.

News Services & Historical Archives

Similar to stock photo companies, some news organizations license secondary use of photos originally taken for and printed in newspapers, magazines and other publications. News services may offer their images as prints, slides or on disk—some even upload photos to online services, where you can pay to download and use them.

Many universities, public libraries, historical societies and other organizations maintain massive collections of photographs germane to a specific field of study or local interest. If you're working on a specific project, many organizations will lend you photos from their archives free of charge.

Appendix

Desktop Publishers' Resources

Mastering design and desktop publishing can't be done in a day, or in a week or month for that matter. Like all disciplines, these too require a long-term commitment to keep looking, keep reading, keep asking, keep experimenting.

The resources listed here will help you locate everything from high-quality design seminars to great books that will help you look good in print.

BOOKS

■ American Press Institute. *Newspaper Design: 2000 and Beyond.* Reston, VA: American Press Institute, 1989.

Contains "before" and "after" versions of some of the country's most famous newspapers, showing how they are adapting to changing reader tastes in the television age. The use of full color throughout this publication adds to its visual impact.

■ Beach, Mark, and Russon, Ken. *Papers for Printing: How to Choose the Right Paper at the Right Price for Any Printing Job.* Portland, OR: Coast to Coast Books, 1989.

Takes the mystery out of choosing paper; contains many samples showing how paper choice affects the appearance of text and illustrations. Help for the stranded newsletter editor with a deadline two days away and three pages to fill.

Beach, Mark, Shepro, Steve, and Russon, Ken. *Getting It Printed: How to Work with Printers and Graphic Arts Services to Assure Quality, Stay on Schedule, and Control Costs.* Portland, OR: Coast to Coast Books, 1986.

Invaluable advice about what to do after the laser printer or phototypesetter has churned out the last page of your brochure, newsletter or book.

Beale, Stephen, and Cavuoto, James. *The Scanner Book: A Complete Guide to the Use and Applications of Desktop Scanners.* Torrance, CA: Micro Publishing Press, 1989.

Describes what to look for in choosing a scanner and how to make the most of it when you get it home. Reviews hardware and software options and shows how to manipulate scanned images on your computer screen.

Binns, Betty. *Better Type: Learn to see subtle distinctions in the faces and spaces of text type.* New York: Watson-Guptill, 1989.

Concise text with numerous illustrations showing how the slightest changes in letter, line and word spacing can have a major effect on a publication's appearance and readability.

Bly, Robert W. *The Copywriter's Handbook.* New York: Henry Holt & Co., 1990.

An entertaining but thorough review of the tools of effective copywriting that can restore vigor to tired copy.

Bly, Robert W. *Secrets of a Freelance Writer.* New York: Henry Holt & Co., 1990.

Although focused on surviving as a freelance writer, many of the ideas in this book can be used by freelance graphic designers and desktop publishers.

Bly, Robert W. *Create the Perfect Sales Piece: How to Produce Brochures, Catalogs, Fliers and Pamphlets.* New York: John Wiley & Sons, 1985.

Bly stresses the importance of project planning before beginning work and lists numerous sources of outside help.

Brady, Philip. *Using Type Right: 121 Basic No-Nonsense Rules for Working With Type.* Cincinnati, OH: North Light Books, 1988.

An entertaining book of tips and techniques for making better use of your desktop publishing or page layout program. Combines concise descriptions of design principles with graphic examples in an oversized format that's a joy to read.

Brown, Alex. *In Print: Text and Type in the Age of Desktop Publishing.* New York: Watson-Guptill, 1989.

Combines concise, highly readable descriptions of the aesthetic qualities of different typefaces and techniques to make effective use of any typeface.

Burke, Clifford. *Type From the Desktop: Designing With Type and Your Computer.* Chapel Hill, NC: Ventana Press, 1990.

A thought-provoking exploration into the world of typography and design. Filled with type examples, this book explores the functions and aesthetics of type.

Cook, Alton, ed. *Type and Color: A Handbook of Creative Combinations.* Rockport, MA: Rockport Publications, 1989.

Previews more than 800,000 possible type/background combinations. Contains more than 100 pages of color samples and removable acetate overlays to let you experiment with black, colored or reversed type on a variety of background colors.

Dair, Carl. *Design With Type.* Toronto, Canada: University of Toronto Press, 1982.

A welcome reprint of the 1960 original, this slim, unpretentious volume contains unforgettable lessons that extend far beyond page design and typography into writer/designer/reader relationships.

■ Finberg, Howard I., and Itule, Bruce D. *Visual Editing: A graphic guide for journalists*. Belmont, CA: Wadsworth, 1990.

More than just guidelines for the effective use of photographs, charts and information graphics, *Visual Editing* thoroughly investigates how computerized publishing is revolutionizing newspaper production.

■ Floyd, Elaine. *Advertising From the Desktop: The Desktop Publisher's Guide to Designing Ads That Work*. Chapel Hill, NC: Ventana Press, 1993.

Put Madison Avenue in your mouse! *Advertising From the Desktop* provides readers with savvy design advice and helpful how-to instructions for creating persuasive ads on the computer. For use with any hardware or software, the book is a unique, idea-packed resource for improving the look and effect of desktop-produced ads.

■ Floyd, Elaine. *Marketing With Newsletters: How to Boost Sales, Add Members, Raise Donations and Further Your Cause With a Promotional Newsletter*. New Orleans, LA: EF Communications, 1991.

Shows for-profit and non-profit organizations how to promote themselves with a newsletter. Includes information on newsletter content, writing and design. Also: information on setting a budget, saving money, developing a readership base, surveying readers, coordinating the newsletter with other marketing projects and finding subcontractors. Over 200 illustrations and sidebars are used to emphasize certain points discussed in the text.

■ Gosney, Michael, Odam, John, and Schmal, Jim. *The Gray Book: Designing in Black & White on Your Computer*. 2nd ed. Chapel Hill, NC: Ventana Press, 1993.

This "idea gallery" offers a lavish variety of the most interesting black, white and gray graphic effects from laser printers, scanners and high-resolution output devices.

Holmes, Nigel. *Designer's Guide to Creating Charts and Diagrams*. New York: Watson-Guptill, 1984.

Well illustrated and written by an innovator in the field of visual information journalism, this book shows how to convert numbers and comparisons into eye-catching graphics.

Hudson, Howard Penn. *Publishing Newsletters*. rev. ed. New York: Charles Scribner's Sons, 1988.

Comprehensive coverage of all aspects of newsletter publishing, by one of the industry's most respected observers and designers, the founder and publisher of the influential *Newsletter on Newsletters*.

Kaatz, Ron. *The NTC Book of Advertising and Marketing Checklists*. Lincolnwood, IL: NTC Business Books, 1988.

A unique, interactive approach to planning advertising design—you learn by answering questions about the desired goals of your advertising.

Kieper, Michael L. *Illustrated Handbook of Desktop Publishing and Typesetting*. Blue Ridge Summit, PA: TAB Books, 1987.

Combines a historical perspective with a carefully annotated overview of just about every desktop publishing hardware and software program available.

Lichty, Tom. *Desktop Publishing With Word for Windows for 2.0*. Chapel Hill, NC: Ventana Press, 1993.

Provides Word users with the design know-how necessary for creating successful, appealing documents. Contains chapters on the use of typography, style sheets, graphic placement and more.

Mansfield, Richard. *Desktop Publishing With WordPerfect 6.0*. Chapel Hill, NC: Ventana Press, 1993.

Offers a wealth of advice and how-to examples for creating appealing documents, working with graphics and creating style sheets. Addresses new tools and techniques available in WordPerfect 6.0, including the GUI, customizable button bar, WYSIWYG editing, dialog boxes and more.

Moen, Daryl R. *Newspaper Layout and Design*. 2nd ed. Ames, IA: Iowa State University Press, 1989.

Detailed analysis of the component parts of a modern newspaper, including observations on current trends.

Naiman, Arthur, ed. *The Macintosh Bible*. 4th ed. Berkeley, CA: Peachpit Press, 1992.

An invaluable aid for both experienced and first-time Macintosh users. Contains capsule reviews of hardware and software plus software-specific practical tips on the most popular programs.

Nelson, Roy Paul. *The Design of Advertising*. 6th ed. Dubuque, IA: William C. Brown, 1989.

A no-nonsense favorite, focusing on effective use of color, space and typography when designing magazine and newspaper ads.

Nelson, Roy Paul. *Publication Design*. 5th ed. Dubuque, IA: William C. Brown, 1989.

This large-format volume focuses on the challenges presented by the various types of publications.

Nemoy, Sheldon, and Aiken, C.J. *Looking Good With CorelDRAW for Version 4.0*. 2nd ed. Chapel Hill, NC: Ventana Press, 1993.

Guidelines and suggestions are offered for taking advantage of CorelDRAW's newest features. Two galleries of annotated artwork feature a stunning array of award-winning black-and-white and four-color illustrations.

One Club for Art and Copy, Inc. *The One Show: Judged to Be Advertising's Best in Print, Radio and TV*. Vol. 14. New York: One Club for Art & Copy, 1992.

The annually published *The One Show* is a lavishly illustrated, large-format book containing full-color reproductions of award-winning advertisements of all types. *The One Show* often provides fresh insight into solutions to your current design problem.

■ Parker, Roger C. *Desktop Publishing With WordPerfect for 5.0 & 5.1.* 2nd ed. Chapel Hill, NC: Ventana Press, 1990.

Desktop Publishing With WordPerfect includes invaluable information on organizing your documents into attractive layouts, working with graphics and creating style sheets for consistency and speed.

■ Parker, Roger C. *The Makeover Book: 101 Design Solutions for Desktop Publishing.* Chapel Hill, NC: Ventana Press, 1989.

Hundreds of actual examples, tips and techniques that let you compare original documents with their makeovers.

■ Parker, Roger C. *Newsletters From the Desktop: Designing Effective Publications With Your Computer.* Chapel Hill, NC: Ventana Press, 1990.

This desktop design guide offers a wealth of desktop publishing techniques and design advice for producing your newsletter, including layout suggestions, creating the nameplate and selecting typefaces.

■ Parker, Roger C., and Kramer, Douglas. *Using Aldus PageMaker 4.* 3rd ed. New York: Bantam Books, 1990.

The latest edition of one of the earliest PageMaker books to appear. Shows how to use the latest 4.0 features.

■ Pattison, Polly, Pretzer, Mary, and Beach, Mark. *Outstanding Newsletter Designs.* Available from: Polly Pattison, 5092 Kingscross Rd., Westminster, CA 92683.

A potpourri of inspirational ideas for newspaper publishers. Any one of its ideas is well worth the cost of this fully illustrated, large-format book.

Rabb, Margaret Y. *The Presentation Design Book: Tips Techniques & Advice for Creating Effective, Attractive Slides, Overheads, Screen Shows, Multimedia & More.* 2nd ed. Chapel Hill, NC: Ventana Press, 1993.

This generic design guide reviews the essentials of creating good-looking slides, overheads, charts, diagrams and handouts. Alerts you to basic pitfalls of producing presentation graphics, and provides examples of how to choose the best medium and tailor it for your audience.

Sitarz, Daniel. *The Desktop Publisher's Legal Handbook: A Comprehensive Guide to Computer Publishing Law.* Carbondale, IL: Nova Publishing, 1989.

A new set of challenges faces writers who become publishers. This concise volume provides copyright information essential to today's computer-based publishers.

Strunk, William, Jr., and White, E. B. *Elements of Style.* 3rd ed. New York: Macmillan, 1979.

Required reading for any publisher, providing an entertaining review of the basics of effective writing, as well as a quick reference for grammar and usage issues.

Swann, Alan. *How to Understand and Use Design and Layout.* Cincinnati, OH: North Light Books, 1991.

This handsomely illustrated volume does an excellent job of balancing theory and practical example. Numerous rough layouts illustrate various formats and ways of placing type on a page.

Tufte, Edward R. *The Visual Display of Quantitative Information.* Cheshire, CT: Graphics Press, 1983.

One of the classics, this book describes various charting and graphing tools and helps you choose the right type of graphic to get your message across. Describes possible pitfalls and ways of maintaining data integrity.

■ White, Alex. *How to Spec Type.* New York: Watson-Guptill, 1987.

Reviews the basics of typography in a straightforward and entertaining fashion.

■ White, Alex. *Type in Use.* New York: Design Press, 1992.

Further explores the seemingly infinite number of ways type can be placed and manipulated on a page. Contains hundreds of thought-provoking examples.

■ White, Jan. *Color for the Electronic Age.* New York: Watson-Guptill, 1990.

Demonstrates, in dozens of examples, many shown in three stages (no color/badly used color/cleverly used color), how color can be used to enhance text, charts and graphs.

■ White, Jan. *Using Charts and Graphs: 1000 ideas for getting attention.* New York: R. R. Bowker, 1984.

Reviews the advantages and disadvantages of the various types of charts and graphs, with an emphasis on presenting data as accurately as possible.

■ Xerox Press. *Xerox Publishing Standards: A manual of style and design.* New York: Watson-Guptill, 1988.

A comprehensive survey of the many design and editorial components involved in establishing a consistent corporate identity throughout a wide range of publications.

■ Zinsser, William. *On Writing Well: An Informal Guide to Writing Nonfiction.* 4th ed. New York: Harper & Row, 1990.

This is a book you'll want to use over and over again, long after you've read it the first time. Emphasizes the importance of clarity and simplicity.

PERIODICALS

- *Aldus Magazine*, Aldus Corp., 411 First Ave. South, Seattle, WA 98104. Bimonthly, with special issues throughout the year.

   Helpful hints and general information for all registered users of Aldus PageMaker and Freehand, by request. One idea can save you dozens of hours of work.

- *Before & After: How to Design Cool Stuff on Your Computer*, PageLab, 331 J St., Ste. 150, Sacramento, CA 95814-9671. Bimonthly.

   This exciting, full-color, bimonthly publication is full of tips and techniques for advanced desktop publishers—and those who want to become advanced desktop publishers. Concisely written and profusely illustrated—not an inch of wasted space.

- *Communication Arts*, Coyne & Blanchard, 410 Sherman Ave., Palo Alto, CA 94306. Eight issues/year.

   Traditional "required reading" for art directors and graphic designers, now devoting increased space to desktop publishing concerns. Special focus issues showcase samples of the year's best designs in advertising, illustration and photography.

- *Electronic Composition & Imaging*, 2240 Midland Ave., Ste. 201, Scarborough, ON M1P 4R8 Canada. Bimonthly.

   Covers mid-level desktop publishing, electronic publishing and prepress imaging equipment, business and design; Q & A section.

- *Electronic Publishing*, PennWell Publishing Co., 1421 S. Sheridan, Tulsa, OK 74112. 18 issues/year.

   Its motto says it all: "No other publication on earth reports as much news about typography and professional publishing." Approaches desktop publishing issues from a typographer's point of view.

■ *Font & Function: The Adobe Type Catalog,* Adobe Systems, P.O. Box 7900, Mountain View, CA 94039-7900. Thrice yearly.

This free publication includes articles on new typeface designs, gives samples of Adobe typefaces in use and shows specimens of all available Adobe fonts.

■ *High Color Magazine,* 21 Elm St., Camden, ME 04843. Bi-monthly.

Heavy technological focus on PC graphics and video applications.

■ *HOW Magazine,* 1507 Dana Ave., Cincinnati, OH 45207. Bimonthly.

Geared to the professional graphic artist, covers graphic design business, production and technology; extensive graphics gallery.

■ *In-House Graphics,* United Communications, 11300 Rockville Pike, Ste. 1100, Rockville, MD 20852. Monthly.

Practical advice for results-oriented graphic designers. Recent articles have ranged from the use of metallic inks and software-specific design techniques to compensation trends for designers and desktop publishers.

■ *Newsletter Design,* Newsletter Clearinghouse, 44 West Market St., P.O. Box 311, Rhinebeck, NY 12572. Monthly.

A visual treat, each month's issue contains illustrations of the front cover and inside spread of over 20 newsletters, along with detailed commentary on their strengths and weaknesses. Provides numerous ideas that can be incorporated in your newsletter.

■ *Newsletter on Newsletters,* Newsletter Clearinghouse, 44 West Market St., P.O. Box 311, Rhinebeck, NY 12572. Biweekly.

Want to know what's going on in the newsletter business? This concise publication contains a capsule look, along with features focusing on graphic, economic, postal and promotional issues.

- *The Page,* P.O. Box 14493, Chicago, IL 60614. Ten issues/year.

  A delightful publication written for Macintosh desktop publishers. *The Page* is an impartial, informed and reader-friendly look at Macintosh desktop publishing from a hands-on perspective.

- *Print: America's Graphic Design Magazine,* RC Publications, Inc., 3200 Tower Oaks Blvd., Rockville, MD 20852. Bi-monthly.

  The techniques and economics of professional graphic design, with an eye on advances in desktop publishing. Its yearly regional design and advertising design issues by themselves justify its subscription price.

- *Publish!* Integrated Media, Inc., 501 Second St., San Francisco, CA 94107. Monthly.

  In-depth critiques of the latest hardware and software, along with design- and technique-oriented articles. Of special interest is its monthly typography column.

- *Step-By-Step Electronic Design: The How-To Newsletter for Desktop Designers,* Dynamic Graphics, 6000 N. Forest Park Dr., P.O. Box 1901, Peoria, IL 61656-1901. Quarterly.

  Advertising-free, technique-oriented advice for advanced desktop publishers and others who aspire to greater expertise in layout and design.

- *U&lc,* International Typeface, 866 Second Ave., New York, NY 10017. Bimonthly.

  This free large-format tabloid contains features written by many of the world's leading typeface designers. It balances a historical perspective with down-to-earth treatment of contemporary publishing issues.

■ *WordPerfect for Windows Magazine*, WordPerfect Publishing, 270 W. Center St., Orem, UT 84057. Monthly.

Features articles and tips and tricks for using all aspects of WordPerfect for Windows, including page layout and publication design.

■ *WordPerfect: The Magazine*, WordPerfect Publishing, 270 W. Center St., Orem, UT 84057. Monthly.

An easy way to keep up-to-date on WordPerfect's growing range of page layout commands and features.

SEMINARS & TRAINING

■ *Career Track*, 3085 Center Green Dr., M/S 15, Boulder, CO 80301. 303-447-2323, or 800-334-6780

Offers seminars, audios and videos on a wide range of desktop publishing and newsletter-related subjects as well as management communication and personal development subjects.

■ *Dynamic Graphics & Education Foundation*, 6000 N. Forest Park Dr., Peoria, IL 61614. 309-688-8800

Sponsors both generic and software-specific workshops throughout the world focusing on desktop publishing design issues.

■ *Electronic Directions*, 220 E. 23rd St., New York, NY 10010. 212-213-6500

Software-specific courses and seminars for desktop publishers.

■ *Folio Publishing News*, Six River Bend Ctr., Box 4949, Stamford, CT 06907-0949. 203-358-9900

Each year, *Folio: The Magazine for Magazine Management* presents a series of two- and three-day conferences around the country, featuring presentations by leading designers and other professionals.

■ *National Association of Desktop Publishers*, 462 Old Boston St., Ste. 8, Topsfield, MA 01983. 508-887-7900

Professional organization for desktop publishers. Publishes *The Journal* (hardware and software reviews, how-to articles, job, show and equipment directories).

■ *Newsletter Publishers Association*, 1401 Wilson Blvd., Ste. 207, Arlington, VA 22209. 703-527-2333

Sponsors seminars and publishes periodicals for newsletter editors.

■ *Newsletter Clearinghouse*, PO Box 311, Rhinebeck, NY 12572. 914-876-2081

Publishes books and newsletters, membership listings and special reports. Sponsors conferences, seminars and design competition.

■ *Padgett-Thompson*, 11221 Roe Ave., Leawood, KS 66211. 913-491-270 or 800-255-4141

A division of American Management Association, the nation's oldest not-for-profit business training organization; offers one- and two-day seminars on desktop publishing, newsletters, copywriting and editing, and proofreading.

■ *Performance Seminar Group*, 31 Main St., Wells River, VT 05081. 802-757-2714

One of the world's largest seminar firms; offers seminars on newsletter publishing and desktop design.

■ *Popular Communication*, Box 21008 S-400-71, Goteborg, Sweden. 031-50-0030

Sponsors desktop publishing design conferences and seminars throughout Europe.

■ *Promotional Perspectives*, 1829 W. Stadium Blvd., Ste. 101, Ann Arbor, MI 48103. 313-994-0007

Offers seminars on design issues for desktop publishers, including newsletter design and more.

■ *Ragan Communication Workshops,* 212 W. Superior St., Chicago, IL 60610. 312-922-8245

Presents seminars and publishes a variety of newsletters specializing in communications skills and newsletter design and production.

■ *Serendal Group,* 8962 E. Hamden Ave., Denver, CO 80231. 303-337-0060

Presents seminars throughout the U.S. and the Far East on desktop publishing design and newsletter publishing. Also, quality management systems in the electronic publishing environment.

Index

the
Ventana Press

Desktop Design Series

To order these and other Ventana Press titles, use the form in the back of this book or contact your local bookstore or computer store. Full money-back guarantee!

Return order form to:
Ventana Press, P.O. Box 2468, Chapel Hill, NC 27515
☎**919/942-0220; Fax 919/942-1140**

Can't wait? Call toll-free, 800/743-5369 (U.S. Only)!

Newsletters From the Desktop
$23.95
306 pages, illustrated
ISBN: 0-940087-40-5
Now the millions of desktop publishers who produce newsletters can learn how to dramatically improve the design of their publications.

The Makeover Book: 101 Design Solutions for Desktop Publishing
$17.95
282 pages, illustrated
ISBN: 0-940087-20-0
"Before-and-after" desktop publishing examples demonstrate how basic design revisions can dramatically improve a document.

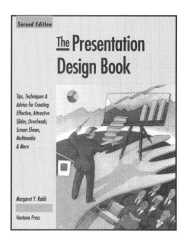

Advertising From the Desktop
$24.95
464 pages, illustrated
ISBN: 1-56604-064-7
Advertising From the Desktop offers unmatched design advice and helpful how-to instructions for creating persuasive ads. This book is an idea-packed resource for improving the look and effect of your ads.

The Presentation Design Book, Second Edition
$24.95
320 pages, illustrated
ISBN: 1-56604-014-0
The Presentation Design Book is filled with thoughtful advice and instructive examples for creating presentation visuals that have the power to communicate and persuade. For use with any software or hardware.

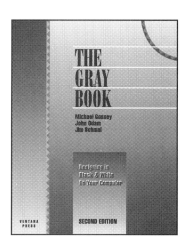

Type From the Desktop
$23.95
290 pages, illustrated
ISBN: 0-940087-45-6
Learn the basics of designing with type from a desktop publisher's perspective. For use with any hardware or software.

The Gray Book, Second Edition
$24.95
272 pages, illustrated
ISBN: 1-56604-073-6
This "idea gallery" for desktop publishers offers a lavish variety of the most interesting black, white and gray graphics effects that can be achieved with laser printers, scanners and high-resolution output devices.

From Ventana Press...

More Companions For Creative Computing

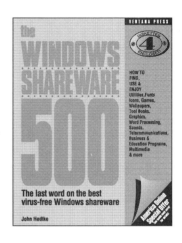

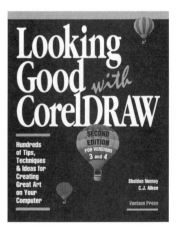

The Windows Shareware 500
$39.95
370 pages, illustrated
ISBN: 1-56604-045-0
The Windows Shareware 500 offers information on finding, select-ing and using the best shareware; reviews of the top 500 pro-grams from a variety of categories; a 4-disk set featuring the author's top picks; and an America Online membership disk with 10 hours of free online time.

Desktop Publishing With WordPerfect 6
$24.95
370 pages, illustrated
ISBN: 1-56604-049-3
The new graphics capabilities of WordPerfect 6.0 can save you thousands of dollars in design and typesetting costs. Includes invaluable design advice and annotated examples.

Voodoo Windows
$19.95
282 pages, illustrated
ISBN: 1-56604-005-1
This one-of-a-kind guide offers a cauldron of Windows tips and tricks that will streamline daily tasks, solve problems and save time.

Looking Good With CorelDRAW!, Second Edition
$27.95
328 pages, illustrated
ISBN: 1-56604-061-2
Guidelines and suggestions are given on how to best take advantage of CorelDRAW's powerful new desktop publishing features for Version 4.

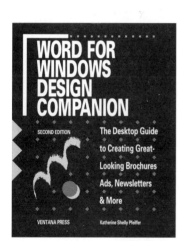

Voodoo Mac
$21.95
307 pages, illustrated
ISBN: 1-56604-028-0
Working with your Mac has never been so easy! *Voodoo Mac* provides never-before-published secrets and tips for maximum productivity.

Word for Windows Design Companion, Second Edition
$21.95
473 pages, illustrated
ISBN: 1-56604-075-2
Filled with innovative design advice and creative examples for getting the most from your Word investment. Covers Word for Windows through Version 6

The Official America Online for Windows Membership Kit & Tour Guide
$34.95
402 pages, illustrated
ISBN: 1-56604-013-2
This book/disk includes the AOL starter disk, 10 free hours of online time for new & current members (a $60 value!), a free month's membership plus your official AOL "tour guide."

TO ORDER additional copies of *Looking Good in Print, Third Edition* or any other Ventana Press title, please fill out this order form and return it to us for quick shipment.

	Quantity		Price		Total
Looking Good in Print, 3rd Edition	_____	x	$24.95	=	$_____
Presentation Design Book, 2nd Edition	_____	x	$24.95	=	$_____
Type From the Desktop	_____	x	$23.95	=	$_____
The Makeover Book	_____	x	$17.95	=	$_____
Newsletters From the Desktop	_____	x	$23.95	=	$_____
Word for Windows Design Companion, 2nd Edition	_____	x	$21.95	=	$_____
The Gray Book, 2nd Edition	_____	x	$24.95	=	$_____
Looking Good With CorelDRAW!, 2nd Edition	_____	x	$27.95	=	$_____
Voodoo Windows	_____	x	$19.95	=	$_____
Advertising From the Desktop	_____	x	$24.95	=	$_____
Desktop Publishing With WordPerfect 6	_____	x	$24.95	=	$_____
The Windows Shareware 500/Mac Shareware 500	_____	x	$39.95	=	$_____
Voodoo Mac	_____	x	$21.95	=	$_____
The Official America Online for Windows/Mac Membership Kit & Tour Guide	_____	x	$34.95	=	$_____

Shipping: Please add $4.50/first book, $1.35/book thereafter; $8.25/book "two-day air," $2.25/book thereafter. For Canada, add $6.50/book. = $_____

Send C.O.D. (add $4.50 to shipping charges) = $_____

North Carolina residents add 6% sales tax = $_____

Total = $_____

Name _____

Company _____

Address (No PO Box) _____

City_____ State_____ Zip_____

Daytime Telephone _____

___ Payment enclosed ___VISA ___MC Acc't # _____

Expiration Date_____ Interbank # _____

Signature _____

Please mail or fax to: **Ventana Press, PO Box 2468, Chapel Hill, NC 27515**
☎ 919/942-0220, FAX: 919/942-1140
CAN'T WAIT? CALL TOLL-FREE ☎ 800/743-5369!